The Soulful Science

The Soulful Science

WHAT ECONOMISTS REALLY DO AND WHY IT MATTERS

Diane Coyle

PRINCETON UNIVERSITY PRESS
PRINCETON AND OXFORD

Published by Princeton University Press,
41 William Street, Princeton, New Jersey 08540

In the United Kingdom: Princeton University Press,
3 Market Place, Woodstock, Oxfordshire OX20 1SY

ISBN-13: 978-0-691-12513-8 (alk. paper)
ISBN-10: 0-691-12513-9 (alk. paper)

Library of Congress Control Number: 2006933326

A catalogue record for this book is available from the British Library

This book has been composed in Lucida

Typeset by T&T Productions Ltd, London

Printed on acid-free paper ∞

pup.princeton.edu

Printed in the United States of America

10 9 8 7 6 5 4 3 2 1

Contents

CONTENTS

Acknowledgements

It's in the nature of this book that I owe a great debt of gratitude to very many economists whose work it describes. I've learned a huge amount from reading so much of the incredibly rich and fascinating literature in economics of the past twenty years, since I finished my PhD. However, I've inevitably had to leave a lot out, so I also owe an apology to all the economists whose contributions or whole fields of research are not covered here.

There are very many people who have talked to me about their research and helped me learn so much over the years. For their generous help with this book, Mike Artis, Will Baumol, Nick Crafts, Bill Easterly, Mike Emmerich, Ben Friedman, Ed Glaeser, Mervyn King, Stephen King, Shirin Madon, Bethan Marshall, Richard Marshall, Paul Ormerod, Paul Seabright, Pat Starr, and Romesh Vaitilingam deserve special thanks. Needless to say, they are not responsible for any of the errors, omissions, or infelicities.

I would particularly like to remember two friends who died while I was writing this book. Paul Geroski helped me shape the original idea and structure before he was taken ill. It would never have got off the ground without his boundless enthusiasm and encouragement. David Walton eagerly discussed it with me whenever we met and was another tremendous source of advice and encouragement. Both were brilliant applied economists, utterly engaged with the question of how to ensure that the relevant evidence could be found and used to make the world a better place. Both are very greatly missed.

This book also owes its existence to the vision of Richard Baggaley and Peter Dougherty of Princeton University Press—I'm very lucky to have such inspiring publishers. As ever, my agent, Sara Menguc, was a wonderful and warm source of help and advice (and pep talks over lunch). And the biggest thanks of all go to my family, Rory, Adam, and Rufus, for putting up with my distraction and the growing mountain of economics books, journals, and papers taking over our home.

Introduction

I want to persuade you that economics gets an unfairly bad press. Economics is entering a new golden age, and this book is about the frontiers of economic research and empirical discovery during the past fifteen or twenty years. Yet these accomplishments are not widely known.

On the contrary, the subject frequently comes under attack, not just in academic journals but also in newspapers and political or literary magazines. Here's a typical example: "For the economists, money is a synonym of happiness... It is their philistine notions of personal and national welfare that have helped to ruin the natural world; confused technology with culture; reduced art to money, time to interest, sexual relations to pornography, friendship to advantage, charity to the charity ball and liberty to shopping." "Economics," he splutters, is "unbelievably crude," and far inferior to a good novel in diagnosing the ills of society (Buchan 1995).

At the same time, there is a widespread perception that economists are extremely powerful. Moisés Naim, the influential editor of *Foreign Policy* magazine, writes: "When economists err in theory, people suffer in practice." He calls us "a smug lot" and urges more humility on our part.[1] It's widely believed by those who credit us with such power that members of the guild of economists run their slide rules over government proposals on just about anything. People are unsure about what this involves—I think many believe simultaneously that economics is both very complicated and just plain common sense—but few would question the importance of economic assessments of public policy, and the role of the profession in government, think tanks, and all the arenas of public policy debate.

Unfortunately, this influence is greatly resented by many people who believe that the economist's mental model or method of analysis is highly

---

[1] In "Economist Class," *Foreign Policy*, March/April 2006 (www.foreignpolicy.com/story/cms.php?story_id=3389, accessed August 15, 2006).

flawed. While they don't always make this critique explicit, those trained in other disciplines believe economics is too narrow in its focus, caring only about money; too dry and robotic in its view of human nature; too reductionist in its methodology. What's more, I think there's also a widespread fear that the influence of economics, perceived to be on the march, has actually been changing the world and is making it more like the arid, calculating, and uncaring domain of Economic Man.

Let me give an example from my own country, the United Kingdom, which illustrates these attitudes. During the months I was writing this book, the British Broadcasting Corporation screened not one but two whole television series about happiness. Their theme was that the thrust of all government economic policies aimed at boosting economic growth was misdirected, because growth doesn't make us happy. A small flock of books about happiness settled in the bookstores, and were widely reviewed in the newspapers and magazines that cover politics and public policy. The government called in "happiness gurus" to run seminars, and even appointed a happiness expert to the Bank of England committee which sets interest rates. It was widely reported that the said guru's research concluded that having more sex made us happier than would a $50,000 pay rise.[2] The flurry of favorable comment and policy interest stemmed, I'm certain, from the belief that the happiness research proves the economists wrong: economic growth doesn't make us any happier, so we can ignore what the economists say about everything!

There's just one catch: economists have been at the forefront of the research into well-being, which is the offspring of a fruitful union between economics and psychology. The number of scholarly articles in the *economics* journals with "happiness" or "well-being" in the title has grown rapidly since the mid 1990s. The most prominent happiness experts being called in by policy makers are economists. The new ideas and findings which have emerged from this overlap between economics and psychology are discussed in this book, along with their implications for the whole subject of economics.

Needless to say, I don't believe this work undermines the foundations of my subject at all. The popular unpopularity of economics rests on perceptions which are twenty or thirty years out of date and were always a bit of a caricature anyway. One of my aims in surveying some of the most interesting areas of new research since the early 1980s is to try to bring the perception of what economists do and say up to date.

---

[2] This is an average across sexual partners, of course.

This is a stepping stone to a more ambitious aim, which is to emphasize to nonspecialists and professional economists alike the importance of this subject for the caliber of public policy and the future well-being of our societies. Reading the publications of the policy intelligentsia— *The New Republic* or *The Nation*, opinion columns in *The Guardian* or *New York Times*, *Le Figaro* or *Le Monde*—or attending policy seminars in these countries, or looking at pamphlets issued by many think tanks, it is clear to me that there has been a kind of romantic backlash against the rationalist foundations of economics.

We economists must take some of the blame. There are too few good communicators among us, and we haven't gone out of our way to explain the fruitfulness of our approach. I admit that many economists are dull and speak in jargon. But there's more to it than our weak PR. This resistance to economics is tied up with the end of the Cold War, the redundancy of the old left–right divisions, and the passing of the Thatcher–Reagan era, which was widely seen as very much a time of triumph for economics and markets. The radical conservatives who were in power in the United States and the United Kingdom during the 1980s drew inspiration and ideas from the strong current in economic research at the time that emphasized the merits of free markets and the rationality of people's expectations and decision making. They were, of course, anticommunists, and it was the era when Ronald Reagan was able to declare victory over communism.

Yet it was not the fall of the Berlin Wall that marked the high tide of this kind of ultra-free-market economics, but rather Reagan's first election victory in 1981. By the time Hollywood caught up, and had Gordon Gekko declare (in the 1987 movie *Wall Streeet*),"Greed is good; greed is right; greed works," leading academic economists had already moved very far from the models of selfish, calculating individuals on which the Gekko view of the economy was based.

My point is not, therefore, a politically partisan one (my personal politics are very much of the flattened-in-the-middle-of-the-road kind). I fear that as long as so many people mistakenly believe economics to be intrinsically right wing, we're in danger of losing the economist's skeptical, empirical way of thinking about society. Unless noneconomists appreciate the vital role of the economic way of thought, we will see increasingly bad, even dangerous, policies.

This is all the more ironic because those scholars working on the frontiers of economics have firmly put behind them the inward-looking reductionism which did indeed sometimes characterize the discipline in the past. Economics is enjoying a spectacularly fruitful period, in particular where it overlaps with other disciplines such as psychology, history, or anthropology. Economists are offering insights and evidence into the organization of human society which are both pathbreaking—because the tools being used were previously unavailable—and controversial—because there is a growing body of evidence challenging embedded political beliefs right across the spectrum. The combination of cheap computing power, the development of new data sets, and innovations in econometrics and in analytical and computational techniques has had a very profound influence on economics, as on other sciences.

This should be of interest to several audiences. Anybody with an interest in politics and public policy should certainly equip themselves with the insights and results I describe here. I hope general readers of books on current affairs will enjoy it too. For professional economists who left the academic world a while ago, this will be a good place to catch up with developments at the frontiers of research, and I give references to further material for those who wish to read more. And I particularly hope researchers in fields other than economics—not only people in the other social sciences or natural sciences, but also our harsh critics in the wider humanities—will be willing to suspend their prejudices about us and find out what we economists are up to these days.

The next eight chapters survey (necessarily briefly) some of the most exciting areas of recent research. They reflect my personal interests—there are bound to be important gaps. The first three chapters (part 1) address the fundamental question of economic development, the wealth of nations as our subject's spiritual elder Adam Smith expressed it. What is the evidence from the past? What does economic theory tell us about how to interpret it? How can theory and evidence inform the current policy debate about reducing global poverty?

Part 2 turns from how economies develop over time to the details (the "microfoundations") of how they operate. What valid assumptions can we make about individual behavior and responses to incentives? Or about what information people have on which to base their individual choices? And what is their motivation—what aims drive their behavior and should be reflected in democratic policy decisions? In other words, do people actually want to get rich or be happy?

The final two chapters (part 3) look at how individual economic choices fit into the world. To what extent and in what ways should economic decisions be interpreted as part of nature, fundamentally evolutionary or biological in nature? And how do our choices aggregate to add up to a social outcome—how do we interact with each other, and what are the links between economics and social organization? This brings the discussion full circle, as social organization is key to questions of economic development.

In the conclusion, I return to the point that economists' way of thinking is both distinctive and essential for good public policy. I hesitate to use the word "methodology," as it's likely to turn off those readers who've made it so far, but there is an important point about the methodology of economics. Part of the critique made of economics by people in other academic disciplines (but especially the humanities) concerns its supposedly false pretensions to scientific status. Many critics, including internal critics, see this as the big mistake made by mainstream economists in the middle part of the twentieth century: we were trying so hard to be a proper science, like physics, that we fell into the trap of a sterile, mechanistic view of human nature and a reductionist vision of society. The mainstream economics of 1945 onwards is often described as "neoclassical." This distinguishes it from the earlier classical economics and signals greater formalism and use of mathematics, and a codification of the standard assumptions made by all economists in their work. These include, for example, the assumptions that people make choices rationally in their own interest, and that aggregate outcomes are the sum of individual outcomes. The term neoclassical is therefore descriptive, but it is also often used by critics of economics as a term of abuse. It's true that there have been plenty of jobbing economists happy to teach and apply unrealistic mathematically based models without thinking seriously about their fit with the "real world"; most of the work discussed in this book has been done by the leading economists, many of them the winners of the Nobel memorial prize, and by no means all of this material has reached current textbooks even at graduate level. I use the term "neoclassical" as a convenient shorthand for the mainstream approach of twentieth-century economics. Part of my argument in this book is that economics has moved decisively beyond the neoclassical assumptions in some areas. We use neoclassical models where it makes sense to do so, for they have proved their worth in many areas, but are no longer restricted by that framework where the evidence is that the assumptions are invalid.

Nevertheless, the distinctiveness and importance of economics remains entirely in its insistence on applying the scientific method to the study of human behavior. However inadequately we put our behavior under the microscope, it is the only valid mode of analysis. In my mind, the most important founding father of economics is the Enlightenment philosopher David Hume, the embodiment of the skeptical method. Although much less well-known now than his close friend Adam Smith, Hume is widely regarded as a more important philosopher. He influenced, among many others, James Madison and Alexander Hamilton, William James, Immanuel Kant, Jeremy Bentham, and Charles Darwin. Usually labeled an empiricist and a skeptic, Hume's declared aim was the introduction of "the experimental method of reasoning into moral subjects," the development of a "science of human nature." In summing up one of his great works, *A Treatise of Human Nature*, Hume wrote:

> It is at least worthwhile to try whether the science of *man* will not admit of the same accuracy which several parts of natural philosophy are found susceptible of.... The sole end of logic is to explain the principle and operation of our reasoning faculty, and the nature of our ideas; morals and criticism as regards our tastes and sentiments; and politics consider[ing] men as united in society and dependent on each other.

He said he wanted to "anatomize human nature in a regular manner" and "draw no conclusions but where he is authorized by experience."[3] This, not the narrow analysis of making profits in the marketplace, remains the aim of economics. Yet it helps to explain, I think, the unpopularity of economists. We economists are unwilling to tolerate imprecision, wishful thinking, or flattering illusion in the study of human behavior and society. I hope this won't deter you from reading on, though, to learn what huge progress economists have made during the past two or three decades in the study of humankind.

---

[3] Hume's 1740 abstract, reprinted in *On Human Nature and the Understanding* (Collier Books, New York, 1972), pp. 289–90. Hume's works are available at www.etext.leeds. ac.uk/hume/.

Prologue to Part 1

The first three chapters start this book with the biggest question of all, the one which has been central to economics since Adam Smith's *The Wealth of Nations*. What makes economies grow, and why do some fail to do so? The latter part of this question has become one of the biggest global public policy issues of our time. In the rich Western countries some people have even rioted in the streets about it, while in the poor countries of the (non)developing world hundreds of millions of other people lead lives of quiet desperation.

There are additional reasons for starting my survey of the frontiers of economic research here. Chapter 1, covering what we have learnt about economic history, demonstrates the importance of new sources of data. Vital new data sets have become available since the 1980s, facilitated by ever-cheaper computer power. They have delivered results which have changed the way economists think about growth, its causes and social mechanisms, which is the subject of chapter 2. The new "top-down" growth theories which have resulted from the historical and macroeconomic evidence highlight the importance of issues such as the institutions and governance of economies. In chapter 3 I look at the implications for poor countries. Development economics has always been a controversial area of research, and that hasn't changed. I would hardly describe the results of recent economic research as amounting to a consensus, even within the profession, never mind in the campaigning think tanks and nongovernmental organizations (NGOs). Still, there has been huge progress in the contribution of economics to analyzing and addressing the challenges of poverty and the failures of growth.

The second part of the book will switch from the top-down, macroeconomic approach to bottom-up microeconomics, and the third part will bring them together, looking at the new microfoundations of the economic study of society. It will bring us full circle, back to the social mechanisms for growth highlighted in this first part.

PART 1
The Mysteries of Wealth and Poverty

The History Detectives

Newcastle-upon-Tyne, in the northeast of England, is the principal town of one of the poorest regions of the United Kingdom. It has in recent times enjoyed a bit of an economic and cultural revival. The sculptor Anthony Gormley created the massive Angel of the North, a twenty-meter-high steel and copper angel with a wingspan of fifty-eight meters standing by the side of the main road into the northeast, to symbolize this renaissance. The Baltic Centre in Newcastle, a converted dockside warehouse, is an exciting arts venue. Nearby Gateshead boasts one of the country's biggest shopping centers. The current buzz harks back to the town's nineteenth-century past, when, as Britain's busiest coal port, it was an industrial hub in the world's leading industrial power. But the Great Depression of the 1930s brought massive unemployment and poverty. People in the northeast, like the other industrial areas of Britain, suffered from extensive hunger and the illnesses of poverty such as tuberculosis and rickets, living in filthy, polluted towns where the grandeur of the Victorian industrial monuments mocked the poor and unemployed.

In this depressing time and place grew a boy whose father was lucky enough to have a steady job as an engineer on the railways. It was an era of street-corner politics: passions ran high, there were mass marches, and even fights between the British fascists and their opponents. This child had a retired uncle, a colorful character living off a pension for injuries received in World War I, who used to stand on a soapbox making speeches advocating socialism. His admiring nephew was often in the audience. The boy also used to attend weekend schools run by the Co-operative Movement, one of the many educational initiatives run by and on behalf of working-class people.[1] As a thirteen year old in 1940, he

---

[1] For a wonderful account of these educational initiatives, see Rose (2001). My mother was still, in 2004, taking courses from the Workers' Educational Association in York, although her latest subject was wine appreciation rather than economics.

heard a lecture that was to set the course of his life. It was given by his school history teacher and was based on a new book, *How to Pay for the War*, by the eminent economist John Maynard Keynes. The boy was hooked on the idea that problems like those he saw around him, unemployment, hunger, insecurity, might have solutions.

From that intellectual seed, Angus Maddison, currently Professor of Economics at the University of Groningen in the Netherlands, went on to become one of the world's leading economic historians. He is little known outside the economics profession but is nevertheless a central character in this chapter because of his definitive work in estimating levels of national output and growth for the whole world from the year 1000 to the present. For we are going to start with something basic: analyzing the history of the world during the past millennium. There is nothing like the grand sweep of history for tempting researchers to develop grand theories. One of the contributions of modern economics is to make it possible to start to weigh one grand theory against another by showing whether some are inconsistent with the historical evidence. And it does so thanks to the efforts of economic historians who apply the weight of statistical theory and computer power to data collected from neglected documents lying on dusty shelves in libraries around the world.

The scale of the task Maddison and other economists set themselves in assembling figures on gross domestic product (GDP) in many countries over many years should not be underestimated. The concept of this measure of the total output of the economy dates back only to 1940.[2] It was not until 1952 that an internationally consistent method of collecting the raw data was agreed and even now many countries, especially poor ones, do not assemble high-quality economic statistics. The formerly communist economies did not start measuring GDP in the same way until after 1990. Prior to World War II no country collected statistics in the right form, and of course the further back in time we go, the less adequate the basic statistical information. What is more, to compare one country with another requires using exchange rates to convert one currency into another: this is particularly controversial and I'll return to it later. So Maddison's estimates of levels of output and growth rates for up to 199 countries since 1000 (although obviously for far fewer countries at the start of that period) is an impressive achievement. For modern times in

---

[2]For an account of the development of national accounts, and for further references, see Stone's 1984 Nobel acceptance speech, at http://nobelprize.org/nobel_prizes/economics/laureates/1984/stone-lecture.pdf.

particular he draws on similar work by other economists, notably the Penn World Tables developed since the mid 1970s by Irving Kravis, Alan Heston, and Robert Summers. The most basic facts about the past and present of the world economy represent a half-century-long effort by very many researchers and have only become widely available since the mid 1990s.

Maddison himself spent much of a long and varied career working for the Organisation for Economic Co-operation and Development (OECD) (based in one of the ritziest *quartiers* of Paris), first on postwar reconstruction in shattered Europe, and later on economic development in other parts of the world. The OECD was the institutional embodiment of George Marshall's famous plan to rebuild Europe in order to create the "political and social conditions in which free institutions can exist." So by no means all of Maddison's career was spent burrowing in the dim stacks of obscure libraries: he traveled widely in Latin America, Asia, and Africa.

One trip, in 1965, took him with three colleagues to Guinea, independent from France since 1958. The French had left in a huff when the country opted for independence, several thousand French administrators, soldiers, and experts simply abruptly leaving a country where only fifty people out of a population of three million had higher education.[3] The new government called in help from the OECD's Development Centre. Its small emergency team of economists found themselves giving a three-week course on how to run an economy to the president, Sekou Touré, his brother Ismael, who was economic development minister, and Keita Fodeba, the defense minister and former professional dancer and founder of the national ballet, Les Ballets Africains.[4] Guinea's soldiers were involved in development work, undertaking tasks such as mending roads and making clothes and shoes. The defense minister was also responsible for policing and had set up a crack unit of traffic police for the capital, Conakry, all glamorous women who doubled as a night-club orchestra. As Maddison puts it, with admirable understatement: "Despite the chaos, it was a lively and interesting place" (see p. 13 of his autobiography (Maddison 1994)). Mongolia was another destination, where the economists stayed in Ulan Bator's only hotel. Its Yugoslav chef

---

[3] The departing French colonialists even took the lightbulbs out of government buildings and smashed windows and crockery when they left (see Meredith 2005, pp. 68, 69).

[4] The company gave its first performance at the Etoile in Paris in 1952, and continues to perform (see www.lesballetsafricains.com). Fodeba was killed, a political prisoner, in 1965.

had gone insane, so bad was the local food, and the British ambassador lived off steak and kidney puddings delivered in the diplomatic bag. He graciously shared these classic British pies with the OECD visitors.

Maddison explains in an autobiographical essay that his involvement with economic statistics, both in real time during the 1950s as countries developed their national accounts and through his work in the 1980s and 1990s developing the historical statistics, emerged out of his engagement with economic policy—which in turn had been triggered by his childhood experiences. The big question, certainly for anyone who has lived cheek by jowl with hunger and poverty as he did, is what makes an economy thrive, or fail to do so? Why *do* economies grow? Is it because of some aspect of culture, as Max Weber suggested in arguing that Protestantism explains the success of capitalism in northern Europe? Is demography destiny, as Robert Thomas Malthus and others since have thought, or is it climate, or ecology? Does colonial exploitation account for the success of the West at the expense of the rest, as many historians, notably Paul Bairoch and Fernand Braudel, have argued (Bairoch 1967; Braudel 1985)? Or does the secret lie, as economists since Adam Smith have believed, in the cumulative gains from the steady specialization of labor and increased trade? And what part is played by technology, which most people believe has an important role in modern growth; how does innovation fit with other explanations? Evidence is needed to start to judge the competing answers: which countries have in fact grown, and when? How do these patterns mesh with the proposed contributory factors, whether population growth or the dates of the Protestant Reformation or colonial conquest?

These are big questions, for the different grand theories of economic history and development are of more than theoretical interest. They point to different policies today for stimulating economic development and reducing poverty. Most of us are far more interested in sweeping arguments than in statistical detail, but it is only by looking thoroughly at the data that we can hope to reject some theories and tentatively accept others, just as scientific debates about the nature of the universe rest on the results of a thousand and one careful experiments. Angus Maddison has assembled much of the necessary evidence, establishing over the decades a network of researchers in the United States, Europe, Japan, and even the Soviet Union (when it still existed) dedicated to collecting the fundamental economic data. He calls it the "Club des Chiffrephiles," or lovers of figures. Maddison's great statistical syntheses of his work were published in 1995 and 2001, updated in 2003, so there has been relatively little time for the data to have changed the academic consensus about the contours of world economic history (Maddison 1995, 2001, 2003). But this will happen. The figures are enriching economists' understanding of what makes economies grow, and may even make it possible to reject some of the most prominent historical explanations.

CONFRONTING BIG THEORIES WITH BIG FACTS

It is possible, with the evidence published in Maddison's *The World Economy: A Millennial Perspective* and *The World Economy: Historical Statistics*, to state several "stylized facts," or valid generalizations, about the main trends in world economic history.

- There was no economic growth before 1000 C.E. This is an exaggeration, as the process of urbanization and improvements in nutrition indicate there must have been some economic progress. But it was too little to register a footprint in economy-wide GDP data.
- "The West" (as it became)[5] but not "the rest" experienced a slow but steady upward crawl in per capita incomes from 1000 up to around 1800. Elsewhere, per capita GDP was the same in 1800 as it had been eight centuries earlier, although quality of life (in terms of life expectancy for example, or new goods) had improved.
- There was a surge in per capita GDP growth after 1820 in all the countries of the West. Britain's surge happened a bit earlier.
- There was no growth surge elsewhere. This includes China, which was the world economic leader in medieval times and still on a par with western Europe at the end of the eighteenth century. Indeed, other researchers argue that China was still richer than "the West" in 1800: this remains an open statistical question. Either way, income per capita in China was about the same in 1900 as in 1300.
- The Western growth surge has continued to the present, with striking ups and downs. Ups include the period 1870-1913 and the 1950-73 "golden age," while there were marked slowdowns in 1913-1950 and after 1973.
- A few non-Western countries have subsequently attained a much faster rate of growth, including Japan and, recently, China.

---

[5] The West includes all of western Europe and the four "offshoots": the United States, Canada, Australia, and New Zealand.

As so many countries have not got to the point of a modern surge in growth, the gap in incomes per capita is the greatest it has ever been, although it increased most rapidly in the early industrial era. In 1000, western Europe lagged behind Asia and northern Africa and far behind China in income levels; by the fourteenth century, on Maddison's figures, it had caught up with world leader China; by 1820 the average Western income was two times the average of the rest, by 1900 six times, and by 2000 the gap was about seven to one.

Everyone would agree that measures of GDP per capita do not tell the whole story about economic development. So, for example, the statement about no growth before 1000 concerns measured GDP growth. It certainly does not deny the evidence of increasing human stature, decreasing infant mortality and improved hygiene, growth of cities, and other indicators pointing to economic development. It's simply that such changes, important as they are in human history, do not leave a footprint in GDP data. The upward creep in GDP per capita in those early times was too slow to register. Economists don't ignore the alternatives to GDP at all. This is a point which will recur in later chapters: many noneconomists wrongly believe that economists only care about GDP, or about incomes measured in money terms, and while this might have been true enough a decade or two ago, it is certainly no longer the case. However, these chapters are about understanding conventional GDP growth, and in this context, the most controversial issues in this list of stylized facts concern the confrontation between the figures and cherished historical theories. The pattern of growth makes grand theories look rather simplistic.

The Search for Turning Points

To take a striking example, the statistical evidence sits uncomfortably with any theory which makes 1500 the key turning point in Western economic development. Maddison's work indicates that there was no acceleration in growth in the West around that time; that came much later, around 1800 or 1820. This should surprise all of us who learnt in high-school history that the Renaissance marked a turning point for western Europe. The flourishing of the arts and sciences, the astonishing technical discoveries such as printing (the Gutenberg Bible of 1455), the great voyages by explorers like Vasco Da Gama and Christopher Columbus, the influx of silver after the conquest of the New World (Pizarro's victory over Atahuallpa in 1532)—none of these triggered accelerated growth in incomes, which continued on a long, slow upward plod for another three centuries. This does not mean that these innovations and explorations were unimportant, that they did not alter the course of human history. For example, it seems certain that access to colonial resources originating in the great voyages of discovery boosted Western growth over time. But that effect came later, in the eighteenth and nineteenth centuries, when faster growth made the additional resources necessary. The earlier era of discovery did not immediately trigger faster growth, although it facilitated it later through the accumulation of human knowledge that made economic growth possible from the eighteenth century onwards.

Yet most accounts still present the Renaissance as a decisive hinge in history. To take a recent example, in his best seller *Guns, Germs and Steel*, the physiologist and biologist Jared Diamond rests heavily on developments around 1500 to build his argument that the combination of their conquest of the New World and technological advances by Europeans explain the subsequent dominance of the West over the rest. While geography and biology made Western success possible, Diamond pegs the *timing* of Western geopolitical advance to the discoveries of the Renaissance. He describes the victory by Pizarro and 168 Spanish troops against 80,000 Indians at Cajamarca in the highlands of Peru on November 16, 1532 as "the most dramatic and decisive moment" in the clash between old world and new (see Diamond 1997, p. 354). Diamond is clearly second to none in his mastery of the sweep of scientific evidence, and there seems no doubt that ecological advantages are vital in explaining the ebb and flow of civilizations; but (even making allowance for rhetorical flourishes) the timing of the trends in his account does not quite tally with the economic evidence. It is not that his argument is incorrect, but rather that, to the extent that conquest laid the foundations for Western dominance, the process took several centuries. There was no billiardball sequence of cause and consequence. The interplay between ideas, technology, conquest, and economic success is more subtle than that.

Another tenacious theory of Western advantage rooted in the sixteenth century is the argument that cultural norms arising from the Protestant Reformation gave northern and western Europe an unsurpassable economic and political advantage. This theory originated with the economic sociologist Max Weber (1999). His famous 1904 essay "The Protestant ethic and the spirit of capitalism" argued that the work ethic and habit of thrift stemmed from the Protestant moral vision; they did not emerge in the southern Catholic swathe of Europe, where the anti-usury teachings of the Church held sway and the workers lacked conscientiousness. Weber singles out the attitude of Italian workers (especially

17

the Neapolitans, and especially the cab drivers of Naples) as a particular obstacle to capitalist development; yet Italy somehow made it into the G7 club of the world's richest economies. Another G7 member, Japan, is not a Christian country at all. So it is evident anyway that a theory pinning economic success on the Protestant religion must be very broad brush. Weber's analysis is also more subtle than many summaries would have it: he is describing a capitalist system of economic organization based on the cultural norms of the mass of the people, which is consistent with isolated eruptions of the capitalist spirit in earlier times and other places. Even so, his argument falls foul of the absence of any evidence of an acceleration in western European (or northern European) growth after 1517, when Martin Luther nailed his ninety-five theses challenging the authority of the Pope to the door of the church in Wittenburg.[6] Again, it is not that cultural change is unimportant, but rather that the role of culture in enhancing or inhibiting growth is more subtle, and gradual, than many discussions of the Protestant work ethic allow.

Theories which see the Renaissance and Reformation as a key juncture in economic history also underplay the evidence of technical improvements and growth prior to the late fifteenth century. Although there is less surviving documentary evidence (after all, the printing press hadn't yet been invented), there were important innovations in agricultural techniques (such as three-field crop rotation), in energy (watermills and windmills), and in some industries (not least in finance, with the development of accountancy and insurance), together enough to contribute to the slow crawl of growth in average incomes per capita. By 1100 the time was ripe for the emergence of the glorious Venetian Republic—not today's theme park, but the richest and most vigorous economy in western Europe between the eleventh and sixteenth centuries, one of the greatest trading nations of all time. Other Italian city states and Flanders were also among the economic leaders of the period from 1100 to 1500.

Few if any modern scholars would anyway put as much emphasis as Weber's original essay on the importance of Protestantism per se as an explanation for economic development, but the idea that growth hinges on culture remains powerful. While there is certainly nothing in the historical growth figures to rule out a role for culture in economic development, culture-based theories need to tally with the growth turning points in the West around 1000 and 1800 (but not 1500) and need to explain

---

[6]Luther (an ex-monk married to an ex-nun) was an advocate of dancing, alcohol, and extra-marital sex, so scarcely a puritan figure himself.

why a few (but not many) non-Western countries have also achieved a surge in per capita income growth subsequently.

If we are looking for simple links in time between growth and culture, the best fit comes from the classical liberal attitudes of the Enlightenment, and the scientific discoveries of the late eighteenth and early nineteenth centuries. As the economic historian Joel Mokyr emphasizes, the scientific discoveries of the Enlightenment and the importance of *ideas* do seem to mark a change of gear in the capacity for economic growth. What seems plausible, and consistent with the evidence, is a complex interplay between the development of ideas and new technologies, the social and cultural changes which accompany them, improvements in living standards which do not register in economy-wide GDP data, and finally measurable increases in the rate of economic growth. For example, for Greg Clark of UC Davis the key is a gradual accumulation of technological knowledge which, combined with fertility control, allowed some economies to escape the "Malthusian trap" at a critical point in the late eighteenth century. He believes that the historical data support a pattern of gradually increasing growth rates, rather than a sudden fissure of no growth followed by a takeoff (see Mokyr 2002; Clark 2005). Cultural influences, whether the influence of Protestantism or something else, will certainly play a part in the control of fertility and the attitude to using new technologies, but it's not a simple story. Culture, social institutions, and technology interact subtly and over long periods during which economic change may be imperceptible in aggregate figures. The effect of even decisive innovations and discoveries can take decades or centuries to appear. Economic historians are now exploring all these complexities—and I return to them in chapter 8—but the grand theories have a tenacious hold, especially outside the economics profession.

THE WEST VERSUS THE REST

One controversial clash of theories fueled by Maddison's data concerns the relative status of the West versus the rest. As we've seen, it was not until around 1800 that an acceleration of growth took western Europe into a different league from the rest of the world. This much is common ground to almost all economic historians. However, there are widely differing views about the relative prosperity of the principal economies of western Europe as against China before this parting of the ways. Maddison's estimates show the West overtaking China by 1400. Adam Smith ranked China behind the industrial leaders of western Europe when he

19

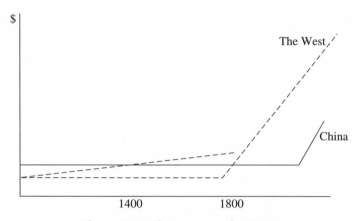

Figure 1.1. China versus the West.

wrote *The Wealth of Nations* in 1759. However, other historians such as Paul Bairoch (1967) and Kenneth Pomeranz (in an influential recent book called *The Great Divergence* (Pomeranz 2000)) rank China ahead until the turning point at the start of the nineteenth century.

This debate might seem a matter of nicety. After all, there is no disagreement about the broad pattern of the West overtaking China and other countries in living standards, and rapidly leaving the rest of the world well behind. Development economist Lant Pritchett observes that we know there has been "divergence, big time" (to quote the title of his article) between the West and the rest since the early nineteenth century (Pritchett 1997). We know today's per capita GDP. Pritchett also calculated, based essentially on the minimum calorie intake for survival, the minimum possible starting level of GDP per capita, converted into today's dollars. These two points are consistent with different growth paths, but constrain their shape. The difference between the two theories is therefore the difference between the two (very stylized) dotted growth paths for the West in figure 1.1, Maddison's being the upper branch and Pomeranz's the lower.

Does this detail of timing matter? It would seem to, because the dispute is in effect a clash of ideologies that offer contrasting explanations for growth, and therefore different conclusions for economic development policies in the future. Those who argue that China remained the world's economic leader until around 1800 see the subsequent Western growth takeoff as the direct result of European exploitation of the resources of the rest of the world, including the European colonies. On the other hand, those who think the West overtook China much earlier see nineteenth- and twentieth-century growth in the West as the acceleration of an internal process, driven by technology and social change, with rapid industrial growth creating additional demand, which could indeed be met thanks to the availability of colonial resources.

The former camp has proven extremely influential outside economics, and in particular among historians and political scientists. Some of these, including Marxist scholars, have followed Bairoch in focusing on colonial exploitation. But for many non-Marxists it is received wisdom too. The eminent French historian Fernand Braudel wrote: "It is virtually beyond question that Europe was less rich than the world it was exploiting" (Braudel 1985, volume 3, p. 533). British historian Mark Mazower argued recently that Western culture and values can have played no part in the political and economic ascendancy of the United States and western Europe since the end of the Cold War precisely because they do not explain past economic leadership. In a newspaper article predicting the end of this Western ascendancy and a return to a world of multiple centers of power, he wrote: "In 1800, China's gross national product was probably still higher than Europe's.... [I]f the West's rise is no more than two centuries old, its success may owe more to contingency and less to values than its cheerleaders believe. For states, as for stock markets, what goes up may also come down" (from "The West needs a new sense of self," *Financial Times*, March 31, 2005). Mazower's concern was to challenge the presumption that economic success depends on the adoption of Western values, a presumption which indeed characterizes the off-putting triumphalism of some Western commentators in recent times.

Kenneth Pomeranz's book offers the most thorough and detailed argument in favor of China's continuing economic superiority up to 1800. He argues that growth processes were similar everywhere up to then, making the world economy "polycentric." About that time, the pressures of growth started to cause widespread ecological scarcity, but the Europeans were able to overcome this barrier through colonization and armed trade, while Britain was uniquely well-placed to industrialize thanks to its coal reserves. His book offers a wealth of supporting evidence on both the Chinese and European economies, emphasizing that calorie intake and other indicators such as longevity and agricultural output (such as the amount of manure used by farmers) point to the Yangzi delta region of China remaining one of the leading world economies up to the end of the eighteenth century.

Maddison is simply dismissive of Pomeranz's claims, describing them as "guesstimates" before going on to say: "He was, in fact, fabricating ammunition for this hypothesis [that China was well ahead of western Europe in 1800]." More politely, he suggests that Pomeranz is misled by his Sinophilia, and concludes that his own work confirms that the assertion of late Chinese superiority or parity is "quite wrong."

What are those of us unable to explore the historical statistics for ourselves to conclude? The balance of more recent evidence on comparative living standards in Asia and Europe tilts in favor of Maddison (Broadberry and Gupta 2006; Allen et al. 2004; Landes 2006). This evidence draws on another international collaboration on the basic statistics of world economic history, in this case collecting price and wage data. The original hero of this piece of detective work is the British economist Lord William Beveridge, better known for writing the blueprint for Britain's welfare system and health service after World War II. Beveridge was a prominent member of the British establishment long before the Labour minister for postwar reconstruction summoned him, in 1941, to chair an interdepartmental committee on social insurance.[7] Born in India (the son of a colonial judge) in 1879, educated at Charterhouse and Oxford, he had been, as well as a leading public servant, a broadcaster and newspaper columnist, an eminent academic, and a social worker and researcher among the poor of London's East End. He had all the confidence one might expect of a man of his talents and his social status in Edwardian Britain. Revealingly, he titled his autobiography *Power and Influence* (Beveridge 1968).

In 1929 Beveridge was director of the London School of Economics. With Harvard economics professor Edwin Gay, he proposed an "International Scientific Committee on Price History," which would collect comparable historical data covering, initially, five countries. The pair put in a bid for funding from the Rockefeller Foundation, and must have been convincing. They were granted $50,000 a year for five years—more than $600,000 a year in 2006 dollars. At once a team of researchers started work collecting figures on wages and the prices of foodstuffs and other goods, starting with Britain, Germany, France, Austria, and the United States (Cole and Crandall 1964). The primary sources included records from medieval manors, from religious and charitable foundations such

---

[7]Beveridge was at first bitterly disappointed to be given this dull task. Although he used the position to reshape postwar British society, he had wanted to be given a leading role planning the war effort instead. For more detail on Beveridge's contribution to posterity, see the outstanding book by Nicholas Timmins (1995).

as Westminster Abbey and Eton College, town corporation accounts from around the country, the Office of Royal Works, and hospitals, including Bethlem Royal Hospital, or Bedlam as it is better known. In time other scholars and countries joined the network. Remarkably, the project had run out of money by 1933, and the events of the 1930s intervened; but researchers continued to collect the data into the 1960s. The results still form the core of modern historical analysis of living standards prior to the nineteenth century.

A recent successor project, aiming to develop global price indices from 1200 to 1950, includes economists from St Petersburg to New York, Oxford to Istanbul. The main challenge is making comparisons between countries, especially for periods when units of measurement were non-standard. The intention is to have data for sixty places in six continents going back to the middle ages, and to include prices for a wider range of goods and services than has been available before. The statistics are being compiled into spreadsheets for the use of other researchers.

Figures on prices and wages give an alternative perspective from measures of GDP per person. Both the purchasing power of workers' pay and national output per capita are (imperfect) indicators of living standards, so data on wages and prices might allow us to adjudicate between the divergent claims based on GDP data concerning Chinese and European economic leadership. Past research has focused on laborers' wages and on grain prices; after all, the ability of ordinary people to buy food seems a fundamental indicator of well-being. However, economic historians Stephen Broadberry and Bishnupriya Gupta have compared Asian and European wages not only in terms of how much grain but also how much silver they could purchase over the centuries (Broadberry and Gupta 2006). They conclude that the purchasing power of wages in terms of *grain* was roughly the same in the advanced parts of China, India, and Europe until about 1800—in effect the same conclusion as Pomeranz, who compared calorie consumption and looked at health indicators related to calorie intake, such as life expectancy.[8] But using Pomeranz's figures on Chinese wages and prices, and the International Scientific Committee's wage and price history evidence for Europe, Broadberry and Gupta show that the amount of *silver* that laborers could purchase was very much higher in northwestern Europe than in the Yangzi delta by 1800. The gap is so large that it cannot be corrected or finessed away

---

[8]Although Maddison argues that the life expectancy figures he used are incorrect (see Maddison 2001, p. 39).

by different statistical assumptions. What does it mean that the "grain wage" was roughly equal in both China and Europe, but the "silver wage" was much higher in Europe? It means that workers in Europe had much greater purchasing power over other goods and services, which might include bread rather than grain in the cities, but also textiles and household goods and a wide range of other items.

Supporting evidence that European consumers were indeed growing much better off in terms of purchasing power over other goods from at least 1500 onwards comes from the new Global Price Project. The prices of luxury goods, such as soap, candles, and writing paper, for example, declined relative to the price of grain throughout Europe. The authors say: "Given that the price of books seems to have plummeted in England and France, it is plausible to imagine the supply of these knowledge goods contributed to the rise of Northwest Europe as a center of knowledge." Whether that is correct or not, the evidence is that northwestern Europe experienced productivity gains outside agriculture that gave people their increasing purchasing power over items other than nonstaple foods. This is consistent with other historical evidence such as higher rates of urbanization in the European core from the sixteenth century onwards—urbanization being highly correlated with economic development—and evidence from wills and other sources that many people were gaining access to a much greater quantity and range of possessions from that time. While the Great Divergence, when European growth accelerated so dramatically, occurred around 1800, its origins lay in the preceding two or three centuries of divergent living standards. There seems only a modest amount of room for doubt that the West, not China, was already the world economic leader when the era of modern industrial growth began.

ECONOMIC LEADERSHIP IN THE WEST

To be precise, a small number of countries in northwestern Europe, notably Britain and Holland, held a clear lead. China resembled the lagging countries within Europe in its standard of living. This early leadership of a small number of countries within Europe opens a route to distinguishing between competing explanations of the sources of economic growth, given that comparable data over a very long period are available for the European economies. Robert Allen of Nuffield College, Oxford, one of the participants in the Global Price Comparison project, has used five centuries' worth of data (1300–1800) precisely in order to rank the favored historical explanations using a small macroeconometric model (Allen 2003). Consisting of five simultaneous equations, and treating potential explanations for growth as exogenous factors, this might seem a rather crude approach to the subtleties of history but has the merit of ruling out explanations which are grossly inconsistent with the empirical evidence. There is sufficient difference between the evolution of what became the leading economies of 1800—Britain and Holland— and the others—Austria, France, Germany, Italy, Spain, and Poland—to make the econometric approach feasible.

What is it that marks out the two leading nations? One feature is that real wages (that is, wages adjusted for price rises) grew more rapidly there, opening up an increasing gap with the other countries in workers' purchasing power. Real wages rose as the population was growing too. This indicates that, for the first time, rapid economic growth had sprung the two countries out of the Malthusian trap. (Malthus, in his hugely influential book, argued that any time wages started to rise, people would have more children, and that increase in the number of workers would in turn reduce wages back to subsistence level. He saw the only potential escape as abstinence from making babies. More on this in the next chapter.)

A second feature of the leading economies is that they had experienced more substantial structural change, in particular a sharp fall in the proportion of the population working in agriculture. Hand in hand with this went greater urbanization, early industrial development (in woollen textiles, for example), and increases in agricultural productivity.

These five economic variables (the real wage, population growth, industrial development, urbanization, and agricultural productivity) are clearly linked, and Allen tests the potential explanatory factors most often put forward:

- the amount of land relative to the population (the Malthusian explanation of limited natural resources to feed the workforce);
- the enclosure movement (usually said to have triggered greater productivity in agriculture);
- literacy (representing increases in human capital);
- constitutional rather than autocratic government (because political institutions might matter for economic success);
- imperialism (exploitation of colonial resources to escape the Malthusian trap);

25

- earlier urbanization (growth and urbanization are linked, but the direction of causality is open to question);
- amount of trade (permitting specialization and the benefits of comparative advantage);
- innovation and productivity in manufacturing (new technologies make it possible to produce more from the same inputs of labor, capital, and land).

It turns out that statistically only the last three variables, and of these primarily growth in trade and productivity gains, explain the countries' different paths of real wages, population, and output growth between 1300 and 1800. Differences between countries in the other variables do not match differences in their patterns of growth.

The satisfying aspect of this result is that it links the analysis of the past to the economics of growth in the present. As we will see in the next chapter, technological change plays the starring role in growth theory now, thanks in large part to the accumulation of evidence from historical statistics. But many historians have emphasized political, cultural, and social rather than technological explanations for economic development in the past. Those who emphasize technology are relatively rare. Two of the best known are Paul David (1991) and David Landes (2003). Another is Joel Mokyr of Northwestern University. In his book *The Gifts of Athena: Historical Origins of the Knowledge Economy*, he writes:

> The roots of twentieth century prosperity were in the industrial revolutions of the nineteenth, but those were precipitated by the intellectual changes of the Enlightenment that preceded them. To create a world in which "useful" knowledge was indeed *used* with an aggressiveness and single-mindedness that no other society had experienced before was the unique Western way that created the material world.
>
> Mokyr (2002, p. 297)

Innovation drives growth. This certainly does not mean other factors are unimportant, just that they are not all-important. Culture, society, and politics have to be invoked to explain why some countries can use new ideas and others cannot, why some do experience a growth takeoff and others do not, but the interplay is likely to be subtle (see Easterlin 2000). Why not China in 1500 or 1800 (and why in 1980)? Why in Britain first, a small, damp, and chilly island at a northerly latitude on the very edge of the European continent? And why just a bit later in some of its neighboring countries—but not elsewhere for another century?

THE INDUSTRIAL REVOLUTION AND BRITISH EXCEPTIONALISM

I have a special enthusiasm for the Industrial Revolution, having grown up in its cradle, the Lancashire cotton textiles city of Manchester in the northwest of England. The spinning jenny and the mule, innovative techniques for spinning, were invented near to my birthplace, and took their place alongside rank upon rank of the new power looms in the huge new factories of Victorian England. More than a century later my parents and aunts and uncles still worked in the cotton industry, although it was declining rapidly by my childhood. We were taught a local pride in Lancashire's industrial past at my school. But now only museums testify to the region's early nineteenth-century world economic leadership. Just as the pitheads are gone from coal mining areas, and the slag heaps landscaped, so the physical evidence of the cotton past has almost entirely vanished, except in the old warehouses converted to expensive apartments.

Cotton and iron; canals and railways; coal mining and steam power—the sinews of the Industrial Revolution. It is accounts of these leading sectors which dominate historical narratives of Britain's economic record, and rightly so. The country had a head start of two or three decades before the rest of "the West" followed it on the path of industrial growth, but only a few decades more before it was overtaken by Germany and, decisively, the United States as the world's leading economy. (We British therefore have a longer tradition than any other nation on Earth of fretting about our economic decline.)

The outline of post-1800 growth set out by Maddison—the sharp acceleration compared with the past, from about 1800 in Britain and from about 1820 in the other northwestern European economies—is widely accepted. Strangely, perhaps, the controversy in this area is about whether British growth during the late eighteenth and nineteenth centuries was high enough, according to the best estimates, to qualify as a revolution. Strange, in the sense that it is completely obvious that whatever the statistics for GDP growth, the economies and societies of Britain and the rest of the world were changed utterly by industrialization. The economic historians associated with the so-called "revisionist" view—that GDP growth was not as rapid as earlier estimates suggested—themselves speak of the "fundamental transformation" of Britain between 1750 and 1850, a transformation so dramatic as to remain historically unique. There is no revolutionary threshold rate of GDP growth: above $x\%$ you have a revolution, below it none. On the contrary, it is more sensible to define revolutionary economic growth as that which involves a restructuring of economic output and therefore of the social relationships which form the context for economic activity. The pace of growth needed to trigger such change might well vary according to time and place.

The leading "revisionists" (although their revisions of the earlier consensus are in fact the new consensus) are Nicholas Crafts, Professor of Economics at the London School of Economics, and C. Knick (short for Knickerbocker) Harley, of the University of Western Ontario. Crafts is a native of Mansfield, a former coal mining town in Britain's Midlands and therefore one of the vitally important cradles of the Industrial Revolution in Britain. Their research (initially separate) shows that those revolutionary changes in technology and the adoption of the factory system, which so captured the imagination of contemporary writers and artists as well as those of our own time, were not widespread. Outside the leading sectors of the economy, there were only modest improvements in productivity. From 1780 to 1830, they conclude, growth in the rest of the economy was very low. They estimate that GDP growth was on average about 1.4% a year from 1780 to 1800, rising to just under 2% a year from 1800 to 1830. These are substantially lower than earlier estimates, which had been widely used by economic historians. Those estimates, produced in the early 1960s, placed too much weight on the rapidly growing new sectors, mainly cotton, in constructing estimates for the output of the economy as a whole.

The earlier figures were published by Phyllis Deane and W. A. Cole in their 1962 volume *British Economic Growth, 1688-1959*. This was a hugely influential book, used by the next generation of economists and historians (and published just as Angus Maddison took a leave of absence from the OECD to write his first book, *Economic Growth in the West*). Its influence was enhanced by the simultaneous publication of *British Historical Statistics*, edited by Brian Mitchell with Phyllis Deane, giving the statistical raw material and describing the sources. It was a pioneering work of quantitative economic history, and one of the first to paint a picture of a gradual acceleration in British growth, dating back to at least the early eighteenth century and gaining momentum later in the nineteenth century. Although the figures turned out to be too high, this is consistent with Maddison's picture of slow, steady growth over a long period, giving way to an acceleration after 1800. In other words, the momentum for rapid growth is internally generated by an initial period of slower growth, and there is no special role for an external trigger.

Although the more subdued Crafts–Harley estimates of British growth were initially somewhat controversial because they overturned a classic text, the finding that new technologies fuel growth in just a few leading sectors is consistent with Allen's findings, described above, on the sequence of the growth takeoff: innovation, trade in manufactured goods, restructuring of the economy toward tradables, induced improvements in agricultural productivity, sustained population growth with rising real wages. Just as in the controversy over the relative position of China and Europe in 1800, the resolution of the academic debate over the rates of growth which transformed Britain into the world's first industrial economy favors conventional economic analysis. What is important is the restructuring of economic activity according to relative productivity changes in different sectors, and the opportunities afforded by trade to exploit the resulting comparative advantage. The West escaped from Malthusian growth, which had been driven by land and population; this gave way to modern growth based on technical change, capital accumulation, and trade. Political and cultural factors, such as religion or colonialism, are not the proximate causes of growth, although they explain the capacity of a society to implement technical innovations or to overcome natural resource constraints as growth accelerates (see Clark (2005) for a recent overview).

The detailed, dare I say dull, work of economists and statisticians in recent decades, rooted in an international effort to collect reliable data on the distant and recent past, has clarified this process. The empirical evidence quite clearly rules out simple grand theories, and demonstrates that economic growth stems from the relative productivity changes and specialization based on technological innovation and trade. Politics, society, and culture matter for growth because they affect the extent to which a particular economy uses its technological and trading opportunities. But they don't "explain" growth.

The next chapter turns to growth theory and the modern experience of growth. But first, one other empirical point is worth emphasizing. Crafts and Harley observe that: "The impact of fundamental innovations on economic growth is often modest for a surprisingly long time" (Crafts and Harley 1992, p. 716; see also Crafts 1991). The conventional measure of the productivity attributable to technical innovations (total factor productivity) does not change very much very quickly in response to technologies and ideas which might eventually have a very large impact on output and prices. The figures for productivity increases might be small even when the eventual impact on growth (and society) is large.

The sense that some numbers are too small to bear the weight of the expectations placed on them reappeared with a vengeance in the late 1980s, when those who were skeptical about the impact of computers argued that the new information and communication technologies (ICTs) couldn't be important because their impact on measured productivity and growth rates was too small. Robert Solow, the jovial, larger-than-life MIT economist, who won the Nobel memorial prize for his work on the theory of growth, famously referred to this as the "productivity paradox."[9] In a revealing paper, Nicholas Crafts (2004) compared the effects of ICTs on productivity growth in their first twenty years with the early impacts of steam in the mid nineteenth century and electricity in the early twentieth century. The figures for ICTs were larger. This makes it hard to sustain the argument that ICTs are economically trivial unless you believe that steam and electricity were also unimportant. In a series of papers Paul David, of Oxford and Stanford Universities, described in some detail the adoption of the cluster of innovations associated with electricity, especially the dynamo. His work confirms that revolutionary innovations have what seem to be small impacts on growth for a long time, for decades. David coined the term "technological presbyopia"— just as middle-aged people find they are too farsighted to read small print up close, and too nearsighted to have good distance vision, people tend to overestimate the short-run impact of new technologies, and expect immediate revolution, but underestimate the long-run impact, which *is* revolutionary. More on the impact of ICTs in the next chapter.

MODERN UPS AND DOWNS

Let me end this chapter by bringing the historical evidence up to date, as a prelude to the next chapter on growth theory. The data on growth are more readily available for more countries in the industrial era. Maddison's division into these periods in modern times is uncontroversial (see table 1.1). (These figures compare with Maddison's estimates of world average growth rates of 0.15% for the period 1000–1500 and 0.32% for 1500–1820.) The fastest world growth, and Western growth, occurred in this "golden age" (the French call the postwar years *les trentes glorieuses*). The following period is widely thought of as one of slowdown and dismal performance—many left-wing or Marxist analysts describe the late 1970s

---

[9]"You can see the productivity miracle everywhere but the statistics" he wrote in his article "We'd better watch out," *New York Times Book Review*, July 12, 1987.

Table 1.1. Growth in modern times.

Years		Average annual world growth (%)
1973–2001	The "neoliberal order"	3.05
1950–73	The "golden age"	4.90
1913–50	War and Depression	1.82
1870–1913	The "liberal order"	2.11
1820–70	The takeoff	0.93

as a "crisis of capitalism"; yet 1973–98 recorded the second-fastest average growth. With the benefit of hindsight, it turned out to be a crisis of communism instead. There has been an acceleration in a few Western economies since 1998; there has been a deterioration in economic performance in the former communist countries and in some African countries. The third-best-performing period was the "liberal order," the first era of free trade and globalization, 1870–1913. The years of war and depression saw weaker growth by comparison, but the weakest period of all came during the "revolutionary" takeoff years of the early nineteenth century.

This helter-skelter account of world economic history has brought us to the twentieth century. During the previous hundred years parts of Europe and then some of its colonial offshoots—especially the United States—had seen the fastest growth anywhere, ever. By 1913 the leading economies had incomes per capita about nine times greater than the rest of the world. That some of them had vast colonial empires reinforced the prosperity of their middle classes. As Maynard Keynes wrote in a justly famous passage:

> Life offered, at a low cost and with the least trouble, conveniences, comforts, and amenities beyond the compass of the richest and most powerful monarchs of other ages. The inhabitant of London could order by telephone, sipping his morning tea in bed, the various products of the whole earth, in such quantity as he might see fit, and reasonably expect their early delivery upon his doorstep; he could at the same moment and by the same means adventure his wealth in the natural resources and new enterprises of any quarter of the world, and share, without exertion or even trouble, in their prospective fruits and advantages; or he could decide to couple the security of his fortunes with the good faith of the townspeople of any substantial municipality in any continent that fancy or information might recommend. He could secure forthwith, if he wished it, cheap and comfortable means of transit to any country or climate without passport or other formality, could despatch his

servant to the neighboring office of a bank for such supply of the precious metals as might seem convenient, and could then proceed abroad to foreign quarters, without knowledge of their religion, language, or customs, bearing coined wealth upon his person, and would consider himself greatly aggrieved and much surprised at the least interference. But, most important of all, he regarded this state of affairs as normal, certain, and permanent, except in the direction of further improvement, and any deviation from it as aberrant, scandalous, and avoidable.

Keynes (1995, chapter 2)

World War I brought this happy situation to an abrupt and bloody end. While economic growth in the leading countries stayed high by comparison with the past for the remainder of the twentieth century, there were also quite striking ups and downs in growth in the West; a few takeoffs, in East Asia, but only a few; and the growth and collapse of the formerly communist planned economies. The next chapter turns to the theory of economic growth, to see how well economists are able to explain these events, and the modern patterns of growth. At the heart of the quest to explain them lies the interplay between ideas and economic activity.

ECONOMISTS: PASSIONATE NERDS

The quest to tackle glaring economic problems—poverty, hunger, human misery—is what makes growth the central issue in economics, and certainly motivates many empirically minded economists. People whose own discipline is nonempirical often misunderstand economists who dive into the statistical detail. After all, there is something unattractively nerdy about this predilection. Take, for example, Charles Fisher, a business historian who founded the study of the North American railroads, collecting timetables, tickets, samples of rails and locomotive bells, and creating the riveting *Rail and Locomotive Historical Society Bulletin*, all while earning a living as an insurance salesman (see Cole 1974). Who would have wanted to sit next to him at a dinner party? Yet it is a mistake to think intense focus on the detail signifies a lack of concern about the big issues. On the contrary, the leading empirical economists are motivated precisely by their engagement with the most profound social challenges; taking the utmost care with statistical evidence is testament to their philosophical and moral engagement and not, as many critics of economics assume, the opposite.

Angus Maddison is one of many whose passion to understand the world and change it (to paraphrase that famous economic *theorist* Karl

Marx) has led them deep into the thickets of statistical evidence. There are plenty of others: I will single out a handful of the best known. One is James Heckman, joint winner with Daniel McFadden of the 2000 Nobel memorial prize in economics for pathbreaking work in micro-econometrics, the application of statistical techniques to large sets of data on individual behavior. Many economists bear a similarity to other nerdy professionals such as computer scientists or engineers, more at ease in front of their computer than at a cocktail party; Heckman, Professor of Economics at the University of Chicago, falls into this category. He is extreme in his refusal to offer conclusions not based on an exhaustive analysis of the statistical evidence, and awesome in his ability to sift and process such evidence. This can make him demanding to work with (as I learnt when commissioning him to write about the economic impact of educational policies in Scotland (Coyle et al. 2005); his demands for data included all possible transport options between Heathrow Airport and Edinburgh, down to alternative car hire details, even though we strongly advised the easy connecting flight).[10] In his Nobel autobiographical essay, Heckman says the shock of moving from Chicago to the American south in 1956, at the age of twelve, and seeing the extent of segregation in his new home was the origin of his interest in policies to improve the status of specific disadvantaged groups in society such as African-Americans (http://nobelprize.org/economics/laureates/2000/heckman-autobio.html (March 21, 2005)). This lifelong vocation still keeps him poring over statistics in a quest for policies which will improve people's lives.

Paul Krugman, another outstanding although controversial empirical economist, attributes his career choice to reading the Isaac Asimov Foundation Trilogy as a shy teenager in the New Jersey suburbs of the 1960s. The heroes of Asimov's series are "psychohistorians," social scientists who use their mathematical expertise and analysis of trends to predict the future and save civilization. Krugman writes:

> In my early teens my secret fantasy was to become a psychohistorian. Unfortunately, there's no such thing (yet). I was and am fascinated by history, but the craft of history is far better at the what and the when than the why, and I eventually wanted more. As for social sciences other than economics, I am interested in their subjects but cannot get excited about their methods—the power of economic models to show how plausible assumptions yield surprising conclusions, to distill clear insights

---

[10]Professor Heckman took the flight.

from seemingly murky issues, has no counterpart yet in political science or sociology. Someday there will exist a unified social science of the kind that Asimov imagined, but for the time being economics is as close to psychohistory as you can get.

www.wws.princeton.edu/~pkrugman/incidents.html (March 21, 2005)

Krugman was also influenced by a trip to advise the Portuguese government in 1976, in the aftermath of a revolution and attempted coup. He says: "My experience in a country in which it was a major challenge even to decide whether output was rising or falling gave me a lasting allergy to models that tell you that a potentially useful policy exists without giving you any way to determine what that policy is."[11]

A third example is Nobel winner Joseph Stiglitz, formerly chairman of Bill Clinton's Council of Economic Advisers and later chief economist at the World Bank. Stiglitz has become a favorite of campaigners on globalization, following his departure from the World Bank and publication of a book highly critical of the Bank and the International Monetary Fund (IMF). This made him popular with left-wing critics of "neoliberalism," although Stiglitz's views are vastly more sophisticated than those of the anticapitalists. Indeed, he won his Nobel memorial prize for his research into how markets depend on flows of information, and sees markets as flawed but all-important. Earlier in his career Stiglitz had spent a sabbatical term at Oxford University. His only teaching burden was to give eight hours of lectures. As Oxford has an eight-week term, it was clearly intended that he would lecture for one hour a week. Instead, in what was no doubt a manifestation of genius, Stiglitz lectured for eight hours in one day to discharge the obligation and have the rest of the term free for research.[12] Stiglitz is driven passionately by a concern to understand why poor countries have not grown, and to change that, which has helped make him so popular among antipoverty campaigners.

It is invidious to single out just a few prominent economists, though. In economics, as in the other sciences, the state of knowledge advances because of the efforts of many researchers. "We are still on that voyage launched by Adam Smith's title, *An Inquiry into the Nature and Causes of the Wealth of Nations*" (Allen et al. 2004, p. 4). All of the evidence described in this chapter was produced as the result of the long and

---

[11]"Why I'm an economist", available at www.pkarchive.org, accessed May 25, 2006.

[12]This anecdote is widely told. It was confirmed for me by Anthony Venables, now of the London School of Economics, who attended the marathon. He says it was a brilliant lecture.

detailed work of teams of researchers. In this collective quest to answer the central questions—What explains growth? Why do I see poverty cheek by jowl with wealth? Why do other women have to suffer the heartbreak of their children dying so often in infancy? Why do other people go hungry?—it is hard to overstate the importance of the painstaking statistical detective work in assembling the figures on past growth performance of many countries. It is the equivalent of the detailed forensic search of the crime scene and the dull door-to-door and telephone enquiries made by the police—this, rather than the brilliant insights of a charismatic detective, is what solves crimes. Similarly, tracking down figures in manuscripts and figuring out how to convert varas into braccios (both units of measurement of cloth around 1600) is what might refute one grand theory of history or offer support to another.

The international networks of economic historians collaborating on collecting data and applying this evidence to competing theories makes economics from the 1930s onwards comparable with many of the natural sciences. The acquisition of historical evidence is fundamental to economic science in the same way as it is to other largely nonexperimental sciences such as geology or ecology. The economy at the aggregate level cannot be understood through controlled experiments (although individual economic behavior and individual markets can and are being experimentally analyzed, as we shall see later). The statistics on output, growth, and other key variables for many countries and for long periods are now publicly available in a standard and internationally comparable format, developed with great rigor through massive international cooperation. It is only in the past decade that this evidence has become available for all researchers to use. The evidence rejects some common historical oversimplifications in favor of a richer and subtler understanding of how economies change. According to Asimov's *Encyclopedia Galactica*, psychohistory is "That branch of mathematics which deals with the reactions of human conglomerates to fixed social and economic stimuli." Although economics is still far from achieving this kind of predictive power, Angus Maddison and others like him have a good claim to be considered the first psychohistorians.

What Makes Economies Grow?

Economic growth is an unusual phenomenon—at least, growth as we normally think about it now, "modern" growth with output expanding fast enough for one generation to have living standards far beyond those of the previous generation, and with extraordinary innovations which improve our health and longevity. It has, after all, only a 200-year record even in the West. What's more, about twenty poor countries have been experiencing declining output per capita, negative growth, since the 1970s. Dozens of countries, including Nigeria and Pakistan, for example, have not yet attained the level of income per capita the United States had achieved by 1870. So one answer to the question posed in the title of this chapter must be that we're not entirely sure, or every economy would be growing.

It might seem dubious to claim any theoretical certainty about the causes, the more time passes without all countries being able to achieve modern growth. Nevertheless, economics now has a theoretical analysis of growth which explains the empirical record reasonably well and also explains why it is difficult for an economy to get to the point where growth begins. It also exemplifies a characteristic new way of thinking about other issues in economics, such as international trade, industrial organization, or geographical location. This new generation of models has moved the economics profession decisively on from the familiar neoclassical framework which dominated for the second half of the twentieth century, a framework much criticized by noneconomists. The new approach in this particular context is broadly known as endogenous growth theory, and will occupy much of this chapter. These growth models are one example of this new generation of modeling in the fields of industrial organization, trade theory, and economic geography.

Readers can be forgiven a natural skepticism about the claim that, after a couple of centuries, economists have finally cracked the mystery of growth, the holy grail of policy makers. If so, why isn't the whole world growing at last? The answer is that getting an economy to expand is more like dancing than cooking. The frequently used metaphor of finding the right "policy recipe" is misleading. Theoretical knowledge is only a small first step toward practical success. It is not possible to set down a simple list of ingredients and a technique anyone could follow. Rather, getting an economy expanding in the way the rich countries already have for the past 200 years depends on a complex sequence of decisions and policies, involving many partners and depending on past choices, current resources, and pure luck.

As for why it took so long for economists to get close to a good theory of growth, one important reason has been the lack of data until quite recently. Over time, it has steadily become more apparent what the empirical predictions of a good theory need to be. The model of growth most economists used through the 1960s into the 1980s seemed to fit the then-available evidence reasonably well. Before the mid 1990s— as we saw in the last chapter—the extensive historical data and cross-country evidence were not available to test and inform the theory. Nor was there enough computer power to make testing theories easy. One of the themes throughout this book will be the importance of new data sets, cheap computer power, and the development of econometric techniques in the current renaissance in economics. That's as true in growth theory as it is in other fields.

A second explanation for the renaissance in growth theory in the late 1980s lies in the renewed interest in the impact of new technologies when it started to become apparent that computer power was becoming cheap and pervasive. Unsurprisingly, the question of the role of innovation came to the fore once again. Growth in the rich industrialized economies had slowed down in the mid 1970s; might the new technologies improve the trend again? At the same time, politics in some big economies—step forward and take a bow Mr. Reagan and Mrs. Thatcher—had taken a decisive turn toward deregulation. Globalization was well underway, with rapid increases in trade and foreign investment. Meanwhile the planned, communist economies were clearly in crisis. The sheer pressure of events always shapes theory, and the unfolding of the 1980s led economists to think once again about the fundamental question of their subject: how does the process of growth work, and can it be influenced by policies? But let's start well before the 1980s.

CLASSICAL GROWTH

With hindsight, the Industrial Revolution is clearly where the explanation for growth must be sought, but that wasn't so obvious in the 1780s.

37

Needless to say, the earliest explanations about why output in Britain, the Netherlands, and France had started to grow much faster than population, and why real wages and living standards were growing, did not have much evidence to go on. Just about the earliest systematic theory was devised by French intellectuals known as the physiocrats or *economistes*, of whom the best known is François Quesnay. Quesnay seems to have been a remarkable character, born into a poor family, illiterate until the age of eleven, orphaned at thirteen. He taught himself medicine and eventually became, by way of being a country surgeon, personal physician to Madame de Pompadour, the influential mistress of Louis XV. He ended his days living at the Palace of Versailles, a member of the Académie des Sciences and a star among intellectuals, the Bernard-Henri Lévy of his day. Quesnay is remembered for his *Tableau œconomique*, a theoretical analysis of the circulation of the country's output among the different classes in society. The physiocrats believed there was scope for productive labor to create an agricultural surplus over and above the nation's subsistence needs. This surplus they attributed to the bounty of nature rather than to productivity gains achieved by the inventiveness of people. They concluded, wrongly with hindsight, that a large agricultural sector was therefore the foundation of economic growth. As we saw in the last chapter, a rapid move away from agriculture as it becomes more productive characterizes the transition to economic growth. Productivity growth in one sector of the economy means it will shrink, rather than grow, as a proportion of the total. Fewer people can produce a given amount of output, so its employment share will shrink. If demand for the output rises by proportionately less than income (the elasticity of demand is less than 1), which is certainly true of food, then its share of total output will also shrink.[1]

Empiricist British thinkers disagreed with the abstract French, despite the deep similarities in their philosophies, firmly rooted in the Enlightenment in both cases. One of the most influential was Robert Thomas Malthus. He was a country parson and Cambridge academic (although he had to resign his fellowship at Jesus College when he got married in 1804, going on to father three children, a modest number for the time). He first published his "Essay on the principle of population" in 1798—with hindsight, again, at exactly the moment in history when it ceased

---

[1] The same arguments apply to the tenacious superstition that manufacturing is now shrinking "too much" in countries like the United States and the United Kingdom.

to apply universally.[2] His logic was that if people were not starving, the "passion between the sexes" would lead to an increase in the rate of population growth. More mouths to feed would at once return people to the serious business of scrabbling for their next meal. Given that yields on land declined the more intensively it was farmed, or the more of the less fertile land was brought into use, at some point increased population growth would exceed growth in food supplies, and population growth would decline again. Not only logical, but also consistent with all of the past. It also earned economics the description "the dismal science" from historian Thomas Carlyle.

Malthus was one of a number of stellar British economists, including David Hume, David Ricardo, and of course Adam Smith, who laid the foundations for classical economics. Smith's views are now claimed by many others in support of their own. To most noneconomists, he is associated with free market, laissez faire, right-wing and minimal-state opinions.[3] It is certainly true that, in common with many Enlightenment thinkers, Smith's aim was to justify individual freedoms and restrain arbitrary acts by the state. In terms of his contribution to understanding "the nature and causes of the wealth of nations," his central point is that growth depends on the division of labor or specialization. The scope for this will vary from country to country, depending on technology and organization as well as the government, although much modern comment on *The Wealth of Nations* focuses on this latter question of whether free competition or government regulation of industry has the upper hand. Smith noted that industry in general offered more scope than agriculture for specialization, and that the richer countries had more industry than the poorer ones. However, even though Smith knew James Watt, who spectacularly improved the steam engine, *The Wealth of Nations* largely ignores the technological innovations of the time—such as the flying shuttle, spinning jenny, and mule—and is rather scathing about innovators in general. Perhaps this is not surprising: there were only twenty to thirty factories big enough to employ as many as 300 workers when the book was published in 1784. Instead, Smith saw growth resulting from the process of exchange in the context of a market, organized by that famous "invisible hand." The fruits of specialization in labor could

---

[2] And indeed, Malthus realized this and changed later editions.

[3] See Peter Dougherty's *Who's Afraid of Adam Smith: How the Market Got Its Soul* for an outstanding analysis of what's wrong with this caricature.

be amplified by exchanging with others in trade. He was right, but he overlooked the role of technology in the tale.

Adam Smith seems to have been, like so many economists today, somewhat awkward socially, happiest poring over his books (there being no computers available at the time). Who knows what he would have made of the modern cottage industry selling ties and mugs bearing his portrait, raising funds for the cause of laissez faire. Yet his work had an immediate impact on opinion and policy at the time, and he remains one of the most famous economists ever. His analysis was greatly extended and updated by the less-famous David Ricardo and John Stuart Mill. Ricardo made familiar the notion of diminishing returns: that bringing additional acres of land into use would generate a diminishing increase in output as a result. Ricardo also extended the analysis of the benefits of exchange to the context of international trade, introducing here the idea of comparative advantage.[4] (The next chapter will return to questions of trade and openness.)

Classical economics was summed up in the bible of late-nineteenth-century economics, John Stuart Mill's *Principles of Political Economy*. It was published in 1848 and was still in use as a textbook in 1900. The analysis of growth was not one of its strengths either. Mill wrote disdainfully: "I am not charmed with the idea of life held out by those who think that the normal state of human beings is that of struggling to get on." He argued that the government should limit the pace of technical change, and was in favor of cooperatives and profit sharing. Like anyone with a shred of sensitivity and imagination, he was clearly moved by the horrors of rapid industrialization, the poverty and misery so visible in the thrusting new cities of Victorian Britain.

So too were Friedrich Engels and Karl Marx. It stirred them to write the *Communist Manifesto*. Engels was a wealthy cotton mill owner, so he knew at first hand observing his own workforce what others discovered from novelists like Charles Dickens and Elizabeth Gaskell. Marx of course drew rather more radical policy conclusions from his observations of the process of industrialization. But in contrast to Mill, and the mainstream economics tradition, he did focus on the process of growth, giving a central role to the accumulation of capital (hence the title of his weighty text, *Das Kapital*), and specifically to technology. This makes him seem rather modern. Paradoxically, there was a revival of interest in Marxist

---

[4]Although the passages in his work on comparative advantage were almost certainly written by James Mill (see Blaug 1996, p. 132).

economics in the dot-com 1990s, just after the collapse of communism, precisely because of this emphasis on technological innovation. Indeed, the relevant chapters on innovation in *Capital* refer to innovations in steam, iron, and steel, and use data provided by Engels on productivity gains in a real cotton spinning mill. Marx as a classical economist was rather prescient, whatever one's views about him as a political theorist.

This canter through the classics has brought the story to the early twentieth century. While there were disagreements between economists before then, it was at this point that the subject divided decisively into a mainstream and a minority view. One of the best-known economists to think seriously about the dynamics of capitalist economies was Joseph Schumpeter, who famously described the process of "creative destruction" whereby a whirlwind of technological innovation sweeps away old methods and businesses, introducing more productive new ones; but his was a minority interest. (I return to Schumpeter in chapter 7.) The mainstream became increasingly formalized and mathematical.[5] It rested the analysis of economic behavior on marginal utility, and the utility- or profit-maximizing behavior of individual economic "agents." So too, in a formal, mathematical way, did the postwar "neoclassical synthesis" set out by Paul Samuelson in his *Foundations of Economic Analysis* in 1947. Yet this mainstream was essentially a static analysis because it was focused on the concept of equilibrium, the state in which the economic system is at rest. For a century, the mainstream neglected innovation and economic growth, only returning to the serious analysis of growth twenty years ago.

Neoclassical Growth

Let's turn now to a more recent era, the early 1950s. A computer was the size of a football stadium, and the total computer processing power available in the world amounted to the power of a single chip in any consumer electronic item today. National accounts were newfangled and available for just a few countries. Historical data still lay in scattered library stacks. How could an economist begin to think about the process of growth? Since the end of World War II, growth rates in rich countries have varied from year to year, and different countries have experienced different average growth rates. The mid 1970s brought a watershed, with

---

[5] One controversial and certainly rather tendentious explanation is that late-nineteenth-century economists were trying to make economics just like physics (see Mirowski 2002).

a faster average growth rate before than afterwards. However, the range of variation between countries and within countries over time is vastly greater for the poorer economies. To mangle Tolstoy's famous phrase, all rich economies are alike; it is poor ones that differ. To an economist in a European or American university looking at experience close to home in the postwar era, it was reasonable to approximate the growth performance of the rich economies as 2–4% a year for most countries and most years, a pattern that has not changed in fifty years. Of course, there has been variability over the course of the business cycle—booms and recessions—so a theory of the ups and downs has been needed on top of the theory of long-run growth. But there was a good workhorse theory of economic growth to explain the long-run stability, initially developed by Nobel laureate Robert Solow, explored and extended by Edward Denison, David Cass, and Tjalling Koopmans in the following years (Solow 1956). Its essence was, reasonably enough, that the growth of outputs depends on the growth of inputs, and on how effectively these inputs are used. This neoclassical model, newly systematized in the postwar years, was the staple until the renewal of interest in growth theory in the late 1980s.

One of its key principles was the concept of diminishing marginal returns. In consumption, this meant each extra apple consumed brought less utility to its eater than the previous apple. In production, it meant each extra unit of input used—land, labor, or physical capital—produced a smaller increment in output. The best land is used first so extra fields have lower crop yields; workers get tired; machines which are run for longer will break down.

Clearly, more inputs are needed for an economy to produce more output. This is bound to be the starting point for any explanation of growth, the accumulation and use of physical capital and human labor. Accumulating physical capital requires that the economy consumes less than today's total output in order to save and invest in new machinery. Human labor depends obviously on the number of workers, how hard they work, and also on their capabilities (which become more important the more jobs involve skills other than muscle power). Decisions to accumulate physical or human capital will depend on the incentives to save rather than spend, work rather than play. Given these decisions, the amount of output produced will increase as the inputs increase, but in diminishing increments. The relationship between inputs and outputs is known as the production function, and will depend on the state of technology or know-how. Some techniques will get more output than others from a given amount of each input (known in the jargon as factors of production); and every technology will require a certain ratio between the different inputs. Say three laborers and three machines can produce twelve chairs a day. But diminishing returns to each input mean that if you add a fourth machine you get only fifteen chairs. Add an extra laborer instead and you get fourteen. But add a machine *and* a laborer, and you'll get sixteen chairs.

What will the aggregate growth rate be for the economy? The answer depends on how fast the workforce and the stock of machines can grow. So how fast is population growth? How much is the economy as a whole saving and investing, and how rapidly does existing capital equipment depreciate and need replacing to keep the capital stock intact? In addition, at what pace does technology progress, as innovations (a better irrigation system, a more efficient dynamo) permit the same amount of inputs to deliver more output?

To start with, let's concentrate on the accumulation of capital. The accumulation of capital seems pretty fundamental to capitalism, and it is natural to think that the rate of saving and investment in new equipment will be decisive for the economy's performance. So assume that the rate of population growth and the pace of technical progress are given and constant. Now, as a thought experiment, suppose that saving and therefore investment in the economy increase significantly (we are assuming away the rest of the world, too, so all investment has to be financed by domestic saving). Extra capital is accumulated, and extra output produced, so growth has accelerated. But in the long run, unless the workforce is also growing faster, the faster growth will not be sustained: diminishing returns to capital will kick in and steadily reduce the gains in output due to each extra increment in capital. The *level of output* per person will be permanently higher than it would have been without the high savings and capital accumulation, but ultimately the *growth rate* will not be any higher. If the ratio of capital to labor is "too high," the return to investment will decline (in line with its diminishing marginal productivity), and capital accumulation will slow down. In the long term—in equilibrium, the economist's metaphorical concept of the state in which the economy will settle down after any disturbance—the growth rate of output will keep the ratio of inputs constant. The long-run growth rate will depend on those things we assumed as givens, namely population and technological change.

Needless to say, I've given a very simple description of the basic growth model. Even so, there is obviously something very unsatisfactory about the Solow model. In effect it explains how economies grow by assuming that they grow. Growth of the labor force is taken as a given. Technical progress is a gift from heaven: the production function is also given. Both are *exogenous*. What's more, every economist handing down this model to the next generation pointed out this flaw. Nor did anybody pretended it was a rounded explanation of the historical experience of growth, despite its tractable equations. There was no room for the drama of the Industrial Revolution or the violent history of empire in what Solow described as "the land of the margin." And to be fair to him, his 1956 article was offering a clear improvement over the previous leading model of growth.[6]

Let's set the theoretical shortcomings to one side, however.[7] How does the neoclassical model fare when it meets the evidence? Obviously, it ignores the overwhelming importance of innovation in the experience of economic growth. Yet the theory had in mind an economy just like that of the United States or the United Kingdom or Germany, a rich economy with a long growth record. In the 1950s and 1960s, although the rich economies were dissimilar, with some experiencing a postwar reconstruction surge in growth, it did not seem unrealistic to suppose that small differences in population growth or the available technology could account for underlying differences in output growth. Empirical research very soon established, though, that the neoclassical framework of the accumulation of capital, subject to diminishing marginal returns, could only explain a small proportion of actual growth in any country. When the inputs were added up, in almost every case their growth proved to be substantially lower than output growth, which therefore had to be explained as the result of "technical progress." In 1956, Solow attributed a full four-fifths of postwar U.S. growth in business output to "technical progress." Of course, this sum depends on how inputs are measured; but even adjusting for improvements in the quality of the inputs—and importantly in the quality of labor, such as more years spent at school on average—all studies have found that (much) more than half of output growth in the developed economies has to be attributed to technical

---

[6]This was the Harrod–Domar model, in which the economy could sustain growth only if the natural rate of growth, which depended on population growth, happened by chance to be the same as the "warranted" rate, which depended on how much people decided to save and invest. The marginal neoclassical framework introduced a mechanism for adjustment of one to the other.

[7]After all, one of the classic jokes in economics is, "That might be fine in practice, but it'll never work in theory."

progress, which is unexplained by the model (Solow 1956; Jorgenson and Griliches 1967; Jorgenson and Yip 2000).

It is worth explaining how the empirical studies do these calculations, which are known as *growth accounting*. Logically, output growth can be exhaustively divided into growth in inputs, plus a residual. The part of growth attributed to labor is its growth rate multiplied by its share in total output, and likewise for capital. The contribution of labor to growth will (or should) incorporate quality changes, such as better schooling, and productivity improvements specific to labor, such as more effective teamwork methods; and likewise for capital. The part left unaccounted for by growth and improvement in inputs is known as *total factor productivity*. It is usually identified with technical progress, although it will also include anything left out of the measurement of inputs, including quality changes not properly accounted for. Such omissions would lead to overestimates of the importance of technical change. On the other hand, productivity improvements due to innovation will increase investment in capital, so part of the growth attributed to capital will in fact be caused by technical change.

While the logic is straightforward, in practice it can be difficult to attribute all changes to the right categories. Even so, there are plentiful studies of levels and growth rates of total factor productivity in many countries. All find that (a) it accounts for a large part of output growth, (b) its level and growth rate vary significantly between countries, and (c) its growth varies over time (see OECD 2001; Helpman 2004).

What is more, as the historical data have become more readily available, it has become apparent that the rate of growth in the industrialized economies has accelerated as the centuries have passed. This can be seen from table 1.1. Although average growth from the 1970s to 1990s was slower than in the preceding decades, it was nevertheless much higher than growth in any period before World War II. Paul Romer (1986) calculated that the probability that growth in a later decade would be higher than growth in an earlier decade was at least 58% and up to 81% for each of the eleven industrial countries he investigated. Given that rates of accumulation have diminished over time, the neoclassical model would imply slowing rather than accelerating rates of output growth, unless the pace of technological progress has been accelerating.

So the evidence from within the rich economies points firmly to the inadequacy of the accumulation of inputs in the context of diminishing marginal returns as an explanation for growth. Theory needs to say something about the forces that shape technology and innovation.

45

Table 2.1. Average annual compound growth rate of GDP per capita (%).

	1913–1950	1950–1973	1973–2001
Western Europe	0.76	4.05	1.88
Western offshoots	1.56	2.45	1.84
Eastern Europe	0.89	3.81	0.68
Former USSR	1.76	3.35	−0.96
Latin America	1.43	2.58	0.91
Japan	0.88	8.06	2.14
Other Asia	−0.10	2.91	3.55
Africa	0.92	2.00	0.19

Sources: Maddison (2003). Western offshoots are the
United States, Canada, Australia, New Zealand.

A second empirical problem for the Solow model is its inability to explain the differences between countries, especially when other, poorer countries are considered. The model implies that, if they have similar technology and population growth, an economy with a high ratio of capital to labor will grow more slowly than one with a low ratio. High capital-to-labor economies are the rich ones: past savings have raised the level of output per capita. So in other words, the theory would lead you to expect poor countries to grow more rapidly than rich ones, and to expect levels of income per capita to converge upwards over time. The reason is that as capital is scarce relative to labor in poor countries, the return to capital is higher, so there is an incentive to save more and accumulate more capital. There's scope for poor economies to catch up until they too attain the steady long-run growth rate.

This implication would have seemed reasonable looking at the postwar experience of the Western economies, with countries such as France and Germany indeed growing rapidly at first and gaining on the United States in living standards, then growing more slowly. However, it is not a good description of a larger group of countries over a longer period. As Robert Lucas has pointed out, if the difference in incomes per capita between the United States and India were due mainly to the difference in their stocks of capital relative to labor, the return to capital in India should be so high that investors would pile all their money into India and none into the United States. Of course, this does not happen (Lucas 1988). Nor has there been any sign of increased convergence since the 1980s, when international barriers to capital mobility started to vanish.

Not only has there been no sign of systematic catch-up by poor countries, but as table 2.1 and figure 2.1 show, the wide variation in growth

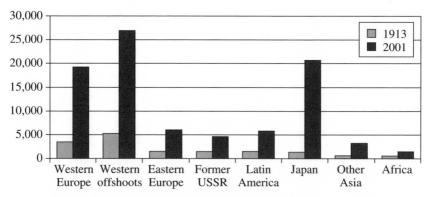

Figure 2.1. Level of GDP per capita (1990 international $).
Source: Maddison (2003).

rates has been getting wider still, and the divergence in incomes per capita has increased. Relatively few countries, including some western European countries in the postwar years and some Asian countries such as Japan and South Korea somewhat later, have followed the implied Solow pattern, growing very rapidly during a period of catch-up and attaining almost the same income per capita as the world leaders.

So in the data on growth and levels of output per capita, there is no evidence of convergence in living standards. There is almost no correlation between a country's initial income and its subsequent growth.

On the other hand, there is firm evidence of what economists call *conditional* convergence in incomes per capita. While there is no correlation between income per capita and subsequent growth, if income per capita is adjusted for ("conditioned on") differences between countries which affect its equilibrium level, then it is strongly negatively correlated with subsequent growth (Barro 1991; Barro and Salai-I-Martin 1995). For example, a poor country which grows very slowly is not converging on the rich countries; but its growth rate may be low because its people have little education, or its fertility and mortality rates are high, or the government makes unhelpful interventions such as spending too much on wars. Adjusting for the effect of such variables, a country's growth rate does tend to be systematically higher, the lower its starting point. By far the most important adjustment to make is the initial level of human capital, the number of workers and their quality.

All this suggests that considering the accumulation of capital is a good starting point for understanding growth. But an improved theory needs to do better at explaining the variations between countries, which the evidence indicates will depend above all on their human capital; and it needs to explain what determines the rate of technical progress. The two *exogenous* variables in the Solow model, growth of labor input and technological change, need to be made *endogenous*.

POST-NEOCLASSICAL ENDOGENOUS GROWTH

May 2, 1997 dawned a brilliantly sunny spring day. Britain had just elected its first Labour government for eighteen years, and the Labour Party's celebrations were still continuing at the Royal Festival Hall by the River Thames in London. A short distance away in Number 10 Downing Street, Tony Blair was forming the first government of his eight-year-plus premiership. Gordon Brown was his Chancellor of the Exchequer (as Britain's finance minister has been known since 1170). Brown turned out to be—as even his political enemies acknowledge—one of Britain's most imposing chancellors. And one of his many gifts to the British people has been to introduce them to the term "post-neoclassical endogenous growth theory."[8] A theory must surely be good if it makes its way into political speeches. So what is it? The "post-neoclassical" bit means it is of 1980s vintage rather than 1950s. And "endogenous" means it offers an explanation for what had merely been assumed in the Solow model. In fact, there are two main flavors of the modern growth model, depending on which previously exogenous variable they focus on endogenizing. One important strand concentrates on human capital, the other on technological innovation. They originate, respectively, in papers by Robert Lucas (1988) and Paul Romer (1986, 1990).[9]

---

[8]In a 1997 speech, written for him by aide Ed Balls, he said: "You wouldn't expect me to talk to you about post-neoclassical endogenous growth theory, and I won't...." Conservative politician Michael Heseltine extended the joke with his pun: "It's not Brown's, it's Balls'." Economist Robert Barro had some years earlier been asked by *The Financial Times* (where Ed Balls worked at the time) to explain post-neoclassical endogenous growth theory to the British public, and was very miffed when the Conservative chancellor Kenneth Clarke poked fun at his article because it used the phrase. Reminiscing about the affair, Barro concluded: "I suppose that I will never understand British humor" (see Barro 1996, p. 22). However, the chasm in understanding may lie not so much between Brits and Americans, or even Conservative and Labour politicians, as between economists and others.

[9]See Warsh (2006) for a history of endogenous growth theory, citing these papers and many other relevant references. Warsh's narrative centers on Paul Romer and consequently downplays the contributions of Lucas and economists working on similar models in other areas of economics, such as Avinash Dixit, Joseph Stiglitz, and Paul Krugman.

The antecedents of these new growth models lay in research in other branches of economics—industrial organization and trade theory—in the late 1970s and early 1980s. The new techniques they introduced abandoned the simplifying assumptions made in all earlier work that firms were identical; that there were constant returns to scale in production (adding the same number of extra units of input increaséd output by a constant amount no matter what the existing level of output); and that there was perfect competition such that no firm could charge a price higher than its costs and make a level of profits higher than the minimum needed to stay in business. The reason for these assumptions had been for the sake of the tractability of the models. But a brilliant technical innovation introduced by Avinash Dixit and Joseph Stiglitz in a 1976 paper spread like wildfire throughout economics (Dixit and Stiglitz 1976). They found a very tractable way of introducing "monopolistic competition." Firms each produce a differentiated product, and thereby have a bit of monopoly power thanks to this bit of distinctiveness. There are also increasing rather than constant returns to scale, which is more realistic as firms in most businesses have some fixed costs which can in some cases be very large. Fixed costs mean that there are economies of scale—the average cost of each item produced will be lower the larger the production run. In some industries, from aerospace to software, fixed costs are large. Paul Krugman took the next step, applying this kind of model to international trade, and subsequently to questions of industrial location in general (Krugman 1980, 1991a,b; Helpman and Krugman 1985). Economists had long realized that increasing returns were an important part of the explanation for why industries tended to locate in particular geographic clusters, or why people tended to congregate in towns and cities, which is where economic growth occurs. Urbanization is intimately linked to growth, and if the account of growth theory which follows ignores the economic geography literature, this is only for reasons of space (see Fujita et al. (1999), which also references this literature, and Glaeser et al. (1995)).

Common to the endogenous growth models of both Lucas and Romer is the introduction of *spillovers*, whereby individual decisions have an immediate effect on others. This is what provides an escape from the realm of diminishing returns, and therefore from the two empirically refuted neoclassical implications of convergence between countries and growth rates which decline over time. Indeed, with increasing returns, rather than diminishing returns, growth can snowball in a virtuous circle, and economies can easily diverge. I'll look at spillovers in human capital and innovation in turn.

My earlier description of the neoclassical model referred to inputs of "labor" and mentioned, fleetingly, issues of labor quality, such as educational attainment. The right kind of concept to use in a theory of growth is not the number of workers but rather a quantity which also takes account of their skills and effectiveness. The term used is *human capital*, the accumulated stock of human abilities, by analogy with the accumulated stock of equipment that makes up physical capital. Lucas adapted the standard model to incorporate human capital explicitly, including individual decisions about how much to invest to acquire knowledge. He argued that such decisions are made in a social context, in a way which has no parallel for decisions to invest in machinery. If I live in a country where average levels of education are low, it is unlikely to pay me to invest heavily in my own human capital because the returns will be low: they will be geared toward the average, which my individual decision cannot affect. So countries can become settled in a low-level trap. Conversely, the payoff to my education will be greater if I'm working with other people who are highly educated. Here is a mechanism which can clearly lead to divergence, not convergence, between economies. In terms of the formal model, Lucas introduced a production function depending on physical capital, aggregate human capital, and average human capital, with diminishing marginal returns to the first two terms, and a spillover from average human capital to the other terms. The incentive for individuals to invest in their own human capital depends on the decisions of others.

It was the introduction of human capital into the theory by Robert Lucas which prompted Robert Barro to compare the growth performance of economies depending on their initial attributes, finding the conditional convergence described above. Starting poor means faster growth, and therefore catch-up to the richer economies as the neoclassical model of accumulation implies, as long as a measure of human capital is included. This result, widely confirmed by other researchers, makes the human capital approach look promising empirically. And of course it makes intuitive sense that improving standards of education are related to better economic outcomes. Barro pointed out that the poor countries which have decisively converged on the rich ones—East Asian "tigers" such as South Korea and Taiwan—had started out with much higher levels of human capital than countries with similar levels of GDP per capita in 1960. So endogenizing the accumulation of human capital in this way is a big step forward. It is likely to be vitally important in thinking about growth in developing countries where initial levels of human capital are low. This is an important theme in the next chapter.

Yet education cannot have been decisive during the Industrial Revolution, when literacy levels were low, and many innovators hadn't been to school at all. So other economists have endogenized technology and the process of innovation instead. In another landmark paper Paul Romer (1986) introduced the economy's stock of knowledge into the production function, alongside the stocks of physical and human capital. In turn there is a separate production function for knowledge, which depends on the inputs each business devotes to accumulating knowledge and—the externality—the economy's total public stock of knowledge. Each business has an incentive to invest in its own knowledge but part of that unintentionally becomes public, not just private, knowledge. New discoveries are to some extent a public good: once somebody makes the conceptual breakthrough, others will imitate. There are diminishing returns to capital and labor but not to aggregate knowledge. Indeed, there are *increasing* returns to knowledge: the same bit of knowledge can be used repeatedly without being used up; and one bit becomes the foundation for the next (no description has been more expressive than Isaac Newton's "standing on the shoulders of giants"). This formalization of growth clearly corresponds to the emphasis some economic historians such as David Landes and Joel Mokyr have placed on ideas and technology.

Romer extended his original model to incorporate research and development (R&D) spending and patenting by businesses. The temporary monopoly offered by a patent gives businesses the chance to profit from product innovation, but the act of patenting in itself puts part of their innovation into the public domain. He wrote: "Long-run growth is driven primarily by the accumulation of knowledge." The beauty of his model and its successors is that they provide a theoretical version of the lesson of history, that growth must be crucially linked with innovation, which can be tested empirically (see Grossman and Helpman 1991; Aghion and Howitt 1998). The empirical evidence certainly supports the importance of such R&D "spillovers" in explaining growth. Indeed, the links between innovation and growth have been explored in detail and there is now a huge literature documenting the existence and size of R&D spillovers in many contexts.[10]

---

[10]For a rich account of the process, see Baumol (forthcoming).

Stepping back from such detail, though, how well do the different endogenous growth models mesh with the very broad contours of economic growth? Do they overcome the empirical shortfalls of the Solow model? And what are we to make of the fact that there are different versions? One point to note before assessing the implications of endogenous growth is that the two models are essentially similar. The stock of knowledge in an economy will be at least partly attached to humans, as part of their human capital; and the parts of human capital which spill over into society, know-how that is "in the air," will be part of the public stock of knowledge. There is surely more progress to be made on understanding these links and measuring human capital and knowledge. But a rounded theory of growth must have room for both human capital and product innovation. Both are empirically important in explaining the growth differences between countries.

THE IMPLICATIONS OF MODERN GROWTH THEORY

Recall that two aspects of reality motivated the introduction of increasing returns to the two types of investment, in human capital and in knowledge. One was the evidence that growth in the rich countries has tended to accelerate over time. The other is that countries' growth records have diverged rather than converged. The basic Solow model, with diminishing returns to the inputs of labor and capital, is inconsistent with these two big facts, whereas endogenous growth models with increasing returns to scale are consistent with them. What are the implications of the presence of increasing returns in the growth process? A world of increasing returns is vastly different from Solow's "land of the margin" with diminishing returns. This step turns out to make size, history, and geography important in theory for economic outcomes: modern growth theory is contingent on circumstances in a way far removed from the abstract world of neoclassical growth.

Size

The use of knowledge is nonrival—ideas don't get used up but can be used repeatedly by many people. Thomas Jefferson famously compared the process to lighting one candle from another. And the more people there are, the more potential inventors there are, the greater the potential contact with new ideas, and the greater the scope for intellectual specialization. In addition, the per capita resource cost of creating knowledge will be lower the larger the population. So the more people there are to use the available knowledge, the greater the economy's output can be. The more people there are, the more knowledge will be added to the public stock. Population growth in itself will spur technical progress and growth in *per capita* output. At least, that's the theoretical implication. It is controversial.

Eyeballing the very-long-term trends in global population and per capita GDP does suggest a link, as population growth started to accelerate around the same time as output. World population climbed slowly from just over a quarter of a billion in the year 1000 to about half a billion in 1600 and just over one billion in 1820, while it has jumped to six billion in the less than two centuries since. In a 1960 paper, three electrical engineers tested the proposition that population growth is proportional to the population level and found that it fitted the historical evidence well. Extrapolating forward, they predicted the world's population would become infinite on Friday November 13, 2026 (presumably an electrical engineers' joke, very much on a par with the sense of humor of a typical economist). Extrapolation is clearly inappropriate—a richer model is needed to predict future population growth.[11] Indeed, in the decades since 1960 the pace at which the number of people in the world is climbing has slowed to be much less than proportionate to the population level. Economist Michael Kremer tested, using a very long run of historical evidence, a model in which more people make for more innovation and faster growth, but in which population growth is also affected by income per capita. In other words, it incorporates the well-known demographic transition of a steep drop in fertility rates in countries which climb above a low level of income (Kremer 1993).

On the other hand, it is not true to say that big economies always grow faster than small ones; there are plenty of small but rapidly growing economies, and small but rich ones. Countries such as Singapore or Switzerland are examples. This fact has made economists a bit uneasy about the first wave of endogenous growth models, with their sizist implications, leading some to develop modifications to limit or eliminate the importance of scale. But, after all, the scale effects were introduced to make the model fit better with the evidence. If human capital is emphasized, the more people there are, the greater the knowledge spillovers

---

[11] One of the important differences between the approach typically taken by economists and those of other disciplines is that economists are far less likely to extrapolate a trend indefinitely forward; economic models inherently include adjustment mechanisms.

in the accumulation of human capital. If innovation is emphasized, the larger the market, the greater the profitability of investing in R&D, and the greater the spillovers. Either way, there is a chain reaction, a virtuous circle which starts slowly then accelerates, related to the scale of the economy. I don't want to overemphasize the importance of scale at all, but it's a wrinkle in the theory which makes some economists very uncomfortable.

Where endogenous growth models have clearly enriched our analysis is in incorporating the real-world complexity of place and time. It matters where an economy is located, and what its history has been. The accumulation of specific experience, reflected in an economy's institutions and norms of behavior, can have extremely long-lasting effects on growth performance. In part 3 of the book I return to these "microfoundations" of macroeconomic performance from the bottom-up perspective of individual choices and interactions. Here I consider their top-down role in growth theory.

Geography

The existence of human capital spillovers, whereby your skills and experience affect my productivity and earning capacity, has other strong implications. If people are free to move, those with human capital that's above average for their location will try to move somewhere with a higher average level. This might account for the enormous pressures for migration from poor to rich countries. It would certainly help explain the tight correlation between economic growth and urbanization. For why do people crowd together in cities, with their filth, congestion, danger, and of course high prices? Costs of production are higher in cities than in less densely populated areas. The only plausible reason for urban concentration is to be close to other people. We learn from others, we exchange ideas, they stimulate us to achieve more ourselves. Alfred Marshall made this argument in a well-known passage, in his 1890 textbook, about the clustering of economic activity in industrial districts:

> The mysteries of the trade become no mysteries but are as it were in the air, and children learn many of them unconsciously. Good work is rightly appreciated, inventions and improvements in machinery, in processes and the general organization of business have their merits promptly discussed. If one man starts a new idea, it is taken up

by others and combined with suggestions of their own; and thus it becomes a source of further new ideas.[12]

Marshall (1920)

The great urbanist Jane Jacobs has long emphasized the economic role of cities, and the importance of the creation of public knowledge in industries such as finance, clothing and textiles, autos, or advertising (Jacobs 1985). And geographers have always, naturally, been interested in questions of location. The introduction of increasing returns in growth theory has generated new insights into the economic analysis of geography, whether that's regional disparities or patterns of trade between countries. As well as addressing the question of how economies grow over time, economists can say more about how they extend in space: for example, why does one city thrive and another decline? The existence of specialized industrial clusters such as shipbuilding or computer software is well-known, but why do they form and why are they where they are? A natural harbor might explain a shipping industry—but a programmer could hunch over a screen anywhere with electricity and telecommunications.

Paul Krugman, although now a famously polemical *New York Times* columnist, made his name applying increasing-returns models to such locational questions, in one of the first examples of how these models came to characterize a new way of thinking about the economy in general (see Krugman (1980), with further extensions and references in Krugman (1991a)). I first met him when I was working as an economics journalist and wanted to interview him about the exciting new developments in economic geography; but setting up the interview was hampered by the fact that, although he knew he was in London, he couldn't tell me his own location. As he'd recently come from giving a lecture in Tierra del Fuego on the far southern tip of Argentina, finding him in my own city seemed feasible, and indeed I tracked him down. Krugman's insight, which sowed the seeds of an intellectual revival in the entire field of economic geography, was that just as increasing returns explain divergent growth histories, they account for divergent geographies as well. The

---

[12]Marshall of course had the sensibilities of his time, but this usage does remind me of one of my favorite cartoons (from *Punch* magazine), of a board meeting with a sole woman present. The chairman says: "That's an excellent suggestion Miss Triggs. Perhaps one of the men would like to make it."

virtuous and vicious circles of growth occur in particular places, in one country (or region or city) rather than another.[13]

To spell it out, knowledge spillovers are made possible by the physical proximity of people, especially when it comes to the sharing and exchange of complicated and abstract ideas, whether in software or a service such as finance or medicine. This is why business executives still fly thousands of miles for face-to-face meetings, why universities exist, and why computer experts cluster together in Silicon Valley. Human capital spillovers (positive or negative) are similarly amplified by the near presence of others. The return to my education is more likely to depend on the educational attainments of other people if we are all present in the same job market. I will only have the prospect of employment in a well-paid job if there is a pool of skilled labor which will attract the kind of employers who want my kind of skills. Places without the skilled people will fail to attract such businesses; and without those good job prospects, few people will have the incentive to ever acquire the skills the high-value firms need. The catch-22 is easy to understand, but very hard to escape. Call it the development catch-22—it sheds new light on the failure of the poor countries to grow, as we will see in the next chapter.

It might seem banal, in that uniquely obscure academic way, to say that economic growth occurs in specific places. However, the analysis of growth up to the end of the 1980s was abstract in the extreme. So one of the spillover benefits of endogenous growth theory, as it were, has been to restore to its proper place the importance of detail. Within a very general analytical framework, you can nevertheless expect a different growth performance from different places.

History

It is not only the accidents of geography that matter, but the accidents of history too. Once a pattern of growth or stagnation becomes established in an economy, whether of an individual town or a whole nation, it takes a lot to make it change. Actually, there is an asymmetry: it's easier to stop a snowball than to start one. Big events such as wars or radical innovations can derail prosperous economies even where the geographical factor is preeminent: for example, the combination of the Civil War

---

[13]His model also included transportation costs, bizarrely ignored in earlier trade theory. *Geography and Trade* (1991) is a very accessible introduction. *The Spatial Economy* (Fujita et al. 1999) is a key textbook. In the context of urban growth and decline, see Glaeser (2003). The business analysis of locational clusters is due to Porter (1990) and Kay (1993).

blockades and the invention of kerosene in place of whale oil destroyed the New England whaling industry. (The final straw came when women dropped the whalebone corset into the dustbin of history (see Menand (2002) for these details).) Setting a snowball rolling, on the other hand, involves the coordination of very many individual decisions to offset adverse spillovers or reinforce favorable ones.

The importance of historical accident in the growth record has come to be widely recognized, and once alerted to this phenomenon, you see it everywhere. In the technical literature, it's called *path dependence*: where you are now depends on how you got there. One very-well-known example is the persistence of the QWERTY layout for keyboards, no longer needed on a modern computer keyboard as opposed to an old-fashioned typewriter, but impossible to change because anybody who has learnt to type is habituated to it.[14] Another is the fact that the early luminaries of the modern computer industry attended Stanford University rather than, say, Chicago or Toulouse. Examples of historical happenstance are widespread in the business economics literature. Almost any industry you care to think of develops in geographical clusters, from the financial center of the City of London in the eighteenth century to ceramic tiles in northern Italy in the twentieth century, to call centers and business-process outsourcing in twenty-first-century Bangalore.

None of this is to say that either history or geography is destiny. How an economy got to where it is today (in both the literal and metaphorical senses) will certainly limit the range of options for tomorrow. But within that range many outcomes may be possible. By definition, if there are increasing returns to some activity such as acquiring human capital, then the more of that activity people undertake, the higher the return they get. There may be many possible paths of growth depending on their choices, or *multiple equilibria*. But what determines the actual collective outcome? One answer may well be the accidents of history, and this is the explanation which has predominated in recent work on growth. On the other hand, sufficiently strong expectations of a different turn of events could prove self-fulfilling: people might be persuaded for any number of reasons that their returns to investing in human capital or R&D in future will be higher than they have been in the past. A sufficiently determined education or industrial policy, for example, might

---

[14] Anybody who doubts the power of this explanation should try typing on the keyboard of a French computer to learn how frustrating it is when just four characters are in a different place. See David (1985), Arthur (1989), and Arthur et al. (1997) on the importance of history for growth.

shift expectations toward such a self-fulfilling growth prophecy. This analysis explains why policy makers have grown increasingly interested in setting out formal growth strategies: they want to persuade their citizens to buy in to a collective vision of a brighter future because if they don't believe it, it won't happen.[15]

Disneyland economics? Well, although self-fulfilling prophesy is theoretically possible, policy makers can't just wish upon a star to get the growth rate they desire. Paul Krugman used a formal endogenous growth model to work out when hopes for the future might outweigh the legacy of the past, and showed that there are three conditions (Krugman 1991c). First, there must be enough interdependence between individual decisions to start with. Second, people must put a relatively high weight on the future compared with the present (there must be a sufficiently low real discount rate), because obviously if they discount the future too much it will not have much influence on their decisions today. Finally, the economy must be able to adjust reasonably quickly, because if it adjusts slowly, the shadow cast by history will always dominate. To put it another way, people must want to change, their wishes must have some traction on the economy, and must be mutually reinforcing. In any particular economy, it will be possible to be more precise about the magnitudes involved. But in any case, these conditions all depend on deep-rooted social and behavioral characteristics, which rules out quick policy fixes.

Institutions

An appreciation that growth is a collective outcome, depending on the interdependence between individuals' choices, in fact makes institutions absolutely central. After all, an institution is by definition a means for people to combine together. The importance of institutions for economic development will be a theme of the next chapter, and I will also revisit it in detail in chapter 8. An economic historian who emphasized the importance of institutions long before it became fashionable to do so in development circles was Douglass North, cowinner of the 1993 Nobel memorial prize (with Robert Fogel). In a much-cited 1968 paper, he showed that productivity improvements in the shipping industry depended more on organizational than technical change (see Fogel (1999) for a review). There are echoes of his historical result in recent

---

[15]See Bradley (2005), for example, for an account of how the Irish government put this into practice in the 1980s, turning the country into the "Celtic tiger."

research in U.S. productivity growth in the 1990s, which also emphasizes the preeminence of organizations over technological innovations
alone (see, for example, Brynjolfsson and Hitt (2000) and McKinseys
Global Institute (2001) and the extensive references contained in them).
In a nutshell, institutions matter because they are the vehicles for
transmitting the legacy of history.

In a brilliant paper Mancur Olson noted that due to their institutional
weaknesses, poor countries have extremely inefficient economies. They
do not use their available physical and human capital or available technology very well. An immigrant from Haiti to the United States becomes
instantly more productive when she lands, indicating that her human
capital was not being fully utilized at home. Returns to investment in
physical capital in developing economies are very high, but the investment doesn't take place. The plausible reason is that social institutions
in poor countries inhibit growth. This fits in with the fact that a few
poor countries do grow extremely rapidly for some period: they have a
catch-up spurt which takes them to the efficient frontier which the rich
countries occupy. At this frontier, endogenous growth models do a very
good job of fitting with the facts (Olson 1996).

The fact that the process of growth is not the same everywhere and
always, that in fact the outcome is highly contingent, complicates giving
policy advice. It is hard to make any generalizations beyond the obvious point that growth depends on the collective capacity of a society,
through its institutions and its current endowment of human and other
resources, to accumulate and combine resources. Indeed, economists
still have some serious disagreements about how high the long-term
growth rate is in the world's most intensively measured and scrutinized
economy, the United States. Table 1.1 indicated that long-term growth
has tended to accelerate over time. Many, but not all, economists would
argue that there has been a further acceleration since the mid 1990s,
thanks to the innovation of the microprocessor.

BACK TO THE FUTURE

Given that how economists think about economies has depended on the
context of their time, it should not be surprising that growth theory saw
a striking revival in the late 1980s. After all, it was then that many people,
especially academics, started to notice the arrival of computers on their
desktops and wonder whether the massive increase in computer power
and declines in its price might have an impact on the economy. A decade

later, nobody, surely, could have failed to notice the "New Economy," an ill-defined phenomenon which nevertheless required everybody to define themselves as either a skeptic or an enthusiast.

New technologies have always given rise to some apprehensions. Mary Shelley played on fears of the power of electricity in *Frankenstein*. It is quite amusing now to come across the description of "The mighty agency of steam, capable of almost unlimited good or evil," in Elizabeth Gaskell's *Mary Barton*, but such views were a Victorian commonplace. While few people seem to fear computers or mobile phones in quite the same way, there has certainly been a clear tendency to belittle their impact.[16] In 1986, Robert Solow (he of the workhorse neoclassical growth model) famously introduced the "productivity paradox": this new technology appearing in workplaces across America seemed to have no impact on productivity and therefore long-term growth. It was not until the late 1990s that measured growth seemed to have increased at all, and it took another few years for a majority of economists to accept that the long-term average for U.S. productivity growth had increased. Indeed, as the evidence that there was in fact a productivity impact from the technologies started to emerge, skepticism took new forms. Robert Gordon, for example, argued that computers alone could never have the impact of past waves of innovation, which had involved more than one new technology emerging at the same time. His example was the combination of innovations in 1860–1900 leading to electricity, motor and air transport, radio and movies, and indoor plumbing (Gordon 1999, 2000).

There are several responses to the argument that computers have not been very important for growth. One is that measuring the impact of steam or electricity in exactly the same way as the impact of computers is measured (using the growth accounting described above), you find that steam and electricity look pretty small too: a "small" percentage point difference in growth rates is the statistical footprint of a large economic and social change (Crafts 2004). (Recall from the last chapter that the Industrial Revolution doesn't look very revolutionary in the GDP growth statistics.) A second is that any radical innovation takes a long time to have a measurable aggregate impact because people take many years to adjust: perhaps new infrastructure must be built, new skills learned, workplaces reorganized (David 1991). Indeed, many people have an incentive to resist innovations. As Niccolò Machiavelli put

---

[16]And some people obviously do have serious apprehensions about biotechnology and genomic research.

it in *The Prince*, "Innovation makes enemies of all those who prospered under the old regime, and only lukewarm support is forthcoming from those who would prosper under the new." And, lastly, although popular attention has focused on computers, there *is* a cluster of new technologies today, including biotechnology, new materials, and nanotechnology. Their combined impact on our well-being is likely to be just as profound as the cluster of technologies introduced around the start of the twentieth century.

I've always been puzzled that some economists have been so skeptical that huge declines in the cost of processing and communicating information will affect the allocation of resources and organization of the economy, when information is fundamental to economic analysis (see chapter 6). Still, this is not the place to tramp further over this already well-trodden ground.[17] Suffice it to say that there is now a consensus that computer-related technologies have led to an acceleration in long-term growth in the United States and a few other economies since the mid 1990s. But there is little agreement about why most countries, especially the other leading Western economies, have not yet shared in this phenomenon. The reasons for the difference must lie in the kind of behavior and institutions which prevail in the United States rather than in Japan or Germany, and attention has focused on factors such as the ease of financing a new venture, patent rules, the science base in universities, and the availability of people with suitable skills. Will Baumol (2002) has used the marvelous image of an "innovation machine" to capture the idea of a whole economic system whose essence is inventing and implementing new technologies. He says of the "unparalleled growth performance of the capitalist economies":

> The free market, once the institutional impediments to its development had been reduced sufficiently, just grew by itself, and by itself became the machine that generates innovation and growth in dramatic profusion. . . . It is clear that innovation plays a far larger role in the activities of many key firms and industries than the current theoretical literature takes into account.
>
> Baumol (2002, pp. 2, 3)

This emphasis on the importance of technological innovation is an overdue return to the lessons of the Industrial Revolution. Increasing-

---

[17]I have already done so myself in two books, *The Weightless World* (1997) and *Paradoxes of Prosperity* (2001). The best recent summary overview is in Helpman (2004) and the OECD has several publications making an empirical assessment of the links between new technologies and productivity growth in member countries.

returns models of endogenous growth theory, along with the emphasis on innovation, now inform an extensive research agenda in many fields of economics. Thanks to the theoretical and empirical advances of the past twenty years, economists now have a good understanding of the process of growth. Although endogenous growth models are even more mathematically rigorous and formal than their predecessor neoclassical version, and for all the jokes about the name, modern analysis of economic growth is profoundly less abstract than it used to be. The realm of endogenous growth theory is a universe away from the neoclassical competitive equilibrium model, as it puts the specifics of time and place, and the grittiest details of particular economies, at center stage. As a result, the new theories have completely changed the focus of economic policy makers when it comes to asking how to boost productivity and growth, with the emphasis now on education, research, innovation, the structural flexibility of the economy, and the quality of economic institutions.

This chapter has looked at some quite general theories of long-run economic growth. These models have their roots in similar models which have transformed just as thoroughly the way economists analyze trade and industrial structure. These concern the fundamental mechanics of the economy and will ultimately be integrated with growth theory, which at present concentrates on ideas and the mechanisms of knowledge transfer. Recall from chapter 1 that there are two keys to modern growth, according to the historical evidence: technical innovation which improves productivity in certain industries, and increasing specialization through trade. How firms in the industries where an innovation becomes available decide what to make and how to price their products and how it comes about that firms in one country or another reap the fruits of their specialization through international trade are vital pieces of the growth jigsaw. In a spectacularly fruitful period of mutual exchange of ideas, the economists working on endogenous growth models and those working on new models in industrial organization and trade transformed all three areas of the subject in the mid to late 1980s. The typical workhorse model of an economist now is a world away from the simple textbook models taught a generation ago. No longer does economics assume identical firms and perfect competition. Firms are typically assumed to be "monopolistically competitive," with a degree of monopoly power gained through differentiation of their products (signaled perhaps by trademarks, or brands) in order to cover their fixed costs of production; but open to competition because entry into the industry by new firms will occur if monopoly profits rise too much. As well as variety, there's innovation. Will Baumol (forthcoming) has integrated the theory of entrepreneurship into these formal models of production, making innovation fundamental to how firms compete with each other. His new textbook based on this modeling approach will take its place as the standard for training the next generations of economists, just as his *Economic Theory and Operations Analysis* set out the state of knowledge on price and production theory for my generation when it was published in 1972 (Baumol 1972). The revolution in the very basics of microeconomic theory has hardly been appreciated at all outside the profession.

In particular—and thanks in part to our recent experience of the ways new information and communication technologies, biotechnology, and other technologies are affecting our own societies—economists have made huge strides recently in analyzing the process of innovation. Will Baumol has explored the differences between radical innovation by entrepreneurs and incremental improvement for the mass market by big corporations, and has brought the process of entrepreneurship within the ambit of standard microeconomic theory. Economists are exploring the process of patenting innovations, the best way to protect intellectual property in order to encourage innovators; the implications for productivity of inward investment by leading foreign companies and the knowledge spillovers which can result; the paths through which research in universities is put into commercial practice by entrepreneurs; and many other empirical details of how it is that technological change turns into aggregate growth.[18] The microeconomic undergrowth beneath the canopy of the macroeconomic growth literature is steadily being filled in by researchers, with important implications for government policy. These processes are amenable to government intervention in ways that a country's history, culture, and geography are not. I'll return to the importance of modern microeconomic research later. But I want to round off this part of the book by applying the lessons of economic history and growth theory to the question of global poverty. What can economics say about why the poor economies haven't grown?

---

[18] The empirical microeconomic literature on innovation and growth, and the behavior of inventors, entrepreneurs, and firms is vast. Literally dozens of new research papers (in English, never mind other languages) are published each week. As a starting point, and for further references, see Audretsch (2006), Jaffe and Trachtenberg (2002), and Jaffe and Lerner (2004) on patents and the papers by Baumol (2002, forthcoming) on innovation and entrepreneurship.

How to Make Poverty History

It is a testament to the adaptability of the British class system that one of the most famous knights of the realm is a foul-mouthed, unkempt former rock star. You can only wonder, listening to Sir Bob Geldof, formerly lead singer of the Boomtown Rats, father of Fifi Trixibelle and Peaches, whether he swore quite as freely while chatting with the Queen during the knighthood ceremony as he does in front of the television cameras. In 2005, Sir Bob, along with other luminaries including rock superstar Bono of U2, film producer Richard Curtis (*Notting Hill, Four Weddings and a Funeral*), and celebrity economist Jeffrey Sachs, decided it was time to tell poverty to fuck off. A series of benefit concerts took place the weekend before that year's annual summit of G8 leaders, named Live8 in an echo of Geldof's Live Aid concert which had raised emergency funds for Ethiopia twenty years earlier. The summer of 2005 was marked by a sustained campaign to "Make Poverty History" by increasing aid spending by rich governments on poor countries, and canceling the foreign debts owed by governments of some of the world's poorest economies. The badge of campaign supporters was a white wristband. Millions wore the wristband and listened to music in aid of the poor, thousands marched ahead of the G8 summit, and a few hundred held a small but nasty riot outside the hotel where it was taking place, before they were upstaged by terrorist attacks in London.

I don't want to sound cynical about the campaign (as opposed to the idiot rioters). Ending the poverty, disease, and hunger which afflicts so many people is a matter of simple humanity. Who could disagree with either the ambition or the sense of urgency? Getting so very many people concerned to improve the world was a great achievement, and essential to stimulate political action by the Western democracies. It is inevitable that a popular campaign will popularize the issues, however, and neither the problems of economic underdevelopment nor the solutions are likely to be straightforward. After decades of effort and hundreds of billions of dollars in aid (two trillion or more calculated at today's prices), even the best-intentioned people should be cautious in making policy prescriptions. As William Easterly (2001, 2006) has pointed out in his excellent books on development policies, there is a long history of panaceas that failed. The Live8 campaigners have fixed on some new panaceas—debt relief, still more aid—but after half a century of failure, a little humility about having discovered the cure for poverty is in order.

Prescribing better policies depends on getting the diagnosis right, which in turn depends on collecting the symptomatic evidence and understanding the workings of the system. This is the metaphor Jeff Sachs adopted in his Live8 book: he described himself as a "clinical economist," just as his wife practices clinical medicine (Sachs 2005). While this sounds straightforward, there is plainly much controversy about the diagnosis of what's wrong with the economies of poor countries. The issue of globalization has become a litmus test of ideological attitudes for many people, with a return among some on the left-of-center of straightforward anticapitalist, antimarket views, and a belief that the world economy is essentially colonial, involving the exploitation of the poor by the rich. At the opposite extreme is the belief that a return to imperialism would be a good thing for countries which have fared so much worse under self-rule (see, for example, Ferguson 2004). Among people of more moderate opinions there is still a division of perception between those who believe global capitalism has been essentially beneficial but needs its problems ironing out, and those who believe it has brought some selective benefits but has essentially operated against the interests of the very poorest countries.

When the evidence available can be used in support of two opposing views of economic development, each held by well-intentioned and intelligent people, we are clearly not in the realm of hard science. This chapter doesn't aim to assess all the arguments and evidence on globalization. There are already many books which offer to fulfill that task.[1] Instead it asks two related questions. What is the nature of the evidence available on the causes of poverty? And does economics today offer the basis for any professional consensus on diagnosis and policy prescriptions? To give you the headline, the answer is tentatively yes: the framework of endogenous growth described in the previous chapter does make sense

---

[1] The professional economists' favorite popular account would be Martin Wolf's *Why Globalization Works* (2004), which has very extensive references, while any bookshop will have a section with plenty of polemical books arguing against globalization, albeit many of them with a hazy grasp of the detailed statistical evidence.

Table 3.1. Extreme poverty as a proportion of population.

	1981	1990	2001
World	40.4	27.9	21.1
China	63.8	33.0	16.6
World excluding China	31.7	26.1	22.5
Sub-Saharan Africa	41.6	44.6	46.4

of the reasons some poor economies don't grow, although development economists have a lot more work to do before they can confidently offer policies to boost growth and cut poverty.

HOW BAD IS THE PROBLEM?

The controversy about economic development is fundamental. Beyond the most basic facts—and even they are often contested—there is no evidence which will not be regarded by some critics as tendentious. What's more, there is now probably more published research on globalization and development than any individual can master. Still, here goes with a brief introduction to the statistics.

The proportion of the world's population living in extreme poverty[2] has declined rapidly since about 1980, as table 3.1 shows. There has never been a faster decline in this proportion at any time in history, and a smaller proportion of the world's population is poor now than ever before (see Bourguignon and Morrison 2002). The absolute number of people living in poverty has fallen by less, because world population has risen from about four billion to about six billion during the past twenty-five years. Most of the decline in extreme poverty has taken place in two populous countries, mainly in China but to some extent in India too. However, poverty (both the number of people and the proportion of the population) has *increased* in sub-Saharan Africa and also in central Asia, in the latter case since the collapse of the Soviet Union.

While the number of people living in extreme poverty has been in decline for many decades now, as indicated in table 3.2, incomes have become more unequal over time. The inequality of incomes can be defined and measured in several ways. Table 3.3 shows two ways. Measured as a ratio of average incomes in the richest countries to average

---

[2] As defined by the World Bank, those who earn less than $1 a day, based on surveys of household consumption and converted to dollars using a measure of purchasing power parity.

Table 3.2. Extreme poverty (millions of people).

	1981	1990	2001
World	1482	1218	1089
China	634	375	212
World excluding China	848	844	877
Sub-Saharan Africa	164	227	313

Source: World Bank World Development Indicators (www.worldbank.org/
data/databytopic/poverty.html#ti, accessed July 8, 2005).

incomes in the poorest, it has never been greater at any time in history. However, the rapid increase in inequality on this measure occurred in the first half of the twentieth century; there has been little change since 1980 by comparison with earlier periods. Some researchers even argue that inequality of incomes has diminished during the past couple of decades. The Gini coefficient is a formula for looking at the whole of the income distribution, giving a value of 0 for all incomes being equal and 1 for all income going to the richest person. This alternative measure can take account of middle-class income gains but doesn't change the picture of a big increase in inequality up to the mid twentieth century which has subsequently stabilized or perhaps reversed in more recent decades.

This question of what has happened to the trend just recently is very controversial.[3] There are disagreements about the correct measurement of income in poor countries, the choice of exchange rate for making comparisons, and the appropriate definition of inequality. If you compare the average income of different countries, which has become more unequal since the early 1980s, it contains little information about inequality between *people*. It speaks instead to the failure of income levels in poor countries to catch up to rich-country income levels, discussed in chapter 2. If you weight average national income per capita by population size, world inequality has probably decreased since the early 1980s because of the great strides made in growth in China and India. However, although some researchers think this is clear, others argue that using market exchange rates rather than purchasing power parity conversions, or using a better measure of living standards than GDP per capita, shows increasing inequality recently. The safe presumption is

---

[3]For an excellent summary of the state of research, and extensive references, see Milanovic (2005).

Table 3.3. Measures of income inequality.

	1820	1870	1910	1929	1950	1970	1992	Later years
Share, top 10%	42.8	47.6	50.9	49.8	51.3	50.8	53.4	
Share, bottom 20%	4.7	3.8	3.0	2.9	2.4	2.2	2.2	
Ratio	9.1	12.4	16.8	17.2	21.2	23.4	23.8	
Gini coefficient	0.500	0.560	0.610	0.616	0.640	0.650	0.657	0.61–0.68

Sources: Bourguignon and Morrison (2002); Milanovic (2005) for "later
years" column surveys a range of studies for years in 1998–2000.

that there has been little change, as the scale of change in the calculated
figures is probably swamped by measurement error.

On the other hand, using average incomes for each country at all,
weighted or not, glosses over the distribution of incomes within each
country, so there is a strong argument that the measurement of inequality should take account of, say, the big increase in inequality within
China. The pattern of income distribution and its recent changes differ
widely from country to country, both within the OECD and within the
developing world, strongly indicating that national political and social
institutions play an important part in determining the degree of inequality inside each nation. The trouble with any measure of inequality is that
it will abstract from the identities of the people whose relative position
is being measured, but when it comes to assessing the effects of policies on people's welfare, statistical anonymity is not meaningful (see
Bourguignon and Coyle 2003). The most thorough attempt to measure
inequality on this concept, looking at individuals, and using surveys
rather than national accounts aggregates to estimate incomes, finds a
small increase in inequality from 1988 to 1993 and an even smaller
decrease from 1994 to 1999 (Milanovic 2005).

Set aside the unresolved debate about the direction of the trend in the
late 1990s. What does this level of world inequality mean? It tells us that
world income distribution is more unequal than distribution within *any*
individual country, reflecting the divergence in economic performance. It
says the ratio of the incomes of the richest 5% of the world population to
the poorest 5% is about 165:1. Putting the spotlight on individuals also
has implications for how we think about aid policy. Branko Milanovic
points out that more than a third of Brazilians are richer than the poorest
5% of French people. He calculates a 10% probability that French aid to

Brazil will be regressive in terms of global income distribution, that is, will be a transfer from a poorer to a richer person. This is a thought-provoking figure.[4]

There is even controversy about how to compare levels of GDP in different countries. The statistics on which these comparisons are based derive from a major international research project, the United Nations International Comparison Project (ICP), run in coordination with the World Bank and the University of Pennsylvania (the output is known as the Penn World Table). The ICP was started in 1968, covering six countries, and with funding from the Ford Foundation. Prior to this there had been almost no systematic collection of international data, although Angus Maddison was working separately on the same task at the OECD in Paris, publishing his results in 1964.[5] Phase 2 of the ICP took it to sixteen countries by 1973, and Phase 3 to thirty-four. The current phase is extending coverage to 150 countries. The project is led by the Center for International Comparisons at the University of Pennsylvania. The founding father in this case was Simon Kuznets, one of the pioneers of national accounts. (He was also winner of the third Nobel in Economics, in 1971; the 1984 prize went to Richard Stone, who co-pioneered national accounting.) Kuznets was on the Penn faculty from 1936 to 1954. His student Irving Kravis was the first director of the UN's ICP, and Heston and Summers (now codirectors of the Penn center) soon joined. There are thus separate but coordinated efforts underway in Europe at Maddison's Groningen Growth and Development Centre, in the United States at the University of Pennsylvania, and with input from the UN, the World Bank, the OECD, the European Union, and statistical offices around the world.

In the years after 1952, when the first international standard for national accounts was published, and prior to 1968 there had been a great expansion in the number of countries collecting data on their GDP. The main analytical challenge was the need to convert national output in different countries into a common currency. Movements in the exchange rate used for this conversion mean that growth rates in the chosen common currency (most often the U.S. dollar) will probably differ from growth rates measured in the national currency. Moreover, the exchange rates observed in the currency markets are not suitable for

---

[4] Assuming the transfer is made by a median-income French taxpayer and randomly allocated in Brazil.

[5] Before the 1960s, the sole attempt to make accurate numerical comparisons between countries was Colin Clark's heroic 1940 book *Conditions of Economic Progress.*

making the comparisons. They are too volatile year-to-year, which would generate meaningless movements in GDP measured in the common currency. And market exchange rates do not measure genuine purchasing power: prices tend to be lower in poor countries, especially prices for nontraded services; the pattern of relative prices is systematically different in poor and rich countries: investment goods are dearer relative to consumer goods in the poor than in the rich countries; and people in different countries buy different goods and services in different quantities. The ICP therefore calculates purchasing power parities, which assess the command the national currency has over goods and services, for each country and uses these to convert national output into international (or PPP) dollars.

This approach is often criticized—on its gritty details by other economists, but often on its principles by noneconomists. The reason is that poor countries' incomes are higher in international dollars than in dollars converted by ordinary exchange rates. The adjustments to reflect actual purchasing power make poor countries look less poor than they would without the corrections. Using exchange rates rather than purchasing power parities to calculate world GDP will also underestimate growth, because it will give too low a weight to rapidly growing poor countries (such as China now). And it will overstate world inequality by exaggerating the difference in ability to purchase goods and services between rich and poor countries. It is evident that some researchers prefer to minimize the estimated incomes and growth rates of developing countries. I would describe some of the assessments of PPPs by political scientists and sociologists as mad conspiracy theories. They do no favors to poor people, even if they do support academic theories of exploitation and immiserization.

Inequality has more clearly diminished when it comes to indicators other than income, however. Compared with 100 or 200 years ago, there are fewer famines, rates of child and infant mortality have fallen, life expectancy and literacy are much increased, and people are spending less time working (for a summary see Kenny (2005) and Crafts (1999)). One widely used measure which incorporates many quality-of-life indicators, and clearly shows the poor countries catching up to the rich ones, is the United Nations Human Development Index. The very first edition of the Human Development Report (1990) emphasizes the convergence in these and other indicators during the previous thirty years (see Human Development Report (1990, chapter 2, p. 17)). World Bank economist Charles Kenny offers historical evidence from India and the

Table 3.4. Human development indicators, selected countries (2004 HDI ranking in brackets).

	Life Expectancy (years)		Adult literacy (%)		GDP per capita (PPP $)	
	2002	1995	2002	1995	2002	1995
Norway (1)	78.9	77.6	100	99.0	36,600	22,427
United States (8)	77.0	76.4	100	99.0	35,750	26,977
Japan (9)	81.5	79.9	100	99.0	26,940	21,930
Russia (57)	66.7	65.5	99.6	99.0	8,230	4,531
Malaysia (59)	73.0	71.4	88.7	83.5	9,120	9,572
Brazil (71)	68.0	66.6	86.4	83.3	7,770	5,928
Bangladesh (138)	61.1	56.9	41.1	38.1	4,550	1,382
Tanzania (162)	43.5	50.6	77.1	67.8	580	636
Zambia (164)	32.7	42.7	79.9	78.2	840	986

Source: UNDP HDR database.

United Kingdom that convergence between rich and poor countries in such indicators of well-being has been occurring for centuries (Kenny 2005). Table 3.4 tries to give a flavor of the components of the index, for three countries in each of the rich, middling, and poor categories. The middle group and, to some extent, Bangladesh look more like the three rich countries in terms of life expectancy at birth and adult literacy—but not in terms of GDP per capita—in the more recent year than they do in the earlier year, even though the table covers only a short period. However, table 3.4 also shows that some countries, almost all in sub-Saharan Africa, have recently fallen back on life expectancy as well as income per capita. The HIV/AIDS pandemic is reversing some of the favorable trends.

In a sense, these bitterly contested facts about comparative levels of GDP and living standards are a mud-churned no-man's-land of development economics. Researchers battle long and hard for small statistical victories that are, when put in perspective, irrelevant. Because there can be no doubt about the big facts: children dying in infancy, readily cured or preventable diseases going untreated, daily hunger bringing despair and vulnerability to illness, the disease and lack of dignity that accompanies a lack of clean water and sewerage systems, and so on. Inequality of incomes within poor countries means the poorest people in the world are even worse off than the statistical averages show. All of these are symptoms of poverty, which is concentrated in some fifty countries, including virtually all of sub-Saharan Africa. Little wonder that Africa has become the focus of so much policy and campaigning effort.

The cure for poverty is economic growth. As table 3.4 indicates, there isn't a one-for-one relationship between growth of GDP and good outcomes such as longer life expectancy and better health. For poor countries, a bit of growth "buys" quite a lot of improvement in other human development indicators, as the annual Human Development Reports show.[6] However, it is quite clear that without growth none of the other improvements occur, while levels of health and life expectancy fall catastrophically in countries where the economy is contracting, such as parts of the former Soviet Union after 1989 or African countries in conflict (Dollar and Kray 2002). The links between inequality and economic growth are hotly debated, along pretty obvious philosophical lines, but a policy of redistribution from rich to poor has never led to a sustained reduction in poverty. Economic growth is necessary (although not sufficient) for this. So the question about causes and cures for poverty is a question about what causes economic growth, or explains its failure.

Even so, we can learn something from looking at simple statistics, at the list of countries which remain poor, for example. Interpreting the data to shed light on the causes of no-growth is much trickier, however. This is why the debates about statistical minutiae are so fraught. If you are inclined to favor global market capitalism, it helps your case to be able to show that poverty and inequality are falling, or vice versa if you're a critic of globalization. But if there can be so much disagreement about whether income inequality is rising or falling, perhaps resolving fundamental questions in political philosophy is just too much weight for the statistics to bear. For politics have long shaped the debate about economic development.

THE POLITICS OF POVERTY

The clash of modern-day views about globalization—good or bad; opportunity or exploitation—continues the tradition of partisanship in development economics. For many decades the subject occupied a mental

---

[6]This is the inverse of the finding that beyond a certain level of GDP per capita, more growth doesn't buy much more happiness, something which has been striking a chord in the rich countries recently (see, for example, Layard 2005). "Happiness" is strongly linked to desirable human development indicators such as health and employment (see chapter 4).

arena separate from the study of the economies of the rich countries. Just as the developing world acted as the theater of the Cold War in real life, the study of development was ideologically riven. Marxist and radical economists explained poverty and the absence of growth as the result of exploitation. Mainstream economists saw underdevelopment as a technical problem to be fixed, and certainly not the inevitable result of colonialism or power politics.

The first article specifically about economic development was written by Paul Rosenstein-Rodan (1943). The first pioneering thing about it was that economists had not previously thought of poor countries in a separate category from rich ones (or thought much about them at all), although it took a while for that thought to extend beyond the poor parts of Europe to the wider world. The article argued that industrial development could not occur without a "big push" because no individual industry would have any incentive to invest and expand unless all the others were doing so at the same time. Certainly in a small country, where any industry's domestic market would be very small, a solo bid for growth would be unprofitable unless other industries were also growing and thereby creating more demand for the products. There needed to be "balanced growth," to use a phrase which became common in the academic literature. The interdependence of different sectors meant there was a need for a coordinated effort, probably with a source of external finance. Similarly, there would need to be government-financed infrastructure because no private industry would risk funding a costly railway or dam by itself, but the existence of the new facility would reduce the costs and increase the profitability of all industries.

The idea planted by this paper that countries progressed in stages from underdevelopment to development took firm hold. One famous exponent was Alexander Gerschenkron, a Russian émigré, whose best-known book, from 1962, has the very politically incorrect title *Economic Backwardness in Historical Perspective* (Gerschenkron 1962). But the most influential text in terms of its impact on policy was a 1960 best seller called *The Stages of Economic Growth: A Non-Communist Manifesto* by Walt Rostow. Rostow was born to a Russian immigrant family in New York in 1916, and named after the poet Walt Whitman. His father had left Russia in 1904 because of his politics—Rostow *père* was a Social Democrat and an opponent of communism. He innoculated his son against Marxism. In an interview printed in the newsletter of the Cliometric Society, Rostow *fils* recalls an ominously charming, leather-jacketed visitor from the Soviet Union calling at the family home in New York some time in the 1920s, and added: "I was anti-Communist from a very early time." (July 1994, volume 9, no. 2; www.eh.net/Rostow.htm, accessed July 13, 2005). Walt Rostow advised Presidents Kennedy and Johnson during the 1960s and was still teaching at the University of Texas, Austin when he died at the age of 86. He saw a transition from stagnation to lasting growth via a "takeoff" which could be ignited by aid. The idea of achieving a takeoff is still influential.

In the brave new world of Anglo-Saxon, neoclassical economics in the 1950s and 1960s, many experts came to think about the absence of growth in poor countries as a simple, technical problem of progressing from one stage to the next. The problem with low incomes was that people did not have enough money to save, and without domestic savings there could be no investment, and without investment there would be no growth. As discussed in the previous chapter, Solow's 1956 growth model implied that higher investment could raise growth only temporarily, but the long-term growth rate would be unchanged given the state of technology and population growth. However, development economists ignored this implication of the cutting-edge growth theory of the time, and instead used its predecessor, the Harrod–Domar model. It *assumed* that output was proportional to the capital stock, so growth in output would be proportional to the change in capital stock, or investment.[7] At the same time, the notion of progress through successive stages of development firmly embedded the idea that poor economies would catch up to rich ones. The convergence predicted by the Solow model was married to the importance of capital investment assumed in the Harrod–Domar model.

To specialist economists, often working in the World Bank or other international institutions, a little bit of theoretical inconsistency was unimportant. The creation of official "development" institutions in the shape of the World Bank, the IMF, and UN agencies for a long time isolated many practicing development economists from the world of academic theory, and encouraged them to create their own body of technical know-how. But in line with the broad intellectual framework of postwar neoclassical economics, they strictly excised any political or historical context from their analysis—which was ironic, as they were almost certainly influenced in their analysis by the political context of

---

[7] Evsey Domar never intended his model to be used as a predictive growth model, and disavowed this interpretation—to no avail for the next fifty years.

these agencies, created in the postwar settlement and based in Washington, DC, and New York.

So in what seems, with hindsight, extreme simplemindedness, these economists calculated the desired level of future output for a particular economy, and worked backwards to calculate the growth and the investment spending which that would require. The difference between the investment spending figure and the country's domestic financial resources was known as the "financing gap." Inspired by the achievements of the space age and the Great Society, Western experts thought that surely it was only a matter of time before poor countries made their way through the stages of development. International donors, from the World Bank to individual governments, poured aid dollars into the financing gap, not only helping the poor but also cementing, it was hoped, a political commitment to the United States and the West rather than the Soviet Union.

Some of the results, from malfunctioning dams and useless factories to presidential Swiss bank accounts, palaces, and fighter jets, are notorious. It took an extraordinarily long time for such scandals to affect the aid-giving business, however. One reason is that development experts built up an institutional self-interest in keeping the money flowing: handing over aid was what they did—and still do. Another is that the Cold War fossilized the development business, as it did so many other institutions of the second half of the twentieth century. It is difficult to be sure what impact aid (and private external finance) has had on developing countries, but it is indisputable that it has not (so far) ended poverty.

But then neither did the radical approach to development. Radical and Marxist economists were inspired by Argentinian economist Raúl Prebisch, who worked for the United Nations Economic Commission on Latin America and later become the first director general of the United Nations Conference on Trade and Development. Prebisch had run the Argentinian central bank during the 1930s, a time of financial catastrophe and economic instability which turned many intellectuals around the world against free-market capitalism. He argued that colonialism had distorted the structure of poor economies (Prebisch 1950). It fossilized them in a pattern of exporting basic commodities to developed countries in return for manufactured goods on unfavorable terms—this is known for obvious reasons as "dependency theory." It lives on in today's debate about "unfair" trade, which I return to below. Increased exposure to international trade only exacerbated this dependency: despite decolonization, third world countries remained peripheral to the first world core.[8] This projected class warfare to a global scale, and echoed the Marxist thinker Rosa Luxemburg's analysis of imperial capitalism.

Prebisch was one of the few development experts of the time to actually come from a developing country. Along with his strong personality and political acumen within the UN bureaucracy, this made him extremely influential in parts of Latin America and some other countries, such as India. The great merit of dependency theory was that it avoided the mechanistic, unhistorical approach of the mainstream development economists who were handing out Western aid. Its great flaw was that it led to disastrous policy advice. This included turning away from trade, and developing domestic industries which in theory would substitute for the expensive imports of consumer goods and machine tools but in practice were inefficient and often corrupt. Soviet Russia was offered as an example of the success of industrialization by design, and the creation of new domestic industries in developing countries often involved centralized economic planning. It was not clear in 1960 or 1970, as it certainly was by 1989, that central planning was the least successful economic system ever devised by humankind. Prebisch died before the fall of the Berlin Wall, but after the failure of past policies had become clear during the Latin American economic crisis of the early 1980s.

Many poor countries adopted planning and other strategies recommended by left-wing economists, with dismal results. At one extreme, the famine in Ethiopia which launched the original Live Aid happened on the watch of a Marxist regime led by Colonel Mengistu. Tanzania, where Julius Nyerere ran a more or less benign socialist regime from 1964–1985, is still one of the poorest countries in Africa. Only Cuba and North Vietnam remain wholeheartedly communist, with dismal economic results, although they combine international isolation with domestic planning. But on the other hand, one of the bitterest experiences of communism has not prevented China from taking huge strides in eliminating poverty since the 1980s. And many noncommunist countries, especially in Africa, remain desperately poor. The choice of ideology in developing countries in the decades prior to the collapse of communism is not a good predictor of poverty and incomes now.

Marxism may be a dead duck, but a clear philosophical divide in thinking about economic development remains. In one of the many little ironies of life, today's radicals have adopted yesterday's mainstream aid

---

[8]Historical note for younger readers: the second world consisted of the communist countries, but the term was never used.

policy. Its most prominent advocate is Jeff Sachs, now Director of the Earth Institute at Columbia University. He was a bearded, precociously young, and brilliant junior professor in the Economics Department at Harvard when I met him—geeky, shambolic, but amiable, lively, and very loud indeed. He'd grown up in Detroit, and was to spend all of the years 1976–2002 based at Harvard, albeit with many trips abroad to offer economic advice, most famously to Poland's Solidarity opposition and then government, and to the new Russian government in the years immediately after 1989.

On the one occasion I've spoken to him since he joined the (small) firmament of economics superstars, he seemed to have changed very little indeed, apart from shaving off the beard. (A good decision.) Rock superstar Bono has described him as an advertisement for why air miles are bad for your health. *The New York Times Magazine* described Bono as "Jeff's sidekick" (November 7, 2004). The late Pope, John Paul II, was a fan (of Jeff, not of U2). *Time* magazine has twice named him (Jeff, not the Pope) as one of the 100 most influential people in the world. In short, Jeff is the hero of all those campaigning to make poverty history. At the heart of his policy advice is writing off debts and increasing aid—a huge increase in the flow of financial resources from rich-country governments to poor-country governments.

The logic is that poor countries are caught in a poverty trap. Incomes are too low for them to save out of their own resources: people have to spend all they earn on food and other necessities. With no savings, there can be no investment. With no investment, the economy can't grow and incomes will stay low. Sachs argues that there is a financing gap to be filled by international donors to enable the world to meet the 2015 Millennium Development Goals. Does this ring a bell? It is the same model that development experts at the World Bank and elsewhere used throughout the 1960s, 1970s, and 1980s.

One of those World Bank experts was William Easterly. Easterly spent sixteen years implementing the aid policies he now believes were badly flawed. As a result, he has become one of the leading critics of the campaign to increase aid. That he has a quirky sense of humor, to say the least, is demonstrated by asides in his curriculum vitae: he says neurosurgery is one of his hobbies, and describes himself as baseball columnist for *L'Osservatore Romano*, the official Vatican newspaper. Easterly left the World Bank on the publication of his book criticizing its *raison d'etre*, namely making grants and cheap loans to poor countries, and now codirects the Development Resources Institute at New York University, just across town from Jeff Sachs.[9] Easterly argues that neither of the links in the chain of reasoning in favor of increased aid are supported by the data on investment and growth. Out of eighty-eight countries over a thirty-year period, there is *no* positive correlation between aid and investment in eighty-four; and out of 138 countries, there is *no* positive link between investment and subsequent growth rates in 134 (Easterly 2001, chapter 2). With rare exceptions, more aid wasn't followed by higher investment, and higher investment hasn't been followed by faster growth.

Easterly also believes the giving of aid creates perverse incentives for its recipients. If funds arrive like manna from overseas, the incentive to increase domestic savings is reduced. Other skeptics about aid put it less neutrally. One long-standing critic of the aid business was the late Peter Bauer, the only prominent right-wing development economist, who said: "If external subsidies were indispensable for economic advance, mankind would still be living in the Stone Age" (Bauer 2000, p. 44). Lord Bauer (he was made a lord by Margaret Thatcher) described aid as "transferring money from poor people in rich countries to rich people in poor countries." He firmly believed it bred corruption and undermined democracy by helping elites stay in power. Atrocious governments can continue to implement damaging policies, and the more they immiserize their countries, the more aid they get in reward, he argued: the incentive aid gives to recipient governments is to prolong poverty rather than ending it. Bauer, who left Hungary for Britain in 1934, stood out as a rather ideological opponent of what was then the mainstream view until the 1970s. He and the American visitor Milton Friedman were snubbed by Keynes and his followers in Cambridge during World War II, excluded from economic seminars. But in recent decades the center of gravity among economists has shifted toward Bauer's view. Although most people, including economists, believe some aid is essential, favoring big increases in aid is now the domain of the fashionable, campaigning left. It should be noted that the logic of one's views about aid should extend to the equally fashionable cause of debt relief as well. William Easterly argues that it is not debt that needs writing off so much as the corrupt elites to whom the relief will be given. Chance are, if the crooks stay, the debt levels will grow again (see Easterly 2006).

---

[9]Its website (www.nyu.edu/fas/institute/dri/literary.html) includes a fine list of fiction and journalism related to economic development, a great introduction for general readers.

Advocates of increased aid or debt relief do of course recognize that in the past the money has not always been well spent. They therefore emphasize the need for what has come to be known as "good governance," spending aid on what it is intended for, and doing it efficiently. Much lip service is paid to the need for recipient governments to crack down on corruption. Jeff Sachs proposes setting up a new UN-run system of aid administration to ensure that the money is well spent on good things like schools and hospitals, a proposal which doesn't obviously add much when there are plenty of existing institutions involved in aid giving, such as the World Bank, IMF, UN, European Union, national governments, and nongovernmental organizations. Besides, you don't have to be a free-market economist like Lord Bauer to be a little skeptical about how well people will behave when faced with free money.

Some abuse of aid dollars wouldn't matter, perhaps, if we could be confident it would lift millions of people out of poverty. We're back with the need to find evidence which helps us judge between two competing diagnoses and prescriptions. Is aid spending essential to end poverty? Or is it, on the contrary, actually bad for the recipient countries? The next section considers the competing explanations for the absence of economic development, and asks whether or not it is possible to adjudicate between them on the basis of the evidence, rather than political philosophy. The last chapter ended with a theory of economic growth consistent with the broad long-term evidence on differences between countries. Can we turn this theoretical approach into a real understanding of why poor countries stay poor? Does economics now offer any hope of a consensus?

IS POVERTY PREDESTINED?

There is almost an embarrassment of competing explanations for persistent poverty (see Collier and Gunning (1999) for a survey). To test between them, economists run growth regressions—statistical relationships between GDP growth in different countries over time and alternative potential explanations. As described in the last chapter, such relationships rule out the Solow growth model because they do not show convergence between poor and rich countries; and they seem to support endogenous growth models by confirming the importance of education levels (conditional convergence). But other variables are thought to be important in explaining how well an economy performs. They can be summed up under the two broad headings of geography and history.

Geography

In a classic paper, Jeff Sachs pointed out that (as the map in figure 3.1 clearly shows) nearly all of the world's poorest countries lie in the tropics, while temperate countries are almost all rich. Singapore and Hong Kong are the only rich, tropical countries, and just a handful of others (Indonesia, Malaysia, Mauritius, and Thailand) have started to catch up (Sachs 2000). Countries which are both tropical and landlocked are the poorest in the world.

Sachs asked whether geography is economic destiny. The question was an obvious extension to the economic field of Jared Diamond's research popularized in *Guns, Germs and Steel*. Sachs identified several reasons for tropical underdevelopment. The most important are related to technology, which is, as we've seen, the main source of long-term growth. Technologies in vital areas such as agriculture and construction do not transfer easily across climate zones. By the start of the modern industrial period the temperate countries had a technological lead. In the case of agriculture, the gap in productivity is now extreme. What is more, there are increasing returns in innovation so the gap between temperate rich and tropical poor has been amplified over time. Social factors, such as a delayed "demographic transition," and the colonial legacy also play a role in amplifying the gap, in his argument. In later work, Sachs went on to emphasize the role of climate in propagating debilitating diseases such as malaria and tuberculosis. There is also a large technology gap in health care between the temperate and tropical countries.

The arguments about disease seem plausible, but on the other hand it is hard to see why Finland's climate should be so conducive to wealth; are Finns really rich just because the cold winters kill unfriendly bugs? And why have tropical countries not separately developed suitable agricultural technologies to increase productivity for their climatic conditions? After all, people born in the tropics are no less clever than temperate zone folk. The geography argument feels uncomfortably deterministic. Nevertheless, the paper had an electrifying impact on the development debate. Many academics have proceeded to test geographical indicators such as temperature and latitude in regressions that also include alternative explanations in order to try and measure the contribution of geography alone to growth. You will not be surprised to learn that the results are (forgive the pun) hotly debated.

Before turning to this debate, I want to mention a second quasi-geographical explanation, which *is* widely accepted: the presence of an

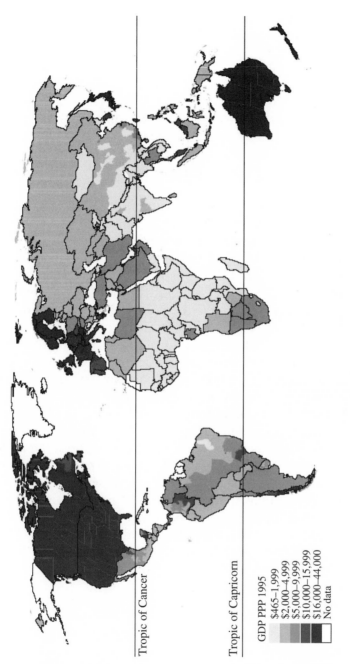

Figure 3.1. Map of GDP per capita. Source: Sachs (2000).

important natural resource such as diamonds or oil. The discovery of a lucrative resource has paradoxically adverse effect on the economy. It's known as "the curse of oil." The curse manifests itself in several ways. In an undemocratic country it enriches only the elite; the poor see few benefits. In an unstable country it is often the cause of conflict as warring parties battle to get their hands on the earnings. For example "conflict diamonds" are one of the causes of continuing fighting in Sierra Leone, 175th out of 175 countries in the UN's 2004 Human Development Index rankings, where people have only just over a two-in-five chance of surviving to the age of forty and almost half the population is undernourished: a curse indeed.

In many countries the discovery of natural resources creates a rich honeypot of fees and revenues for corrupt officials. Poor countries do not often have political institutions which can cope with the flood of revenues. And even in the least corrupt, most stable democracies, it harms the economy anyway. Large prospective export revenues from oil or natural gas raise the real exchange rate of the country blessed with the resource. The exchange rate is the price which brings into balance exports and imports—what one country wants to sell overseas with what other countries have to sell to it in return. Discovering oil tilts the balance, so the exchange rate must adjust. Unfortunately, that makes all the lucky country's *other* exports more expensive in terms of foreign currencies, so those export sales go down. And it makes imports more expensive in terms of domestic currency, so prices go up. What's more, the additional revenues at home from the resource discovery will boost the consumption of goods and services. The price of those not traded in global markets will rise, but the price of anything exported cannot go up because it's set in world markets. This too increases the exchange rate in real terms, another blow to local exports. In the developed world the curse of oil is called "Dutch disease" because it happened in the Netherlands when large reserves of natural gas were discovered in the 1970s. It happened to the United Kingdom and Norway too because of North Sea oil. British manufacturing industry has never really recovered from the blow of the resulting recession.

History

One of the explanations for the failure of growth most often offered as an alternative to geographical destiny is the importance of history. History manifests itself in a country's existing capabilities—the number of factories, the quality of the electricity or road network, the skills of the people, the level of savings accumulated, and so on. If you want to be rich, it helps not to start out poor. One particularly important aspect of a country's legacy is the level of education and skills attained by its people. This is, as we saw in the last chapter, central in growth theory now. Much empirical research confirms the importance of education (see, for example, Easterlin 1981; Ljungqvist 1993; Ray 2000). But perhaps more important still is a country's institutional legacy. We've already briefly met Douglass North, who emphasized in the historical context the vital importance of institutions for growth (see North (1990) for a summary of his earlier work). A pathbreaking piece of research by 1998 Nobel winner Amartya Sen established that democratic institutions can prevent famines (Sen 1981). A massive literature has since established the importance for the economy of institutions and politics, ranging from high-level political structures such as democracy or dictatorship, the type of legal system, the strength of property rights, the absence of corruption, all the way to the number of small organizations including churches that people join and the arrangements in villages for managing the irrigation system (see Przeworski and Limongi (1993) for an overview of the varying interpretations). The latter kinds of institution are often said to make up something called social capital, in analogy with physical and human capital, and we'll be returning to them too in chapter 8.

In the case of developing countries, flaws in political, legal, and economic institutions are increasingly thought to play an important part in the failure to grow. This is difficult to test statistically. How do you measure institutions? And which ones matter? Three aspects of institutional structure have gained particular attention. One is corruption. Pretty much everyone with advice on how developing countries can grow faster starts with the warning that no policies will be effective unless governments stamp out corruption. For example, it's part of the first recommendation of the thoughtful 2005 report of the Africa Commission.[10] Much research effort has been put into testing this theory, the trick being to include in the regression tests other influences on growth in order to measure the separate effect of corruption, however that is measured. Even then, care must be taken to check the direction of causality—it might be that poverty breeds corruption rather than the other way round.

Figure 3.2 does not represent a careful assessment of this kind, but it does give a good impression of the relationship being tested: in the high

---

[10]Set up by the United Kingdom as part of its G8 presidency that year.

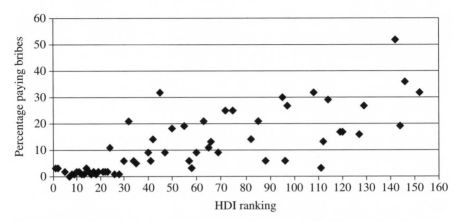

Figure 3.2. HDI ranking versus corruption. Sources: UNDP Human Development Report (2004); Transparency International (2003). Note: "GDP PPP" denotes the GDP per person in purchasing power parity international dollars.

human development countries on the left of the chart, there is next to no corruption (measured here as the proportion of respondents in the annual Transparency International (TI) survey who said they had to pay a bribe in the previous twelve months); beyond about number 25 in the HDI ranking, the degree of corruption tends to rise the lower the level of human development. (In this sample of sixty countries, the bottom three are in sub-Saharan Africa and the next lowest group in eastern Europe. If the TI survey covered more African countries, the relationship shown in the scatter plot would be much clearer.) This is an impressionistic illustration, but there is also good evidence based on careful statistical work that the economic cost of corruption in developing countries is very high, and the presence of corruption pervasive (see Transparency International 2003; Lipset and Lenz 2001).

A second debate about institutions concerns the absence of clear title to property for poor people in developing countries. A book by Hernando de Soto drew on an experiment he'd had researchers conduct in countries such as Peru, Haiti, and the Philippines, trying to register legal small businesses (de Soto 2000). In all the experiments, the number of steps, the bribes needed, and the bureaucratic incompetence involved made legal registration next to impossible. In real life, many would-be entrepreneurs opt to operate in the shadow economy instead. That means, however, they cannot raise external finance and don't hold the correct legal title to the assets they build. Growth is severely inhibited. De Soto's book was very influential, reflecting his prominence in public life in Peru as well as his record as a respected economist.

A third specific aspect of institutional legacy which is relevant to developing countries is the colonial experience. Distant history can explain poverty today if it still shapes the political system and institutional structure. A problem with the geography hypothesis as it stands is that countries' fortunes have ebbed and flowed, but their latitude doesn't change any faster than the continents drift. Of course climate and ecology have changed over long periods—this is part of Jared Diamond's (2005) account of the collapse of ancient societies. But tropical countries have stayed poor while temperate countries have become rich during the past 250 years. This is too short a time for geographical factors to have changed much but just about coincides with the age of empire and its aftermath. One influential paper notes that the countries which were relatively rich in 1500 were tropical; they are relatively poor today (Acemoglu et al. 2002; see also Easterly and Levine 2003). The reversal of fortunes occurred in the nineteenth century and is obviously related to industrialization, or the lack of it. It argues that the tropical colonies failed to industrialize because of the colonial institutions through which they had been governed. European settlers found tropical countries uncomfortable and disease prone, so they set up institutions such as plantations or large-scale mining, extracting the resources with relatively few European managers and administrators. On the other hand, many western Europeans settled in the colonies they found comfortable, such as North America or New Zealand, and created political and legal institutions very similar to the ones they had at home. The econometric research indicates that geography in itself does not help explain growth when institutions are included in the regression too. The weather and the germs do matter, but indirectly, through the history of colonial institutions and their political legacy.

There's an echo in this of the radical argument that poverty is caused by exploitation: it's just the long shadow of past exploitation, embedded in the institutions through which people interact and the patterns of behavior and association which are normal in their societies. It's clear there must be some truth in this. In his history of postwar Africa, Martin Meredith explains how newly independent Africans continued to see the state, inherited from colonizers, as an alien imposition, with the result that many didn't hesitate to cheat the government (see Meredith 2005, chapter 9). Corruption spread far and fast, with disastrous economic results. Still, like the pure geographical explanation, the historical explanation is a somewhat fatalistic account of growth and poverty. Many of us might feel uncomfortable with the determinism involved in linking growth to any kind of external or immovable factor, whether that's distance from the Equator or past history or even something less tangible such as a culture which predisposes people toward corruption. Is poverty really predestined, which would be one interpretation of the results of growth regressions? After all, some poor countries have grown their way to wealth. And besides, doesn't the answer that it's all because of their institutions just push the question one remove further back? What prevents the institutions from changing?

ENDOGENIZING POVERTY

In the light of these questions, endogenous growth theory is having an impact on development economics. We saw in the last chapter how the interaction between individuals' decisions, or feedback from one person's choices to another's, made multiple economic outcomes possible. This suggests looking at lack of coordination in key decisions as the reason for growth failures. And as people relate to each other through the social and political mechanisms we call institutions, this approach should be consistent with the evidence from regressions.

For example, the empirical evidence linking education, or "human capital," to growth is robust. As people in a poor country have, very reasonably, low expectations about future prospects, perhaps they are unwilling to take the risk of setting up a business, or investing in their children's education. Why spend money on school fees, and lose the child's potential income from working, when he (and certainly she) is unlikely to get a job good enough to repay the investment? After all, it's a poor country and there are hardly any good jobs to be had. Moreover, the family probably will not have the money to pay for schooling or cover the loss of income, and is very unlikely to be able to borrow it on the hope of a higher income years ahead (Ljungqvist 1993). I find this a compelling account of the failure of economies to grow because it tallies so much with my own family experience. Thirty years on, my older brothers and sister can still remember their struggle to convince my father, who'd left school at fourteen to work in a factory, that it was worthwhile going to university. He'd have much preferred them to be turning over part of their pay packets to their parents. (Luckily my eldest brother already had his doctorate from Oxford by the time it was my turn to have the argument.) If this was a common enough attitude in the United Kingdom in the 1970s, it is surely still common in many much poorer countries. If almost every family thinks like this, none will educate their children; but unless most children are better educated, nobody will ever set up businesses needing skilled labor and paying higher wages.

NYU economist Debraj Ray has pointed out that the old idea of balanced growth captures some of this flavor of self-fulfilling outcomes. Rosenstein-Rodan was describing a complementarity between the investment decisions of one firm and all the others (Ray 2000). None can profitably expand alone, so the likelihood is that none will; but if they all invested, they would all find it profitable. But as Ray points out, we do not understand at all well why an economy settles in one of these multiple potential grooves rather than another. What can jolt a population from self-fulfilling pessimism to self-fulfilling optimism? As soon as you make the plausible assumption that the process of moving from one groove to another involves some time lags between people's choices and better outcomes, the transition becomes extremely difficult. What can motivate the first brave souls to abandon traditional ways and try something new when they won't even get an immediate reward for it (Adsera and Ray 1998)?

In addition to expectations about the future, the historical legacy will certainly also explain why some countries end up with low-growth outcomes. History will have shaped expectations and beliefs. It will also have created today's starting point: the level of GDP and of physical and human capital in the economy. One part of the historical legacy highlighted by Ray and other development economists is the degree of inequality within the country. High inequality might lock in economic stagnation. Unsurprisingly, the empirical question of whether or not inequality hinders or helps growth has been trampled over, inconclusively, by an army of researchers. Some Latin American economies are extremely unequal but they are middle income rather than very poor; China has become more unequal as it has grown explosively; Russia has become more unequal too but its growth has tanked. Still, the most unequal countries are in general the poorest countries (or vice versa). One obvious channel through which inequality can hinder growth is that, where there is no way to transfer the resources from the haves to the have-nots through credit, because of an inadequate banking system, poor people are unable to afford to invest in the education that could make them better off. Both the inequality and the low growth are set in cement. You can see Hernando de Soto's point about the lack of title to property as an argument about the absence of mechanisms to overcome inequality: owning property is all the more important if it is not possible to borrow money from the bank.

WHICH POLICIES WORK?

Why is this endogenous growth framework of self-perpetuating poverty any different from the kind of poverty trap described by Jeff Sachs in making his case for massive increases in aid? Poor people have low incomes, so they can't save, so they can't invest, so growth and incomes stay low. The difference lies essentially in the consequent policy prescriptions. Thinking about the absence of growth as endogenous points to policies which are geared at producing changes in attitudes and behavior and might therefore be one-offs rather than permanent correctives. For example, a big increase in government spending for a period of some years might be earmarked to get everyone into secondary education, in order to jump-start the process whereby employers create enough good jobs needing high-school graduates to encourage everyone to want to complete high school because there are jobs paying higher wages; but a permanent increase in the general level of aid, on the other hand, would not obviously set the economy on a virtuous growth circle. Of course, donors do try to specify what aid should be used for but this does, uncomfortably, involve instructing recipient governments what to do.

Perhaps the key lies in aiding individuals, not governments? The endogenous growth framework suggests looking for policies designed to coordinate individual decisions, creating suitable incentives for everyone to invest, and seeking to overcome barriers such as the absence of banks and credit for poor people. It isn't at all noninterventionist, but rather differently interventionist. William Easterly uses the language of aiding "searchers" rather than "planners." The aim is to alter the incentives affecting individual behavior. One might describe it as the "clever push" rather than the "big push." Needless to say, designing clever policies is the hard part. While they will conform to certain principles, the details will depend on the institutional, historical, and even geographical specifics of each country.

Suppose a benevolent economist, a wiser and humbler figure than the economists from the World Bank and IMF who dished out recipes for growth with such confidence in the 1960s and 1970s, takes over a developing economy today. Her task is to jolt the country from one growth equilibrium to another. She knows that such jumps from vicious to virtuous circles are hard to achieve, but is encouraged by the fact that when they occur the results are so startling everyone will describe it as a "miracle." Hence the Japanese miracle of the 1960s, followed by the East Asian miracle, and also the Irish miracle, and perhaps now the Indian miracle. Can we say what policies she should introduce to work a miracle in a small and extremely poor sub-Saharan African country or a larger but stagnant South American country?

Some prescriptions are both banal and extremely difficult to implement. Most of what comes under the heading of "good governance" is in this category. Democracies tend to have better economies than those run by murderous kleptocrats. Civil war is bad for growth. Governments should clamp down on corruption, ensure that the legal system is fair and honest, and that officials are capable of doing their jobs. Institutional reform is important but extremely difficult because, as we'll see in chapter 8, institutions are aggregations of millions of individual decisions and the way they interact with each other.

Almost as important, and somewhat easier to implement, are some basics of macroeconomic policy. Governments need to run their finances and set interest rates so that inflation stays low and the budget deficit never gets too big. High inflation is extremely bad for poor people, whose incomes can never keep up with rising prices, and also destabilizes the economy. It is only relatively recently that the governments of rich countries have figured out how to keep macroeconomic policy stable, and most of them find it hard to control their budget deficits. The task is all the harder for the governments of poor countries, who usually have few sources of tax revenue and little capacity to collect the money. It doesn't help that many development campaigners have demonized the idea of macroeconomic stability. They refer to it as "the Washington Consensus," implying that it's a conspiracy on the part of Wall Street financiers in cahoots with the IMF, rather than a solid professional consensus among economists. IMF advice to governments to cut out-of-control and inflationary budget deficits (often referred to as "structural adjustment") is particularly controversial among leftist critics, who think all government spending is good, and less government spending will hurt poor people disproportionately. However, in many cases profligate developing-country governments are not spending on poor people, but rather on the middle classes and elites, or even of course on themselves (Alesina et al. 1998).

Is Globalization Good?

Other parts of the IMF's advice have been even more controversial, and none more so than the pressure it put on developing countries in the 1990s to open their economies to flows of capital from overseas as well as to trade in goods and services. The buzzword for the dramatic increases in trade and foreign investment was globalization. Trade had been growing steadily since the end of World War II thanks to policies of liberalization in imports and exports, and the new policies of capital liberalization helped encourage a big increase in cross-border investment of various types during the 1990s. Then 1997–98 brought a serious financial crisis to the East Asian countries which had gone furthest down this path. The crisis in effect launched the campaigns which led to Live8 and Make Poverty History. There was a backlash against both trade in goods and services and international capital flows. Does economics have a verdict on international openness?

One of the core beliefs of most economists is that international trade is a good thing. The essence of economic activity is mutually beneficial exchange between people who have different things to offer. The benefits of the division of labor stood at the core of Adam Smith's appreciation of the market. International trade extends the benefits of specialization across borders. Globalization has intensified the process.

As described earlier in this chapter, one strand of the development literature has long challenged this. Following Raúl Prebisch, dissenting economists tended to favor import protection for domestic industries. They pointed to the examples of successful catch-up countries such as Japan and South Korea, where the government was careful to nurture domestic industries up to the point where they could compete in world markets for consumer goods, for example. This group criticized the conventional policy prescription in favor of freer trade. Convention won the day, and the liberalization of trade in goods was extended in successive trade "rounds" under the General Agreement on Tariffs and Trade (GATT), the set of rules established after World War II for negotiating on trade issues. The World Trade Organization took over from the GATT in 1995 and has spent nearly a decade trying to agree another "round" of liberalization.

There is little dispute that many economies have benefited from ever-freer trade. The question concerns the impact on poor countries. The "fair-trade" argument, which is the successor to dependency theory, is that the WTO's rules do not give poor countries reasonable access to world markets. In particular, agricultural subsidies in Europe and North America distort global food markets so much that other food producers are harmed. EU farm subsidies are certainly grotesquely large: over €300 billion a year, more than the GDP of all of sub-Saharan Africa, and said to be enough to fly all of Europe's cows around the world first class. The effect is particularly severe for Southern Hemisphere producers of agricultural commodities such as sugar and cotton. This is a good argument. However, the fair-trade community takes its arguments further than many economists would go on the basis of the evidence. For the impact of trade rules and protectionism is more opaque in the case of other commodities; and some fair traders just don't like businesses, regardless of what they do. They wrongly imply that international trade, and particularly its regulator, the World Trade Organization, is somehow by nature "unfair."

There have been two important lines of argument making an economic case for caution about freer trade. The first one was a call for "managed" trade made by Paul Krugman in particular during the 1980s. The argument is related to the new generation of models described in the last chapter. Increasing returns to scale imply that there are large gains to specialization, so that geographic clusters of activity emerge. In this case it might be better for global welfare, and will almost certainly be better for a country which can specialize, if policy is directed toward this kind of clustering rather than favoring international exchange between many competing companies doing the same thing in different countries. The applicability of such arguments is clear in thinking about, say, competition for global market share between Airbus and Boeing. When it comes to a developing country thinking about its food processing or textiles industry, though, it is less persuasive. In fact, it looks a lot like the old arguments in favor of protection of domestic industries and import substitution. In the end Krugman himself reached the conclusion that managing trade was simply too vulnerable to lobbying of government by special-interest groups, and it is therefore better not to try—although of course governments do all still favor major national companies in trade talks (Krugman 1994a,b).

A more recent note of caution has come from Harvard economist Dani Rodrik. He (rightly, I think) believes that the kind of growth regressions in which researchers so often try to weigh one explanation for growth against others are flawed (Rodrik 2005). It is easy to get misleading results if important variables are left out (so something that's included might be reflecting the influence of whatever's excluded), or if

a measure trying to capture a policy—How protectionist is the country?—
is misdefined (Rodríguez and Rodrik 1999). Correcting for such issues,
he reported that there was no sign that countries grew faster because
of more-open trade policies. In subsequent research, Rodrik has argued
that openness to trade is in fact important for economic growth, but
indirectly so. Countries which are open to international trade have a
firmer rule of law, and it is the rule of law which raises growth (Rodrik
2004a; Rigobon and Rodrik 2004). Few economists fully shared his earlier reservations anyway. The overwhelming weight of evidence is that
trade is beneficial.

When it comes to capital flows, the balance of evidence lies with critics of the speed of liberalization during the 1990s. Not surprisingly,
there was much soul searching in the IMF and among economists generally after the 1997–98 global financial crisis. It is now widely accepted
that developing countries should move very cautiously when it comes to
allowing the free flow of some kinds of investment, especially short-term
financial investments, aptly described as "hot money."

THE VERDICT ON AID

There is a lot of political momentum behind the campaign to increase
aid spending. At the 2005 G8 summit, Western leaders promised to write
off large amounts of developing-country debt and increase aid, to the
tune of an extra $50 billion a year (on top of the existing $79 billion a
year). The additional money has a string attached, which is that recipients must ensure the aid is being "well spent." Certainly none of the
personal extravagance or secret bank accounts which were so common
in the past. The money must be earmarked for specific projects, and
carefully monitored.

This nannying insistence on spending the money properly stems from
one particularly influential piece of research. This research, which supports the claim that "good" aid is extremely effective in raising growth
and reducing poverty, was published in 2000, and circulated in development circles as a World Bank working paper before that (Burnside and
Dollar 2000). Twice a year the World Bank and IMF hold joint meetings,
usually in Washington, DC. The events, which feature set-piece meetings
of finance and economy ministers from around the world, became notorious for the lavishness of their cocktail parties. Politicians and officials
were gathering to discuss poverty while unashamedly guzzling cham-
pagne and canapés. So controversial did the parties become that by the

time I started covering the events as a journalist they had been, sadly, very much toned down. I can clearly remember chatting at one of these duller cocktail parties to a senior British treasury official who was clutching a glass of warm white wine in one hand and a thick printout in the other. "This is it," he said. "It's the aid bible."

"It" was the research of Craig Burnside and David Dollar, two World Bank economists. They had looked at the impact of aid spending in different developing countries and found that it boosted growth in those countries which had "good" economic policies. Good policies involved keeping the government's budget deficit low, keeping inflation low, and opening the economy to foreign trade and investment. Happily, these were exactly the policies the World Bank had been recommending. The research was so enthusiastically welcomed because it validated the Bank continuing to do what aid officials wanted: giving aid to the governments of poor countries as long as they did as they were told. I'm putting an unkind gloss on the paper, which is a substantial and serious piece of research. Nevertheless, it did have a clear institutional benefit for the World Bank.

Several researchers have since called the Burnside and Dollar results into question, however, finding that with small changes in the data used—the countries included, the years, the definitions of how policies are measured—the link between aid, policies, and growth vanishes. Most economists cannot find a robust link between more aid and faster growth. Down the road from the World Bank in Washington, DC, at the IMF, economists Raghuram Rajan and Arvind Subramanian have recently made the disturbing finding that aid has had adverse effects on the economy even when given to a government with good economic policies. They point out that even if every single aid project is beneficial in itself, large aid flows could have damaging systematic effects on the economy. Ignore the criticism that aid makes governments dependent on foreign assistance and has a corrupting influence. Even without any other drawback, inflows of foreign exchange will tend to raise the exchange rate of the recipient country. This makes its exports less competitive in world markets.

If this sounds familiar, it should: this is the same phenomenon as "the curse of oil." Is there a "curse of aid" too? Rajan and Subramanian find that recipients of large amounts of aid do indeed experience this effect. Their export sectors grow more slowly than those of countries which don't receive much aid. Not only does this hit growth directly, but the export sector is also typically the source of skills and productivity

93

improvements which spill over to the rest of the economy. Interestingly, private inflows of foreign currency do not seem to have the same effect. Remittances sent home by nationals working overseas do not send the exchange rate higher and hamper competitiveness. The reason seems to be that remittances are self-correcting: people don't send so much money home if the exchange rate is rising.

> In sum, then, the bad news is that even if delivered with the best intentions and used carefully by recipient governments, there are side effects like adverse impact on competitiveness which can offset aid's beneficial effect on growth. This may well explain why it is so hard to find robust positive effects of aid on growth. The good news is that by paying careful attention to macroeconomic management and issues like absorptive capacity, perhaps aid may have a better chance of success. We have to be careful, however, given the past checkered history of aid, that we do not place more hopes on aid as an instrument of development than it is capable of delivering.
>
> Rajan and Subramanian (2005)

In practice, very few development economists would argue against substantial aid for poor countries. There are many basic humanitarian needs to be met, for example in cases of floods, famine, and war. And many would be optimistic that it is possible to spend the money better in the future than in the past; it could hardly be spent worse in many cases. But a diminishing proportion would share Jeff Sachs's optimism that massive aid spending will be enough to set poor countries on the path to sustained growth.

AND SO THE ANSWER IS?

The campaign against globalization was catalyzed by the financial crisis of 1997, and nurtured by a wider sense of disappointment that the promise the underdevelopment could be fixed was never realized. Mainstream economists had a clear idea of what policies governments ought to implement—and the results were pretty disappointing. Although a smaller proportion of the world's population is living in poverty, we hoped for more. Although China and India have made giant strides, Bangladesh and Malawi have not.

The high-level principles underlying the mainstream view have not changed. Macroeconomic and political stability, and the rule of law, are fundamental to economic growth. All economists would agree that institutions are important, and as chapter 2 describes there has been a lot of recent progress in analyzing what exactly it is that's important. The innovation in development economics has been to start to assess in detail which policies can jolt an economy from no-growth to growth. In a recent paper, Rodrik uses the same metaphor as Jeff Sachs in his book: the aim is economic diagnostics. However, he draws a contrasting conclusion. Where Sachs and the campaigners recommend the same policies for all—cut debt, increase aid, spend the money on investment—Rodrik concludes that all developing countries have different problems, and a list of identikit reforms will not make a difference. More and more economists are coming to this conclusion. After all, the success stories—Japan, South Korea, Ireland, China, perhaps now Poland—have all taken different paths. Rodrik writes: "Sound institutional arrangements have large elements of indeterminacy and country specificity. Policy experimentation therefore becomes a necessary component of institutional development" (Rodrik 2004b). Do these involve a lack of skills? If skilled workers are paid a high premium relative to unskilled workers, the answer is probably yes. Does the country have poor infrastructure relative to other countries at similar levels of development? If so, the social return to investment is probably too low.

A massive amount of research is underway on detailed policies in the specific context of particular countries. This doesn't set the pulse of campaigners racing: it's hard to draw in the crowds for a big concert with a slogan about teaching assistants and class sizes in Vadodara and Mumbai in India (Banerjee et al. 2005). Even so, development economics is using new growth models, the new techniques of econometrics, and the increasing availability of data to make rapid progress in devising policies which will, one day, make poverty history.

Prologue to Part 2

A change of gear. The first three chapters addressed the really big question in economics, looking at theories and evidence on how economies in the aggregate grow over time. Economists have made huge strides in the past twenty years on both the empirical and theoretical fronts. I want to turn in the next three chapters to the perspective of individual behavior. Here too there have been amazing discoveries in economic research. Then in part 3 I will aim to show that the microfoundations of social organization join up with the macroperspective of part 1, adding up to a very rich and ever-improving understanding of why economies prosper, or why they do not. To get there, part 2 takes a detour into the basics of microeconomic theory.

I imagine that courses in introductory microeconomics form the major hurdle that deters many students from majoring in the subject. The novice is asked to take as given all kinds of implausible assumptions about how people behave. We assume that consumers want to maximize utility (what's that?), that they calculate their choices (using differential calculus!) in order to do so, that their preferences have all kinds of happy mathematical properties explained away as common sense and convenience (convexity, reflexivity, continuity, transitivity, monotonicity, and local nonsatiation). We assume, without even noticing, that everyone knows everything they need to. Some equations and proofs later, and hey presto, we have derived a demand curve. We go through the same process for firms producing goods and services, in order to derive a supply curve, and then other proofs to establish that demand and supply curves will cross at a market equilibrium with pleasing properties for our welfare.

However, what I aim to do in the next three chapters is not at all make fun of the use of mathematics to describe how people make decisions. On the contrary, although I'll hide it from you, microeconomics is more mathematical than ever. What is more, despite the strong assumptions that we make (and which we economists are quickly socialized into accepting as normal), conventional microeconomics is an extremely powerful tool for analyzing and changing the real world. This is thanks in no small part to the creation of rich new data sets about individual behavior and choices, and new econometric techniques for assessing the evidence and thus devising better policies or court judgements with clearer impacts. The joint development of better-quality data, richer theories, and sophisticated econometrics since the mid 1980s has closely paralleled what happened in the top-down approach described in part 1.

What I also address in this part at some length is how fascinating areas of economic research are testing and sometimes abandoning the restrictive assumptions we always used to make because that was the only way we were able to use the mathematics. Chapter 4 looks at the assumption that we maximize utility as conventionally captured in a monetary measure such as income or profit. Chapter 5 describes the fruitful marriage between economics and psychology, exploring what assumptions we could validly make about how people choose. Chapter 6 looks at the way economists are abandoning the old, convenient assumption of perfect, or at least symmetric, information.

PART 2

Are Individuals Free to Choose?

What's It All About?

Jeremy Bentham died on June 6, 1832 at the age of eighty-four. The eminent philosopher left his body to a disciple, one Southwood Smith, who dissected the corpse before an audience of Bentham's friends at the Webb Street School of Anatomy. It was the first known example of such a bequest to science. Smith passed the preserved head and body to University College London (UCL) in 1850. Bentham's remains are still on display there, or rather the body is displayed with a wax head, topped with a floppy hat. The real head lies locked up in the vaults as it was so often stolen by students from rival colleges (www.answers.com/topic/university-college-london-1). Bizarre as his bequest seems, Bentham hoped to demythologize the human body by creating what he called an "auto-icon." However, he managed instead to create a rich personal mythology. It's said that the body is wheeled out to attend important UCL meetings, where it is recorded in the minutes as "present but not voting." Bentham is notorious, too, for the idea of the panopticon, a prison built around a central observation point for the effective supervision of prisoners who would not know when they were being watched; he believed the design would create a "sentiment of an invisible omniscience." This is the suffocating concept Michel Foucault (1977) used as a central image in *Discipline and Punish: The Birth of the Prison*, his assault on modern society's controls on individual autonomy.

In fact, Bentham was an all-round eccentric. He was ahead of his time in wearing knitted woollen underpants (so it was discovered post mortem by Mr. Smith): most Victorian men simply tucked their shirt tails between their legs. And, whether or not due to the scratch of wool on his testicles, Bentham was the intellectual father of utilitarianism, the philosophy that can be summed up as "the greatest happiness of the greatest number." Utilitarianism formed one of the key foundation stones of economics. It gave us the concept of marginal utility, the extra benefit gained as the result of one choice rather than another, which in turn ultimately underpins the theory of rational choice and the efficiency of the price mechanism and markets. In the years since the development of these concepts in classical economics, their philosophical basis has got lost. Few economics students learning about indifference curves read Bentham's *Introduction to the Principles of Morals and Legislation* or John Stuart Mill's *Utilitarianism*. However, economics is getting back to basics. There is a growing body of research into whether or not economic success makes us *happy*. If not (and the suspicion is that it doesn't), should economic policy only or mainly be concerned with growth? The program of research brings economists into partnership with psychologists, epidemiologists, and public-health experts. At present it has had little influence on current economic policy, but this seems to be changing—many people would argue for the better.

The issues in trying to understand whether economists can make us happy can be divided into two groups. One concerns whether the target of economic policy can be improved. We measure growth as the increase in GDP per person. But does this make sense? GDP is a specific accounting concept which is only a proxy for things we really care about such as the ability to purchase goods and services but also health, longevity, friendship, and quality of life. It is not real in the way that the number of cars produced within certain geographical boundaries is real, although GDP certainly incorporates measures such as the physical output (and price) of cars, cornflakes, insurance policies, houses, and the million and one other products and services created in the economy. Many people in the West are asking whether we don't have enough of all of these already, and whether the social and environmental price for further growth might not be too high.

We—humans and economists alike—only care about GDP as an indicator of things that do matter. Contrary to popular impression, some economists at least have been well aware of the limitations of this particular statistical measure, and we will explore some of its shortcomings below. The Human Development Index, discussed in the previous chapter, is one widely used indicator of economic progress which incorporates, in addition to GDP, measures such as life expectancy, infant mortality, literacy, and calorie intake. So the question is whether there is a better measure to use as a target in order to assess the effectiveness of economic policy. A second area of research involves looking directly at evidence about what improves well-being using surveys asking people how they feel, with results which turn out to raise some fundamental questions about how we organize our societies. This is a live debate in the wider world as well as within the subject, so new findings on what makes people happy—and suggestions as to how to improve well-being—are being published all the time. The number of articles in the EconLit database referring to "subjective well-being" (as happiness is referred to by academics) climbed from four in 1991–95 to twenty-nine in 1996–2000 and one hundred in 2001–5 (and there was no significant upward trend in the total number of articles over those years).

So happiness is worth a chapter for two reasons. The first is that it links to a series of earlier debates in economic research about defining the purpose of economic policy, and measuring the policy targets correctly. The second is that the new focus on happiness is an important part of the emerging intellectual framework in economics, which is steadily replacing some of the unsatisfactory parts of the twentieth-century neoclassical approach. The next three chapters look in different ways at this important aspect of modern economics, and its fruitful overlap with psychology. What do we humans care about? How do we take decisions? And what do the answers to these two questions imply about how economic policy can improve our well-being?

What Are We Measuring?

When a finance minister presents his budget with the boast that his policies have increased growth, he clearly expects his listeners and voters to be impressed. Pretty much every national economy now collects statistics, however imperfectly, to measure GDP; and the complicated methodology for doing so is agreed internationally by statisticians and revised every so often. There are three ways to measure total GDP: add up all the incomes in the economy; add up all the output; or add up all the expenditure. When proper account is taken of both the future and the rest of the world (in the form of savings and the balance of payments) these three approaches should all give (roughly) the same figure. One might imagine that this task is complicated in practice but straightforward in principle. Not so: even the principle is fraught with complexity.

There are several complications, some of which relate to the practicalities of constructing the GDP statistics, and others which concern whether GDP is the right thing to measure at all. Starting with the first category, one is a flaw which has become particularly acute recently: namely, how to account for new or much better types of product such as microfiber underwear versus woollen undergarments, or electric lights rather than oil lamps, or more powerful and faster computers. GDP measures the volume and price of goods: bushels of wheat and price per bushel, number of light bulbs and price per bulb. Of course, the mix of goods constantly changes, so it no longer includes crinoline hoops and carriages—today it will include jeans and computers instead. In general, quality improvements are ignored. But new technologies such as computers present a special problem because of the scale and pace at which their quality has improved and their price declined. We are buying many more of them than we did twenty years ago so their *real* (volume) contribution to GDP has been rising. But a $1000 computer of 2005 is also a vastly better product than $1000 worth of a 1995 or 1985 computer. The staggering quality improvement is not captured in the statistics.

Or at least it wasn't until statisticians started estimating "hedonic" prices: that is, not the price anyone might pay for an actual laptop, but a construct measuring the price per unit of a given quality of computer services. A hedonic price index is constructed from regressions that attribute elements of the actual price paid to different quality characteristics—processing speed, DVD drives, memory size, and so on. These equations are then used to track continuing changes in the quality mix. Nobody ever pays a hedonic price for their computer and yet dividing the total amount spent on computers by a hedonic price index gives the best estimate we have of the volume of real computing power in the economy. While the computer example is extreme, there are many, many goods whose quality improves so profoundly that measured prices will understate the "real" growth of the economy. In a famous 1997 paper economist William Nordhaus of Yale University calculated that the price per lumen of illumination had declined by more than 99% since 1800, taking into account the technological shift from tapers and candles to oil lamps to electric light, whereas the measured price indices for lighting equipment had risen by 180% (Nordhaus 1997). One 1996 survey estimated that the omission of innovation and quality improvements had understated real U.S. GDP growth by 0.6-1.5 percentage points a year, over a period when measured GDP growth was usually 2-3% a year (Shapiro and Wilcox 1997). At about the same time, the Boskin Commission in the United States estimated that official statistics overstated consumer price inflation by 1-1.5%, and correspondingly understated real GDP growth by the same amount (Boskin Commission 1996). The Bureau of Economic Analysis now uses hedonic prices for a number of high-technology goods.

This was a live issue during the New Economy boom of the late 1990s, when it became popular in countries like France and Germany to argue that their GDP growth was so much lower than that of the United States largely because of the different approaches to calculating prices and real GDP; but other national statistical offices are now following the lead of the Bureau of Economic Analysis. The adjustment for innovation and quality improvement is starting to be incorporated into the statistics. Even so, it is very unlikely that GDP will ever capture the full impact of the number and variety of new products and services in the economy: there will never be hedonic prices for toothpaste or tights or sliced bread, but mundane innovations such as these have made a vast contribution to the ease of everyday life.

A second problem of GDP measurement is that most economies have governments which provide services and employ workers. If the government just acted like a big company, charging a price for what it provides, it would be simple to measure both the volume of output and the value in the same way as for privately provided services and goods. But many public-sector services are provided free or subsidized to users: there is not always a market price available. There are some ways round this problem. Statisticians might be able to use school fees in the private sector to estimate the value of public-school lessons, for example. Other government services, such as local administration or the administration of justice, may be much harder to find comparable market prices for, however.

Even so, accounting for the public sector is not a serious hurdle in itself. But it is just one example of the difficulties which arise in measuring the contribution of services not bought and sold in a market. There are many other nonmarket services which are simply omitted from GDP. The most glaring example is household production, as the statisticians call it: all the domestic services needed to run a home, the cleaning and childcare and gardening and cooking. Again, there are private-sector versions of these services: it would be possible to use the prices of these comparators to include an estimate of household production, as well as government production, in GDP. Britain's Office for National Statistics (ONS) has in fact carried out this exercise. Time-use surveys are based on diaries kept by a large number of people who recorded how they spent every half hour of their days. These provided estimates of how much time was spent carrying out domestic tasks. Private-sector equivalent jobs were used to calculate the value of this unpaid work. Adding household production would roughly double conventional GDP, the ONS found (see www.statistics.gov.uk/timeuse/default.asp). In a country like the United Kingdom this might be seen as no more than a nice feminist point, as women spend much more time than men on such tasks. In poor economies, though, the point is harder to dismiss because so many of the activities which take place in the market in developed economies are instead performed by the household in developing countries. Not only cooking but the growing and processing of food might be carried out at home. Construction of dwellings, provision of water, entertainment— these are all examples of the many activities which are counted in GDP in some countries and not in others. So the location of the boundary between market and nonmarket activities is problematic for the concept of GDP.

This takes us on from the measurement to the definitional issues. As well as omitting many goods and services which clearly ought to be included in the sum total of economic activities we value and would like to increase, GDP includes many things we'd all like to see less of. If someone provides a service, it's in there. More crime can increase GDP if it means there has been growth in the services provided by lawyers. More ill health increases use of medical services, which adds to GDP. Oil spills lead to GDP growth because of the clean-up operations. A hurricane or earthquake boosts growth too because there is a reconstruction boom: we measure the increase in activity but not the loss in current wealth and future potential caused by deaths and damage to infrastructure.

One key omission of this kind is an assessment of the environmental impact of GDP growth. The construction and operation of a new factory are clearly good for conventional measures of growth: more jobs and wages, more goods bought and consumed. If the factory pollutes the local river, however, that could be measured as a plus, too: another business might get the job of cleaning up. The "externality" imposed on nearby residents (bad smells, toxic effects) is not accounted for in practice, although in principle one can imagine deducting the amount by which residents might need to be compensated for the pollution. Nor is the full environmental impact of the energy and materials used by the factory accounted for. The monetary cost of energy use is counted, but not the depletion of the finite resources of oil or coal used in generating the energy: here too the current gain is measured but not the future potential loss. For example, one economist has estimated that the depletion of minerals has cost the equivalent of about 1% of global consumption each year (Weitzmann 1999). Politicians still talk to voters in terms of boosting growth in GDP, however, which has led some economists and environmentalists to regard economic growth as actually a bad thing rather than a benefit or a mixed blessing, arguing that growth can diminish economic well-being if environmental impacts are properly accounted for. One well-known advocate of this view is Herman Daly, who introduced the term "uneconomic growth" (see Daly 1996).

An increasing number of national statistical offices are very alert to these environmental considerations and now collect figures relevant to making an assessment of the environmental and resource impact of economic activity. But these are usually kept as "satellite accounts" and not included in GDP. Some researchers, mostly inspired by the environmental considerations, have therefore tried to devise alternatives to GDP. Well-known examples that try to capture all of these considerations in an improved measure of the economy as a whole are the Index of Sustainable Economic Welfare (ISEW) and the Genuine Progress Index (GPI). These indices differ in detail but they all start with GDP, make an addition for unpaid household work, and deductions for environmental bads. Other adjustments are included. For example, GDP is reduced when there is an increase in income inequality. Calculations for eleven countries can be found on the Friends of the Earth website. In the case of the United States, conventional GDP per capita increased fourfold between 1950 and 1995; but there was a two-fifths decline in the GPI per capita. The pattern is the same in every case.

Interestingly, the website allows users to calculate their own measure of economic well-being by changing the weights assigned to different parts of the calculation. It is possible for a very gloomy person to work out that the United Kingdom's ISEW has fallen to zero (www.foe.co.uk/campaigns/sustainable_development/progress, accessed September 15, 2005). On the other hand, it is not possible for a Pollyanna (one who cares not at all about the environment but wants to add a high value for domestic labor) to construct an ISEW which matches or outpaces GDP. The alternative index is defined and constructed to make optimism impossible. Yet there *are* reasons to be cheerful, and to believe that conventional GDP overstates well-being by leaving out environmental impacts but underestimates economic well-being in other ways. The introduction of new and better-quality goods, as we just saw, is one reason. Another, discussed in the previous chapter, motivated the construction of the Human Development Index (HDI). There have been huge improvements in well-being, over time and in most countries, such as greater longevity, reduced infant mortality, and better health, which are omitted from the national accounts. The HDI is similar in its construction to the GPI but includes different variables: infant mortality and literacy, for example, and women's empowerment. In contrast to the GPI, growth in the HDI has exceeded growth in GDP.

The HDI approach has been extended by economic historian Nicholas Crafts, who calculates the index back to 1870 (including GDP per capita, life expectancy, literacy, and school enrolment). Unsurprisingly, the HDI going so far back into the past displays the same phenomenon as the HDI post 1960: it grew much faster than GDP per capita. Crafts then compares the HDI with GDP per capita adjusted for the value people place on reduced mortality rates and reduced working hours. The adjustments could be introduced to the existing measure of GDP to reflect a broader understanding of living standards, rather than replacing it. They too indicate that conventional GDP underestimates "true" growth, with more of the increment coming from reduced working hours, at least since 1950.

Perhaps you begin to see a flaw with all of these alternatives to GDP. Each approach calculates an index composed of sometimes wildly non-commensurate indicators. GDP is already counting haircuts, food, cars, insurance, and all of the huge variety of goods and services produced in a modern economy, adding up the amounts spent on each to get a measure of nominal GDP and dividing by a price index to work out the volume of economic output, or real GDP. This is weird enough. But the alternative indices are mixing together conceptually different items: income inequality, greenhouse gas emissions, life expectancy, and output of food and haircuts are just different, and are not measured in the same kind of units.

Moreover, the alternatives, such as the HDI and GPI, include only the things of interest to their creators. But why? What is the rationale for including pollution but excluding literacy rates? Which index can be justified as the ultimate target of policy makers? Defining an alternative index to conventional national income or output involves value judgements about the weight to be put on other components apart from economic growth. Surely it makes more sense to stick to GDP as an economic target, and consider explicitly any trade-offs between growth in economic output and the quality of the environment or the quality of health, rather than submerging them in a single index? This was the approach adopted by the Australian Bureau of Statistics (ABS) in its publication *Measures of Australia's Progress*, launched in 2002 (see www.abs.gov.au). This annual assessment of whether or not life for Australians is getting better includes fifteen headline indicators that almost everybody accepts as important, chosen in a national consultation, plus an accompanying suite of several hundred indicators that some people thought important and others didn't. The ABS notes that it is not for statisticians to make value judgements in constructing indicators.

There is indeed little policy value in a mix-and-match policy target which can be made to say whatever reflects the biases and concerns of its creators. Some omissions, notably of environmental impacts, certainly overstate real GDP; but a majority of economists would probably accept that the omissions which understate GDP are bigger, and probably very much bigger. In which case, faster growth in GDP remains a good target for economic policy. We can be confident that people will be growing better off even faster than the statistics indicate.

Or can we?

DOES ECONOMIC GROWTH MAKE US HAPPY?

Richard Layard was thirty-one when he was asked to become a researcher for a major U.K. inquiry into the higher education system, the Robbins Committee, which set the stage for a huge expansion of university education in the 1960s. He was asked whether it would be better to spend extra public money on universities or on regeneration of the kind of depressed northern towns like Newcastle where Angus Maddison grew up. Realizing he had no idea how to go about tackling the question, Lord Layard (as he has become) started to learn economics. It came as a shock—he'd studied history and sociology in his own student days—but he learned to love the analytical power of the rational-choice framework, and also the empiricism of economics, the insistence on making theories testable and finding the relevant evidence. In his recent research, as founder of the Centre for Economic Performance at the London School of Economics, Layard turned his quantitative spotlight onto what seems to be an intrinsically qualitative question: what makes us happy?

As it happens, over the years a number of surveys have asked thousands of people in many countries exactly this question. To be precise, the question is typically: "Taking all things together, would you say you are very happy, quite happy, or not very happy?" In the United States and the United Kingdom just over half say they're quite happy, and only a small proportion say they're not very happy. The responses are very different in other countries, though. The average happiness level reported in such surveys is lower in countries such as Greece or Hungary, and lower by far in poor countries such as Tanzania or Pakistan. In general,

109

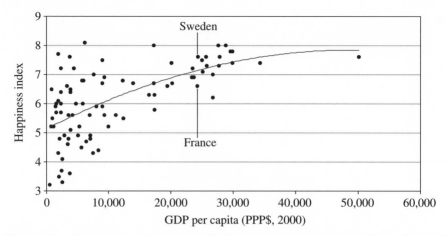

Figure 4.1. Happiness index versus GDP per capita. Sources: World Database of Happiness (www.eur.nl/fsw/research/happiness, accessed October 14, 2005); UNDP Human Development Indicators database. The "happiness index" ranges from 0 to 10, derived from the World Values Survey. The figures are for 1990–2000.

a higher level of GDP per capita corresponds to a higher average level of happiness.[1] No surprise here, surely?

However, there are puzzles in the happiness data. As figure 4.1 also shows, some countries are much less happy than others with similar levels of income: for example, France and Sweden have similar levels of income, but the French are much less happy. In general, it is hard to explain the big differences in reported happiness from country to country, which might reflect on linguistic and cultural differences in responses to surveys. Furthermore, the extra happiness added by every extra dollar of GDP declines as countries get richer, as the estimated trend line on the chart suggests. Within any single rich country, such as the United States, the surveys show that happiness has risen very little while GDP per capita has increased several times over. In a well-known paper which helped launch happiness research, Richard Easterlin found that average self-reported happiness in Japan did not increase between 1958 and 1987, yet GDP per capita increased fivefold (Easterlin 1995; see also Easterlin 2001). In poor countries this is not so: happiness is clearly rising hand in hand with GDP. There seems to be a threshold of around $15,000 per person per year: beyond this, there is no strong link

---

[1]The research literature refers to happiness as "subjective well-being."

between higher GDP and greater well-being. So higher incomes do make people happier—and then they don't, at least not much.

This in itself surely isn't surprising: one would not expect human happiness to increase without bound, whereas GDP can and does carry on increasing year after year. It's designed to be that kind of variable. Mr. Micawber famously observed (in *David Copperfield*): "Annual income twenty pounds, annual expenditure nineteen pounds nineteen and six, result happiness. Annual income twenty pounds, annual expenditure twenty pounds ought and six, result misery." Nobody would extend this to say: "Annual income twenty-one pounds, result joy. Annual income twenty-five pounds, result earthly bliss." Yet this does not imply that taking away income would not make people more unhappy. At the same time, there are other indications of anomie in the rich countries, signs that the vast prosperity of the late twentieth century has unexpectedly brought dissatisfaction with life in its wake. For example, in several countries there is evidence of a rising incidence of depression, alcohol and drug abuse, and in some cases crime rates and suicide rates have gone up too.[2]

Richard Layard explores these conundrums in his book *Happiness*. Why doesn't being richer make us happier? One possibility is that the question is flawed—perhaps people mean different things by happiness. For instance, it has been discovered that replies to surveys are affected by the weather: people say they're happier if answering the question when it's sunny—although they then correct their answer when the bias is pointed out to them. To tackle this possibility, researchers have begun to try to measure happiness more carefully, through diaries, or even through brain scans. It has emerged already that people report the emotions they feel at the peak and the end of different experiences, and do not adjust for duration. In addition, some people are extremely unhappy, while most do not feel an extreme of emotion, and few are extremely happy.

If we assume that answers to the question are meaningful, two psychological mechanisms seem to come into play, once people get beyond being able to satisfy their basic needs such as food and shelter. One is quite rapid adaptation to circumstances. The other is known as "the aspirational treadmill," psychologist-speak for the rat race: what we care

---

[2]The evidence is cited in Layard (2005), which contains comprehensive references, including to earlier econometric work by Bruno Frey and Alois Stutzer (Frey and Stutzer 2002), and by David Blanchflower and Andrew Oswald (Blanchflower and Oswald 2004a,b).

about is not our absolute standard of living but how we compare with other people.

Evidence of swift adaptation to a new level of income is found in many studies. Studies of lottery winners indicate that the happiness effect of a big win lasts only about two years. People who are badly injured and become paraplegic as a result of accidents are very unhappy—for a while, but then their reported level of happiness climbs back toward its previous level. Not all experiences are subject to adaptation: being mentally ill makes someone permanently unhappy, for example. But people certainly adapt quickly to having a higher income, a process described as the "hedonic treadmill" because it takes more and more money to generate an increment in happiness. When people at different levels of income are asked how much extra they think they need, the answer is at least an extra forty cents needed for every dollar actually earned. Getting an extra dollar this year makes you want more next year. Richard Layard describes this as an income addiction. Unless people understand that working harder and earning more won't make them happier, they will continue to struggle for no resulting improvement in their well-being. He, and some other economists, believe people need to be forced off the hedonic treadmill. Layard advocates raising income tax enough to discourage people from working extra hours: the psychological characteristic means they need to be forced to choose an appropriate work–life balance. Robert Frank of Cornell University takes a different tack. In his book *What Price the Moral High Ground* (2003) he recommends punitive taxation of luxury goods like fancy cars and designer clothes, as these are only bought in the psychologically barren pursuit of additional consumption.

The second reason for buying luxury goods can be found in our concern with relative status. We evaluate our happiness relative to our expectations, and our expectations change depending on what we see others consuming. This sounds like an old insight dressed up in new clothing. The economist Thorstein Veblen coined the phrase "conspicuous consumption" in his classic book *Theory of the Leisure Class* to describe the element of rivalry, of keeping up with the Joneses, in economic life. He wrote:

> The standard of expenditure which commonly guides our efforts is not the average, ordinary expenditure already achieved; it is an ideal of consumption which lies just beyond our reach, or to reach which requires some strain. The motive is comparison—the stimulus of an invidious

comparison which prompts us to outdo those with whom we are in the habit of classing ourselves.

Veblen (1994, p. 103)

Veblen, wisely, analyzes the phenomenon without feeling the need to offer advice to policy makers. The growing pro-happiness lobby's various proposals for shaking the rest of us off the hedonic and aspirational treadmills are ominously puritanical. Richard Layard writes that he grew up in a house without central heating, and was perfectly happy despite having to warm up his frozen feet by putting them in a bowl of hot water from time to time. It brought to mind at once the famous Monty Python sketch in which four millionaires outdo each other in their boasts about their tough childhood: "We were so poor, we 'ad to live in a cardboard box... But we were 'appy." I grew up in a cold and damp house too, one where I woke to find ice on the inside of my bedroom window in winter, and as a result I'd rather work hard enough to keep on paying the central heating bills. The problem is identifying the right level of habituation that a policy of enforced work–life balance for each of us should aim for. It doesn't feel like an appropriate issue for the government, or its clever advisers like Lord Layard, to pass judgment on, at least in a democracy.

A related strand in the recent research on the psychology of well-being is the "paradox of choice," the title of a book by Barry Schwartz (2004), professor of social theory at Swarthmore College. Professor Schwartz caught the popular mood with his description of how too much choice stresses us out. It certainly stresses him—the book opens with a description of the trauma of choosing a new pair of jeans at Gap. Would buying "relaxed fit" mean he'd grown too fat? Did he want stonewashed or distressed? Why had buying a pair of blue jeans become such a big enterprise? Professor Schwartz goes on to describe at length the psychological characteristics which make it impossible for us to choose rationally—I return to these in detail in the next chapter. The psychological benefit of choice rests in the fact that choice gives us control over our lives. Too much choice returns us to helplessness, though. We become overwhelmed by the extent of choice, just as the professor did in the changing room at Gap.

Policies aimed at discouraging us from buying luxury goods or restricting our choice have an alarmingly authoritarian, not to say puritanical, ring, however. After all, Chairman Mao wanted everybody in China to wear the same style clothes as he did. I'm not at all sure I share Professor Schwartz's sartorial preferences. As it happens, I don't spend much

113

on clothes but I do love to buy designer shoes, and I don't want Professor Frank making me work harder to be able to afford a new pair. If we left the selection of luxuries to a popular vote, I doubt it would coincide with the selections made by a panel of economics professors.

POLICIES FOR HAPPINESS

There are two types of evidence which give much more specific insights into what improves people's well-being. Do they have any useful policy implications? One type is the growing number of psychological surveys which ask people detailed questions about what they do during the day and how they feel as they're doing it. For example, one well-known study asked 909 Texan women to keep a diary dividing each day into episodes, and to report how much of various emotions they felt during each episode. Their answers were converted into an index of feeling good or bad. The women liked sex best, followed by socializing and relaxing. Praying, eating, exercising, and watching television also scored quite highly. They liked commuting and working least, followed by housework and childcare. They loved being with friends and hated being with their boss, coworkers, and customers; husband and children were in the middle. These are hardly surprising results. Nor do they lead to any obvious policy conclusions about how to improve national well-being either, however amusing it might be if a political party were to campaign on a platform of more sex for more people.

An additional obstacle to drawing up a national happiness policy is the suspicion that differences between countries are so large that the surveys are misleading. The results of psychological experiments do indicate that people are very bad at making an accurate assessment of experiences which extend over time. They remember either the peak of the experience, or their most recent experience. Many irrelevant factors also affect how people report their life satisfaction. In particular, how the respondent feels when asked the question influences their assessment of how they felt during a previous experience. Actually, we don't need psychologists to tell us this: few women are happy during childbirth, most forget their unhappiness right afterwards, and many mothers have more than one baby. So surveys which ask people to recall their feelings are fraught with problems.

However, there is an alternative approach which involves directly measuring national well-being using a new tool developed by a team led by Daniel Kahneman, a psychologist based at Princeton University who was the winner of the 2002 Nobel memorial prize in economics (see Kahneman et al. 2004). Professor Kahneman will star in the next chapter. For now, I just want to describe the indicator his team are developing, thanks to funding from the National Institutes of Health. The diaries kept by 909 Texan women, described above, were trialing a technique called the Day Reconstruction Method (DRM). A close alternative is known as the Experience Sampling Method (ESM), in which people are prompted (by a Palm Pilot or similar device) at random times in the day to record what they're currently doing and how they are feeling. The ESM is regarded by psychologists as the best way to measure how people feel, but it is expensive and may also lead to underreporting of the kinds of feelings people have when doing something they don't want interrupted. The data collected through the DRM can be used to characterize how people typically feel in certain kinds of activities.

This average "affect" (as psychologists term it) can in turn be combined with measures of the time spent doing different things. Several national statistical offices including the Bureau of Labor Statistics in the United States and the ONS in the United Kingdom have begun to introduce periodic time-use surveys for large samples of the population. The goal is to develop National Well-Being Accounts. While these are unlikely to displace the conventional National Accounts, measuring GDP, they will be an important supplement. And statisticians are taking their development seriously, discussing the statistical hurdles at their regular meetings in fora like the OECD and the United Nations. It will not be long before National Well-Being Accounts are a reality. Note, though, that Nicholas Craft's relatively simple adjustments to GDP, described earlier in this chapter, go a long way toward measuring the same thing. He adjusted GDP for changes in longevity and hours worked, both linked to the time people have available for pleasurable activities rather than work.

More useful for policy making for the time being at least is evidence from yet more surveys, such as the General Social Survey in the United States and the British Household Panel Survey in the United Kingdom. A handful of factors stand out, from regression analysis, as contributing substantially to respondents' reported levels of satisfaction with their lives. These are marital status, being in work, family financial situation, community environment, health, political freedom, and personal or religious values. There are some surprising gaps here—for example, education is uncorrelated with life satisfaction, and so is climate. Although Finns, who live in one cold, dark, northern place, have a high suicide rate, Minnesotans, living in another cold, dark, northern place, are among the happiest people in the United States. In the regressions, then, the divorce rate, the unemployment rate, the level of trust, membership of organizations (other than religious ones), the quality of government, and the proportion of the population believing in God together account for 60% of the difference in happiness between countries. Individuals are less happy if they are in their 40s, divorced or widowed, the children of divorced parents, not white (in the United States and United Kingdom), or not male (see, for example, Blanchflower and Oswald (2000); Andrew Oswald's website, www2.warwick.ac.uk/fac/soc/economics/staff/faculty/oswald/, has extensive links to this literature). Again, many of these are not amenable to policy intervention. The government cannot legislate for happy marriages (although it can make it harder to get a divorce), or for the inner meaning people find from their religion or personal philosophy. However, the list does highlight a few areas of policy intervention. For example, as unemployment clearly makes people very unhappy, high and stable employment is a good policy target. Another is prioritizing good health. As mentioned earlier, people do adapt, to some extent, to physical ill health. But they never adapt to mental illness or chronic pain. This argues for putting a higher priority on the relief of these conditions, whereas mental health in particular is usually an underresourced area of health care.

Government policies might also be able to improve the level of community cohesion and trust, often referred to as social capital. The level of trust is often measured by the proportion of the population choosing the positive option in reply to the question, "Generally speaking, would you say that most people can be trusted, or that you can't be too careful in dealing with people?" The proportion of positive responses ranged from 5% in Brazil to 64% in Norway. While it is not obvious how to improve levels of trust, it is certain that government policies can and do have an impact. How to measure and improve social capital is a hot area of research, covered in chapter 8.

Finally, governments can very directly affect personal freedom. People in the communist countries before 1989 were clearly much unhappier than people living in Western democracies. People are very happy in Swiss cantons where they have the right to demand frequent referenda to decide policies. Results like these suggest that democracy, including local democracy and decentralization, can have a direct impact on wellbeing.

I am much happier with a policy prescription that requires my government to improve the quality of democracy and keep unemployment low than one which requires my government to tax or restrict goods regarded as luxuries by its economic advisers. One might think at this point that it has taken a whole lot of economic research to get to an obvious conclusion: good government and lots of jobs are good for the national level of well-being.

Earlier in this chapter I suggested that it made sense for policy makers to monitor all the indicators which were important to the national well-being. Rather than ditching GDP and ceasing to try to increase economic growth, and instead adopting an alternative indicator such as the GPI or ISEW, politicians should encourage GDP growth at the same time as monitoring what is happening to environmental quality or income distribution or any of the other measures important to their voters. The research into happiness confirms this strategy, as GDP *is* correlated with happiness, albeit only weakly in rich countries. In poor countries, increasing GDP is strongly correlated with well-being, so the conventional focus on economic growth is absolutely appropriate for them.

What's the answer to the critics who regard economic growth as an inappropriate metric for how society is doing? One of the favorite icons of the pro-happiness lobby is Jigme Singye Wangchuck, King of Bhutan. Ascending the throne in 1972 at the age of seventeen, his majesty has been something of a modernizer from day one. A selected number of foreign dignitaries were invited to attend his coronation in the formerly completely isolated mountain kingdom. He has reduced the scope of the monarchy's absolute powers, introducing a governing council. Television and the Internet were legalized in 1999 and recently Bhutan has gained its first ever telecommunications, as mobile phones can reach terrain which was inaccessible to fixed-line networks (www.pbs.org/frontlineworld/stories/bhutan/gnh.html). But perhaps his lasting contribution to the Bhutanese, and the rest of us, is the concept of gross national happiness (GNH). In an interview, King Wangchuck said: "Happiness takes precedence over economic prosperity in our national development process" (Schell 2002). In February 2004 the Centre for Bhutan Studies held a conference at which invited foreign guests discussed how to implement a measure of GNH to guide policy, and a follow-up conference took place in Nova Scotia in 2005. GNH has four "pillars": the environment, equity, cultural values, and good governance. Egalitarianism is a central value in Bhutanese society, and the government spends a full 18% of its budget on health and education, a high proportion for a poor country.

Nevertheless, Bhutan, I should point out, ranks 134th out of 159 in the United Nations HDI ranking, and had annual GDP per capita of just $1,969 in 2003. It is just as well that his majesty is more concerned about GNH than these other indicators. The king is a man of simple tastes (no doubt formed during his years spent in an English public—that is, private—school): he reportedly leads an ascetic life in line with Buddhist values, preferring a log cabin in the mountains to the splendid royal palace. However, his four queens, all sisters, live in the palace, so no doubt he visits often. Public life is tightly controlled. The sole Internet service provider, DrukNet, bars access to inappropriate websites. Since 1988 everybody has been required to wear the national dress in public, on pain of arrest, so Professor Schwartz would find shopping easy in Bhutan. While sympathizing with the desire of a small landlocked country to maintain its cultural identity, one should perhaps be a little skeptical about the policy proclamations of an absolute monarch whose family has run Bhutan for a century. Yet Bhutan is indeed Shangri-la to many of those Western researchers keen to enhance concern for the environment and equality in economic policy making. They should pause to reflect that, whatever their political preferences, the research into the psychology of happiness does *not* find that a more equal society or unspoilt forests make us happy, or at any rate not directly. On the other hand, freedom does improve our well-being directly. Different values can conflict, and the links between values and indicators are not straightforward. Increasing happiness is, unfortunately, not easy. Devising a measure of GNH doesn't offer a shortcut through moral philosophy.

HUMANIZING ECONOMICS

The happiness agenda is humanizing economics by restoring morality to economic debate, after a half century in which professional economics lost contact with the question of values. However, I'd caution against rushing headlong into happy-think. Conventional economic growth is without question desirable. There is no doubt that the vast majority of people in the world will be made happier by increases in GDP per capita. In the rich economies as well as the poor ones, people want higher incomes, even if some intellectuals think they ought to know better. Moreover, we should be cautious about assuming there's a trade-off between growth and moral values, which is very much the approach taken by some critics of pro-growth economic policies. Those who emphasize the use of alternative indicators to GDP, or who argue we should concentrate on happiness instead of GDP, tend to claim there is a choice between the materialism of the conventional approach and the alternative which would sacrifice additional growth for a greener or simpler life. However, as Benjamin Friedman (2005) argues in a fascinating book, growing economies are essential if we're to realize other values, such as tolerance, democracy, social mobility, and fairness. Stagnating economies experience the opposite. There might be a trade-off, but it is not materialism versus morality but rather the inherent tension between different moral values. So it would be rash indeed to counsel the abandonment of policies to grow GDP. At the same time, the recognition and improving understanding of environmental and social impacts of economic growth must be welcomed, and we can hope that this might lead to improved policies in future. Putting a human face on economic policy is overdue.

Suppose we were to take the happiness research absolutely at face value. What makes people happiest of all? Well, sex. The straightforward policy implication is that to increase national well-being, more people need to have more sex. This doesn't sound like a reasonable economic policy prescription, however. Without happiness-neutral or happiness-damaging activities like work, or the restless ambition to innovate or make money, we'd have fewer creature comforts like central heating, we'd lead unhealthier and shorter lives, and eat boring and inadequate food. A return to the kind of society and economy we had at the $15,000 per capita level of GDP would not be a vote winner. The quest for happiness is a fundamental human drive, perhaps, but there are others. John Stuart Mill addressed this conundrum in chapter 2 of *Utilitarianism*:

> A being of higher faculties requires more to make him happy, is capable probably of more acute suffering, and certainly accessible to it at more points, than one of an inferior type; but in spite of these liabilities, he can never really wish to sink into what he feels to be a lower grade of existence. We may give what explanation we please of this unwillingness; we may attribute it to pride, a name which is given indiscriminately to some of the most and to some of the least estimable feelings of which mankind are capable: we may refer it to the love of liberty and personal independence, an appeal to which was with the Stoics one of the most effective means for the inculcation of it; to the love of power, or to the love of excitement, both of which do really enter into and contribute to it: but its most appropriate appellation is a sense of dignity, which all human beings possess in one form or other, and in some, though by no means in exact, proportion to their higher faculties, and which is so essential a part of the happiness of those in whom

it is strong, that nothing which conflicts with it could be, otherwise than momentarily, an object of desire to them. Whoever supposes that this preference takes place at a sacrifice of happiness—that the superior being, in anything like equal circumstances, is not happier than the inferior—confounds the two very different ideas, of happiness, and content. It is indisputable that the being whose capacities of enjoyment are low, has the greatest chance of having them fully satisfied; and a highly endowed being will always feel that any happiness which he can look for, as the world is constituted, is imperfect. But he can learn to bear its imperfections, if they are at all bearable; and they will not make him envy the being who is indeed unconscious of the imperfections, but only because he feels not at all the good which those imperfections qualify. It is better to be a human being dissatisfied than a pig satisfied; better to be Socrates dissatisfied than a fool satisfied.

In other words, he argues that well-being has more than one dimension. Perhaps the happiness research is only capturing the contentment dimension? Without further surveys and psychological research we're not in a position to know. But other areas of psychological research into economic decisions raise equally difficult questions about what it is that people *really* want. This is the subject of the next chapter.

Economics for Humans

What would you get if you crossed the Vulcan Mr. Spock from Star Trek with Hercule Poirot, the crime writer Agatha Christie's little Belgian detective? The answer is the economist's idea of a normal human being. Both characters are, of course, famous for their logic and rationality. Spock is contrasted with the impulsive Captain Kirk, intuitive and emotional. In the film *The Wrath of Khan* Spock sacrifices himself for the sake of the rest of the crew of the Starship Enterprise. In a direct reference to classical utilitarianism,[1] he explains that the needs of the many outweigh the needs of the one. Poirot can solve mysteries simply by making logical deductions on the basis of the available information, without ever leaving his room (see, for example, *The Mystery of Hunter's Lodge*, in which Poirot solves a murder committed in Derbyshire without leaving his flat in London). "Remember always the little grey cells, *mon ami*," as Poirot puts it. His foil is the illogical but sensitive Captain Hastings. Sherlock Holmes, another *homo economicus*, has his Dr. Watson.

This contrast between cold, calculating rationalism and impulsive, emotional responses is a very familiar one. It's the difference between logic and intuition, between prose and poetry. In his poem "The Vision of Sin," Alfred, Lord Tennyson wrote:

> Every minute dies a man, Every minute one is born.

Charles Babbage, the famous Victorian scientist and forefather of the programmable computer, wrote to congratulate him on the poem. Babbage added:

> I need hardly point out to you that this calculation would tend to keep the sum total of the world's population in a state of perpetual equipoise, whereas it is a well-known fact that the said sum total is constantly on

---

[1] Not to mention the self-sacrifice of Sidney Carton in *A Tale of Two Cities* by Charles Dickens.

the increase. I would therefore take the liberty of suggesting that in the next edition of your excellent poem the erroneous calculation to which I refer should be corrected as follows:

Every minute dies a man, And one and a sixteenth is born

The actual number is much longer but I believe 1-1/16 will be sufficiently accurate for poetry.

For those trained in the humanities, it may be poetry which expresses the deeper truths of life. But economists tend to be in the Babbage camp. My own sociological observation of my profession over the years reveals that many economists read crime fiction and science fiction. Books in both genres often create an ordered and self-contained world, where the application of logical decision making leads to desirable outcomes. James Mirrlees, awarded the Nobel memorial prize for his work on economic behavior when there is incomplete information, was asked in the subsequent blaze of media interviews how he relaxed. Reading detective novels, he replied without hesitation. William Sharpe, an earlier Nobel laureate, was asked how he came to choose his specialism. "At many points in my decision tree, fortune decreed that I should take the branch on this path rather than another. To get here, one must have the good luck to draw a great many favorable random numbers." In the same vein, one of my fellow graduate students contributed a cookie recipe to the department newsletter which read, "Form the dough into small convex sets and place on a greased separating hyperplane in the oven for 20 minutes." The voice of Mr. Spock echoes eerily here.

Does it matter that economists think so differently from the norm, that their cultural references are Star Trek and the mean streets of detective fiction? Economists do, in some experiments and surveys, reveal that they are more rational and calculating than the average. Whether they select the subject because of their personalities, or are changed by its study is not clear. Whichever way the causality runs, critics accuse economics of a lack of psychological realism, a lack sufficiently grave to undermine the usefulness of the subject in the study of human society or formation of public policy.

Does this shot hit home, or is this chasm merely another manifestation of the division between the scientific and artistic cultures, accusing each other, respectively, of a lack of realism and a lack of rigor? That's the question this chapter addresses. Psychology does present a challenge to economics, because emotions and other gaps in rationality demonstrably affect people's decisions.

Consider how difficult it is to give away free money. That people will accept something for nothing is a basic prediction of economic theory. A bank that offered passersby £10 in cash as a marketing stunt found that none would take the money: they all suspected there was a catch. And they were entirely rational, because in fact they had to take a voucher inside the bank to claim the £10, and suffer a marketing pitch first. The money wasn't really free, but cost time and aggravation. But other examples demonstrate rather less rational behavior. Take the ultimatum game. In this experiment, one person has £100 to share with another; the second person can either accept or reject the first person's offer, but there is no negotiation. Experimenters have consistently found that people will turn down offers of less than £30–40 as unfair. They would rather have nothing than £10 or £20 for free. It shouldn't, in theory, happen.

The sense of fairness these participants so firmly demonstrate has long been taken into account by practicing economists. Adam Smith himself was well aware of the influence of "moral sentiments" in the organization of society. The work of David Hume, another of the founding fathers of economics, centered on exploring the limits of reason, the imperfections of human perception and understanding. Economists in the 1930s paid great attention to psychology. Keynes offers the best-known example, with his emphasis on the importance of "animal spirits" for investment, and his comparison of the stock market to a beauty contest in which each judge is trying to guess which candidate the other judges will choose.

Postwar neoclassical economics broke from this richer psychological tradition and placed rational "Economic Man" center stage in the so-called Standard Social Science Model (SSSM), as if we all behaved like Vulcans. This assumes that people are self-interested, know what their preferences are at all times, and always act to maximize their own utility. Yet although rational-choice behavior formed the basis of all their workhorse models, in general economists well appreciated its limitations. Back in 1977 Amartya Sen, a Nobel prize winner, famously described the selfish, calculating agents of economic theory as "rational fools." More than twenty years ago George Akerlof and Janet Yellen proposed the "efficiency wage" hypothesis, a theory which tried to explain why real wages didn't fall during recessions in order to prevent unemployment. The argument was essentially that workers felt cuts in wages for putting in the same effort were unfair, so employers would not cut pay in a business downturn because it would lead to reduced effort by the remaining workers.

123

So an awareness of the psychological limitations of the SSSM is longstanding and widespread in economics. In many contexts, most economists do not consider this lack of psychological realism to be a problem at all. Conventional microeconomic theory has proven to be extremely fruitful in predicting the behavior of consumers and businesses. Certainly with the kinds of modeling innovation described earlier, in chapter 2, and the new economics of information described in the next chapter, today's workhorse microeconomic models fit the data extremely well and are widely used in practical policy making, in the commercial courts, and in business. The list of useful applications of everyday microeconomics is endless. Each week I receive emails listing about thirty new empirical papers by economists working in the United States and Europe on competition economics and industrial organization. There are similar quantities of applied research in other fields, such as education economics, public economics, labor economics, and all the other specialisms. Almost all of this work assumes rational and self-interested behavior by individuals. In most contexts, this is how we behave. The experimental work of economists such as Vernon Smith and Charles Plott, described in more detail below, confirms that the conventional microeconomic model of a market equilibrium based on rational individual behavior is an accurate portrait of what actually happens in real markets.

The danger in devoting a whole chapter to psychologically richer models is that I'll give the impression that they are more important for the future of economics than is actually the case, and correspondingly underplay the massive contribution of conventional, mainstream approaches. There is now a flourishing program of research in economics, using results from psychological and neurological studies and laboratory experiments to explore the ways in which real humans differ from these ideal rational economic agents. Its aim is to see whether there is systematically nonrational (as opposed to utterly irrational and unpredictable) behavior, taking account of which could improve economic theory and policy. These fields, behavioral and experimental economics and neuroeconomics, are producing fascinating results. However, the applicability of the results is narrow, and economics as a whole doesn't need the psychological research to restore its worth as a subject.

There are two key areas, though, where richer psychological insights are improving economic models. One is finance and the other is consumer behavior in other areas concerning decisions about the uncertain future, such as saving for old age. There is no question that psychological insight is needed to understand, or predict, or work in the financial markets. A wonderful and accessible introduction to behavioral finance is Robert Shiller's best seller *Irrational Exuberance* and herd behavior in financial markets has become a popular research topic (see, for example, Banerjee 1992). The rest of this chapter concentrates more on consumer decisions.

The roots of behavioral and experimental economics go back at least to Nobel laureate Herbert Simon's concept of "bounded rationality." Arguing that people mostly did not have enough time or information to maximize their utility in the way a rational economic agent is supposed to, he suggested that they "satisfice," following rules of thumb which produce a good enough outcome rather than the absolutely best one in all circumstances. The baton was picked up by others from the 1960s onwards, leading to further Nobel memorial prizes for Vernon Smith and Daniel Kahneman (whose coauthor Amos Tversky died before their Nobel was awarded in 2002).[2] Smith created the field of experimental economics, overturning the presumption that it could never be a "proper" science because of the impossibility of performing controlled experiments. He pioneered the use of experiments in decision making to design ways of making markets work efficiently, including Treasury bond auctions, or designing new institutions such as carbon-emissions trading schemes. Kahneman and Tversky applied psychological results in economic contexts, mainly through experiments such as the ultimatum game, to uncover systematic departures from rational behavior: when did people optimize and when did they satisfice?

Even more recently, the field of neuroeconomics has emerged, using new medical techniques. Practitioners of neuroeconomics use functional magnetic resonance imaging (fMRI) scans to monitor people's brains as they take economic decisions. This strongly suggests that different parts of the brain predominate in different types of decision making—decisions about the present and the future, for example. It looks as if we have several inner Mini-Mes tussling internally, with a rational economic agent inhabiting the cortex, fighting it out for control of decisions with

---

[2] The fact that so many of the Nobel memorial prizes in economics have been awarded to economists whose work departs from the assumption of rational maximizing behavior by individual agents should perhaps in itself give pause for thought to the critics who criticize economics for being unrealistic. This chapter draws on several surveys including Camerer (2003), Camerer et al. (2004a), Kahneman (2003b), Rabin (1993, 1998), Smith (2003), and Thaler (2000) as well as the collection of essays edited by Camerer et al. (2004b). All contain plentiful further references.

gamblers, nervous wrecks, and compulsive shoppers elsewhere in the brain, in the older (in evolutionary terms) limbic system.

This fifty-year research pedigree means that by now behavioral insights are affecting policy. For instance, the 2005 Pensions Commission report in the United Kingdom recommended that people should have to opt out of pension savings schemes rather than opting in to them, drawing on experimental results which demonstrate the sheer degree of inertia and shortsightedness in our financial decisions. Participation rates in opting-out schemes run at about 70–80%, compared with 20–30% for opting-in schemes. This is useful knowledge, and it's steadily catching on in policy circles. And although behavioral economics hasn't yet made it into many college textbooks, which still teach theory based on rational, optimizing, individualistic behavior, it can't be long before this starts to change, as it already has in some specific areas of the subject such as finance.

This chapter looks at what behavioral economics and neuroeconomics tell us about how we make decisions when the future is uncertain. Seasoning economics with psychological insight will perhaps lead to better policies but at the same time leaves some as-yet unanswered questions. What we don't yet know is how to tell when psychologically richer assumptions about behavior are more valid than the good old neoclassical assumption of self-interested calculation. This is partly an empirical question, but in addition we have no overarching model which encompasses the whole variety of human decision taking, just a growing body of experimental evidence. Until there's enough to allow a more systematic categorization of decision taking, it's hard to feel entirely comfortable with the benign paternalism of behavioral economists: the expert in the white coat knows what you want better than you know yourself, you quirky human.

How Irrational Are We?

Perhaps the experts do know best. Does this sound like you: lacking in willpower, unable to resist the piece of cake you know you'll regret next time you step on the scales; a bit impulsive; unable to resist a bargain even though you know that it's not as great as the marketing pretends; definitely above average in your intelligence and your driving ability? Yes, that makes you a human. We all know we're like this, to greater or lesser degrees. As Daniel Kahneman has put it: "People are not accustomed to thinking hard." Reasoning takes a deliberate effort and is hard work. Most decisions are taken spontaneously and intuitively. The acquisition of a certain skill, whether it is playing tennis or stitching wounds or manipulating software, is a gradual process of translating repeated effort into something so familiar that it becomes effortless in the end (Kahneman 2003a). Even when people are trying to reason, they are prone to certain biases, especially when it involves making predictions about the future. Many of us are overconfident, for example, or wrongly inclined to assume that others share our opinions. And even if we don't make such errors of judgement, we're not necessarily consistent in what we want, lacking willpower for example.

Despite this, conventional economic models often start out with general statements of the form: assume N identical independent agents who maximize $U(x)$ over every future time period subject to not spending more than their total future income. $U(x)$ is their utility function, a summary of the preferences they have for fast cars versus family holidays, and all other goods and services, or whatever it is they care about. The direction of the program of research in psychology and economics has been to develop modifications of the assumption that every person has stable and consistent preferences, in line with which they will seek to maximize their level of utility. How can economics be made more realistic without denting its analytical strength? The findings can be divided into several principal areas, most of them understood and appreciated by many economists but not so far incorporated into the subject systematically. The behavioral critique has three elements. The first challenges the conventional assumptions about what people really prefer, and tries to describe a more realistic form of the utility function. The second asks how competently people actually make calculations about their utility in practice. The third challenges the very idea of a stable and consistent set of preferences at all.

Realistic Preferences

The conventional textbook economic model has derived its powerful analytical muscle from making certain assumptions about the form of individuals' utility functions. Utility is assumed to depend on the level of income. There is assumed to be a smaller and smaller addition to utility (diminishing marginal utility) from each additional unit of income. The relationship between utility and income is assumed to be smooth and continuous. Oh, and (usually) everyone is assumed to be identical. Nobody ever thought all of this was realistic, but it has the great merit

127

of being extremely easy to handle mathematically, and of delivering analytically clear results. So one of the first questions is how far does this set of assumptions about the utility function differ from reality—what is sacrificed for the sake of theoretical clarity?

One central finding is that people care very much more about their position relative to a reference level, rather than in an absolute sense. In experiments most people choose a lower income rather than a higher one if, in the case of the higher income, someone else would be getting much more than them. This would not have been surprising to Thorstein Veblen. It is not the consumption of goods in their own right that we care about, he argued: "the motive that lies at the root of ownership is emulation." But the importance of assessing utility according to a reference level goes well beyond status envy. We care too about our level of future consumption in the light of past and current consumption. We are very much more averse to losing something we have than we are attracted to the possibility of making the same size of gain. Tversky and Kahneman have even put a figure on it: in monetary terms we estimate a loss as roughly twice as large as equal dollar gain.

Related to this marked loss aversion is the endowment effect, whereby people value something much more as soon as it is theirs. In a well-known experiment, one group of students were given $5 mugs and asked how much they would sell them for, while another group were asked how much it would take for them to choose cash rather than the mug. The choosers preferred anything over $3.50 in cash, but the owners wanted $7 on average to part with their mugs. A similar phenomenon leads to status quo bias, whereby people tend to stick to the combination of goods they own already even if offered alternatives where some gains offset other losses.

A further consequence of assessing utility relative to a reference level is that we perceive a greater impact on our well-being from changes close to the reference level. This is known as diminishing sensitivity, and it is pervasive in human perception. For example, we are much more sensitive to the difference between an increase in temperature of three degrees (fahrenheit) and six degrees than to the difference between an increase of twenty-three and twenty-six degrees. Applied to economic decisions, this leads to some decidedly nonrational choices. Although people tend to be both loss averse and risk averse, many prefer to take a gamble combining a high chance of losing nothing and a small chance of losing a lot to a gamble combining a smaller chance of losing nothing and a larger chance of losing a smaller amount, where both gambles are set up to give the same expected outcome. We are more sensitive to the smaller losses.

In addition to the findings about the nature of people's preferences—the importance of reference levels and loss aversion—it is also clear from experimental evidence (not to mention experience of life) that our preferences are not purely self-interested. This is not to challenge Adam Smith's famous assertion that: "It is not from the benevolence of the butcher, the brewer and the baker that we expect our dinner, but from their regard for their own interest." Still, there are clear departures from self-interest in our behavior, much in evidence when it comes to questions of distribution or allocation of resources.

In short, we have a strong sense of fairness, which can trump self-interest. It is not necessarily the same notion of fairness for everyone. Some see equal shares as fair. But many people seem to apply an alternative which shares improvements in welfare equally, regardless of the starting point. In other words, they do not weigh up the justice of the overall distribution in considering how to share out new gains, so much as the piecemeal changes themselves. Loss aversion also influences our notions of fairness: many people feel it is unfair to deprive others of what they already have, such as a job or a piece of property. Just as in the case of assessments of our own utility, changes (from a reference level) seem to matter more than absolute levels. Furthermore, the reference point for assessing fairness can change over time: hence "squatters' rights."

Our views about allocation are also strongly influenced by a sense of reciprocity toward what we take to be other people's motivations and intentions. This is very apparent when it comes to public goods. For example, in a drought a self-interested rationalist would not bother conserving water whatever others were doing, a self-sacrificing altruist would conserve as much as possible regardless of what others chose, and normal people conserve water if they think almost everybody else is doing the same, but not if they're not. This kind of behavior is widely appreciated in game theory (and evolutionary biology), where it's known as a "tit-for-tat" strategy. It is also the kind of behavior assumed in the efficiency wage models I looked at as a young student, where firms pay higher wages than they would if they were pure profit maximizers, and workers reciprocate with greater effort than they would if they were pure utility maximizers. The importance of motives is clearly demonstrated by ultimatum game experiments in which subjects will accept "unfair"

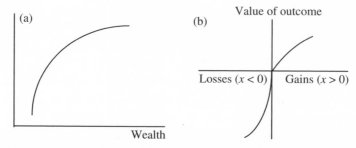

Figure 5.1. (a) Conventional utility function. (Expected utility is smoothly increasing in the level of wealth, with diminishing marginal returns, and no "kinks" at specific levels.) (b) Utility function, prospect theory. (People evaluate risky prospects on the basis of losses or gains relative to a reference level. The kink at the reference point indicates loss aversion. Diminishing sensitivity moving away from the reference point indicates that people value large gains less than proportionately but are risk loving toward large losses (i.e., value large losses less than proportionately).)

offers if they come from a computer but not if they come from another human. Social relationships affect the psychology of choice.

These characteristics—loss aversion or reciprocal altruism—imply a different sort of utility function than the type used in economic models. It is often referred to by Kahneman and Tversky's term *prospect theory*. The differences between the conventional and prospect theory utility functions is illustrated in figure 5.1, which show the level of utility on the vertical axis. The utility function of prospect theory will bend around a reference level, it will weight losses and gains differently, and it will weight them less the further away they are from the reference level. It will not be independent of the utility of others, either.

Biases in Judgement

The second set of issues concerns the process of maximization, and the plentiful evidence that we are in general not very good at doing it, mainly because of the inevitable uncertainty about the future. By now there is a lengthy list of our systematic departures from rational calculation in the face of uncertainty. Many concern the difficulty we have in understanding and applying probability theory. Here are some of the most striking.

The law of small numbers. People expect a small sample to reflect the total population, or infer too much from short sequences of events. A stellar example of this bias is given by Nassim Taleb in his 2001 book *Fooled by Randomness*: a stock market analyst who gets his market predictions right three times in a row is thought to be a genius when the result is likely to have been a fluke. A gambler who gets a few tails one after the other reasons that it will be heads next time, whereas equal numbers of heads and tails can only be expected in a very large number of coin tosses. Even lengthy streaks of events can be purely random.

Confirmatory bias. Once people have formed a firm belief, they will not pay attention to information disproving it. What's more, some of the psychological experiments indicate that people will actively misinterpret evidence which doesn't confirm their initial view. This can explain why a fresh pair of eyes is so often thought to be helpful in solving a problem: these fresh thinkers will not have their assessment of evidence clouded by old hypotheses they can't set aside. It also explains why beliefs can sometimes polarize, as people use all new information as support for their prior views.

Anchoring. In making numerical assessments, we look for a starting point or anchor for our estimate. In one experiment subjects were asked, after a spin of a wheel of fortune, for the proportion of African countries that are members of the United Nations. Although the number generated by the wheel was clearly random, it influenced the answers given.

Hindsight bias. As it says, we exaggerate after an event the extent to which we believed it would happen beforehand. Anybody who watches the news will be familiar with this one.

Biases in memory. We give too much weight to particularly vivid or memorable experiences even if we have superior sources of information. If we were mugged in a particular city, we will think it is dangerous even if it has the lowest crime figures in the land. We similarly remember the peak of events, or the end, rather than their duration or middle: long and uneventful minor operations do not stay in the memory in the same way as much shorter ones which involve a moment of acute pain.

Overconfidence. This is perhaps the best established of all the human biases of judgement, and completely pervasive. We all think we're better, smarter, or more talented than average, at least in any dimension we care about. This includes all those stock market analysts with only a weak grip on probability theory.

One interesting question is whether knowing about all these biases in judgement makes people less prone to committing them. Nassim Taleb

131

set up his own hedge fund to exploit his understanding of probability theory, taking account of the random nature of long sequences and also the much higher probability of extreme events than most people appreciate. The fund trades options based on the calculation that there are "fat tails," a higher probability of extreme events in the markets than is assumed by conventional options pricing.[3] The fund's returns are not public, but according to its founder, the gains it made during extreme events entirely unexpected to most traders, like the October 1987 crash or the 2000 stock market dive, were large enough to keep it profitable for decades. Experimental evidence indicates that experts do take account of statistical reality in circumstances where outcomes are predictable, but are if anything more prone to biased judgements when circumstances are inherently unpredictable—such as the future of the stock market or the outlook for the U.S. economy. They are more overconfident or more extreme in their views precisely because they *are* experts and have hung their views on a scaffolding of lengthy training and reasoning. On the other hand, professional training can make a difference in one respect: in all the psychological experiments, students of economics are more likely than other students to act on the basis of self-interest alone. This takes us into neuroeconomics, which uses physiological studies of the brain to shed light on economic decision making. I return to this below.

The Concept of Utility

A third area of behavioral research questions the very concept that each of us has a stable utility function to maximize. For preferences seem to be inconsistent over time. Experimental evidence suggests that sometimes we can't perceive what we will want in future. For example, referring back to the previous chapter you might remember that we are not very good at predicting our own future happiness. We fail to take into account the likelihood that our reference points will change, that we'll adapt to new circumstances. Thus winning the lottery doesn't, after a year or two, make you happier. As an adolescent, it's impossible to imagine that a quiet evening at home listening to classical music might ever be more enjoyable than a late night at a deafening rock concert.

Another problem with the concept of a utility function is that our preferences are in some ways inconsistent or unstable. For example, people

---

[3] There's a marvelous Malcolm Gladwell profile of Nassim Taleb at www.gladwell.com/2002/2002_04_29_a_blowingup.htm.

make inconsistent choices when logically equivalent choices are presented or *framed* in different ways. Of 100 people treated, 90 survive surgery and 34 are alive after five years, whereas 100 survive radiation therapy and 22 are alive after five years. And what about this case: 10 die during surgery and 66 die within five years, whereas none die during radiation therapy and 78 die within five years. Is surgery or radiation treatment better? Framed the first way only 18% of respondents favored radiation treatment, but framed the second way, in terms of avoiding immediate death, this proportion rose to 44%. The problem for expected utility theory is that the frames seem to determine people's preferences.

Worse still, people's preferences can flip or change with context. I might choose red shoes ahead of blue ones when the choice is red, blue, or brown, but out of black, red, and blue choose the blue ones. The menu of choice often affects consumers, as marketing experts well understand. If my choice is only two items, a $20 or $40 bottle of wine, say, I might choose the cheap one, but if an even more expensive one is added to the list I'll opt for the $40 wine.

Another challenge to the concept of a stable utility function comes from looking at the ways we assess likely future outcomes. Often we underestimate long-run effects on our utility, giving greater weight to more immediate factors. And the future needn't be very far away. After being stranded one day in the rain with no cabs in sight, Colin Camerer decided to study taxi drivers in New York. They turned out to have a daily target for their takings, and stopped driving when they reached it. In the rain they were busy, and hit their target early. Even the prospect of making two normal days' takings in just one day didn't override the rule of thumb.

In general, people have a strong urge toward immediate gratification and lack self-control. Internet retailers rely on this when they offer next-day delivery at a premium price. Addicts of tobacco or other drugs are often well aware that they are doing themselves long-term harm. It's not that they are making an incorrect risk assessment. They know the likely effects—and go ahead and take the risk anyway. Most of us understand that we should save more. Often, we have quite a sophisticated understanding of our lack of self-control; we have devised ways of committing ourselves to overcoming it. Regular savings schemes straight out of the payroll cheque are one example. Joining Alcoholics Anonymous is another. So is making a New Year's resolution and telling all our friends about it. Rational Economic Man would have no need of such devices.

133

Using Irrationality Rationally

Psychological and behavioral insights are still almost entirely absent from economic textbooks, but they are having an impact on policy applications. This is surely good news? Policies which work with the grain of human nature will be more effective than those which work against it. So shouldn't policy makers recognize the flawed reality of humankind?

Advertising agencies have long understood the power of appeals to emotion. For example, in 1989 the State of California took a new tack in addressing smoking, especially among young people, by using clever ads in its Tobacco Control Program, portraying the threat from smoking as much more immediate than the danger of lung cancer years in the future. The ads appealed to short-term preferences such as appearing cool or avoiding impotence, to young people's rebelliousness, and to strong emotions such as the love for one's children. Several evaluations suggest the campaign had a significant impact on health outcomes.[4] The marketing and advertising industries evidently have a better grip than economists on the foibles of human behavior.

Is it possible to apply psychology equally cleverly in economic policy? Two areas where psychology plays an extremely important role concern the labor market and personal finance. In the former, people's decisions are strongly influenced by their strong sense of fairness and reciprocity. In the latter, people are making very-long-term decisions in the face of great uncertainty about the future, so our urge for immediate gratification and our lack of consistency in preferences can cause many people to make choices which are not in their own best long-term interest.

The conventional neoclassical framework has a hard time explaining many aspects of labor-market behavior. One mentioned earlier is the fact that employers don't cut (real) wages during a downturn; instead they will lay off workers. A possible explanation is that they do so because workers whose wages are cut will respond by reducing their effort—less money for the same work is unfair. Truman Bewley researched this question very directly by surveying managers and workers. He found that workers said they would be willing to accept pay cuts if it would help colleagues keep their job, but managers said they feared cuts would

---

[4]For example, 33,300 fewer deaths from heart disease between 1989 and 1997 than if the previous trend had continued (see http://content.nejm.org/cgi/content/abstract/343/24/1772). In addition there was a 14% drop in lung cancer rates in the state compared with a 2.7% drop in the rest of the United States (Centers for Disease Control and Prevention).

reduce morale and productivity. Bewley's research has also found that, contrary to conventional theory, the risk of being laid off does not make people work harder; on the contrary, threats decrease productivity. The explanation is that workers are not purely selfish, but rather identify with the firm and believe the firm should reciprocate, and identify with them. Work is a social activity as well as an economic one.

Some European governments have taken this to heart and concluded that unemployment can be reduced by work sharing. For example, the French government introduced a thirty-five hour limit to the working week on January 1, 2001, reasoning that employers would not cut pay, while workers would increase their effort and become more productive. On balance, the assessment of French economists is that this was correct (although the thirty-five-hour limit did reduce firms' profitability and has since been relaxed by a right-wing government). Yet there are other aspects of labor-market behavior where rational choice triumphs over human psychology. For example, employers respond very rationally indeed to taxes on labor by hiring fewer workers. There is a lot we still need to learn about how to humanize labor economics.

Clearer examples of the potential contribution of behavioral insights come in the case of savings and insurance, financial decisions involving complicated assessments of likely outcomes far into the future. In all Western economies, where populations are aging, many people are saving too little for their retirement. All of us know that saving is good, but shopping is more fun. Policy recommendations on how to increase pension savings get tangled up in politics, with conflicting views as to whether governments should be getting more involved in providing pensions to save us from our own foolishness, or on the contrary less involved so we realize we have to save for ourselves. Both sides of this debate assume that people are rational, conventional utility maximizers. Yet when it comes to making decisions about saving long term for their future, the evidence is clear that most people are pretty bad. They certainly don't maximize their long-term utility. Thus the status quo bias makes people reluctant to change existing arrangements. The framing of choices has a big influence on how people act. The difference in participation rates in opt-out rather than opt-in pension schemes, mentioned on p. 126, is a very good example of this. One obvious, and easy, policy step is therefore to change the frame to make long-term saving an opt-out decision.

Insurance decisions are equally fraught with nonrationality. Framing matters here too: a majority will opt for default choices, in selecting an

135

insurance scheme for example. New Jersey has a default car insurance scheme which sets a low insurance premium payment with the option of purchasing the right to sue; neighboring Pennsylvania's default scheme sets a high premium with the right to opt for a lower payment removing the right to sue. In the two states 80% and 75%, respectively, choose the default. The starting point anchors their choice when they are uncertain what to do. Another example is people's tendency to over-insure themselves for small risks and under-insure themselves for large ones, compared with *homo economicus*. This is a reflection of the combination of loss aversion and increased risk taking over large losses. One product which relies on these behavioral characteristics is the kind of warranty you can buy to cover loss or damage to consumer electrical items. When I looked at this in detail as a member of a Competition Commission inquiry into the sale of these warranties, we found that about a fifth of consumers paid premiums as high as 40% or 50% of the price of a product that had a very low probability of breaking down. Looking at how to remedy the competition problems that we found, we spent a lot of time discussing how retailers should be required to frame consumers' choices when they shopped (www.competition-commission. org.uk/inquiries/completed/2003/warranty/index.htm).

Long-term savings decisions affect my income in retirement, and the kind of fiscal burden I will impose on future taxpayers. There's a strong case for governments to try to tackle this issue. Few people would object to the use of framing mechanisms such as opting out versus opting in to try to steer us into making wiser choices. Many economists are keen to develop other policies which are made more effective by the use of psychological research. A report of a conference on the policy implications of behavioral economics, held by the Federal Reserve Bank of Boston in 2003, notes that:

> Most participants were persuaded that normal people make decisions they regret in predictable ways, that policy makers can often identify "true welfare" from among the competing versions, and that collective actions and institutions sometimes emerge to exploit cognitive mistakes. Thus the concept of "benign" or "libertarian" paternalism met an enthusiastic response.

Personally, I'm only semi-enthusiastic about paternalism. I suspect that the number of no-brainer behavioral policies like the savings scheme example above might be quite small, and that policy makers might over-paternalistically feel it was in people's best interest to be compelled to do some things and not to do others. Even where there is no question of compulsion, the idea of politicians embracing the techniques of advertising and marketing even more than they already do is pretty unappealing. Is paternalism the only way that clever experts can design policies to overcome human psychological frailties? Perhaps not: another area of research into the overlap between psychology and economics points to the use of better-designed markets to achieve better outcomes.

EXPERIMENTING WITH MARKET DESIGN

Let's step back and remind ourselves why economists are so keen on individual choice in free markets. One of the main reasons for the kind of unrealistic assumptions the subject makes about individual behavior is that, if everybody is a rational, self-regarding, utility-maximizing clone with stable and consistent preferences (and some other conditions hold too), then it is possible to prove a number of neat conclusions, one of which is that the competitive market outcome is efficient. It is the best solution to the problem of allocating scarce resources among competing uses, and it will deliver the greatest possible amount of welfare. This is a powerful conclusion, and almost worth the array of unrealistic assumptions.

What's more, there are many contexts in which the laws derived from the conventional neoclassical assumptions work terribly well. Higher prices often do reduce demand. Indeed, some experiments appear to establish that the laws of economics apply in monkey society as well. Capuchin monkeys taught to use money (silver tokens) to buy food obeyed the laws of demand and supply: when the price of grapes fell, they bought more grapes and less Jell-O.[5]

So, while aware (in the recesses of their minds) about the restrictiveness of the assumptions on which this conclusion is based, economists are typically very strong supporters of market solutions to a wide range of problems. One topical example is congestion charging in city centers. In 2003 London's mayor introduced a congestion charge for driving into the central area of the city between 7.00 A.M. and 6.30 P.M. in order to reduce the number of vehicles clogging the streets and polluting the atmosphere. It worked extremely well, with a 30% reduction in (nonexempt) traffic volumes after six months (www.tfl.gov.uk/tfl/downloads/pdf/congestion-charging/cc-6monthson.pdf). Londoners

---

[5] Equally, they behaved like humans in showing loss aversion and failing to save enough for the future (see Dubner and Levitt 2005).

are for the most part happy with this initially controversial use of the price mechanism, to the extent that the mayor has raised the charge and plans extended coverage. Economists see it as a triumph for their profession. Economists typically also favor using markets to allocate other scarce resources such as radio spectrum, or permission to emit greenhouse gases.

Other people don't always agree, however. The economist Alan Blinder once conducted an informal survey among his acquaintances, asking whether there should be two lines or one line in a crowded cafeteria at lunchtime: one long and slow line with everyone paying the same price; or two lines, one of them an express till with higher prices. All of the economists he asked said two and all the noneconomists said one.[6] This is an everyday example of the uniformly shared view among noneconomists that during wartime the government should ration scarce essential goods such as food, clothes, and energy, because it is unfair for the rich to be able to buy more through paying higher prices in such circumstances. Similarly, most Europeans believe access to health care should be rationed by the government rather than the price mechanism, although beliefs on this differ in other countries.

Economists might not be typical—but are they right? And if only sometimes, when? When does the efficiency of the price mechanism overcome normal psychology, such as the instinct for fairness or the influence of reference levels? This is the kind of question addressed by the program of research in experimental economics launched by Vernon Smith, cowinner with Daniel Kahneman of the 2002 Nobel memorial prize in economics. Smith was launched on his pioneering work in experimental economics by his Harvard teacher, Edwin Chamberlin. Chamberlin set up a classroom game where he had students try to buy and sell a fictitious good in pairs. Each pair came up with a different price, and Chamberlin regarded this as proof of the failure of the conventional competitive equilibrium model. Smith, when he became a teacher himself, set up an experiment where a group of sellers traded with a group of buyers and called out the prices at which they were willing to trade—the pattern used in old-fashioned open outcry financial and commodities markets.

To his surprise, he found that in this more realistic experiment the trading prices quickly converged to the theoretical competitive equilibrium. From this starting point Smith and others conducted many

---

[6] *New England Economic Review*, First Quarter 2004, report of a conference "How Humans Behave" held in June 2003. Papers available at www.bos.frb.org/economic/conf/conf48/index.htm.

experiments which demonstrated that markets do produce the results predicted by economic theory. People's behavior gets them to the same outcome as predicted by the unrealistic theory, through a process of trial and error. From this starting point, Smith developed a hugely influential program of research using laboratory experiments to design markets by seeing how people responded to different types of rules for making their decisions. As he described it:

> The important thing that laboratory experiments bring to the table is that you can study things which are not. You see, with econometric studies, you can only study what is because it's the systems that exist now that are generating the data that is the input to econometric applications of economic theory. What you can do in the laboratory is think about completely different arrangements, entirely new institutions, entirely new kinds of markets that have never been tried before.

> BBC radio interview with the author, *Analysis*, December 2, 2004

This program of research has become well-established and influential in public policy. Many governments hire economists to design markets to achieve specific purposes: sell Treasury bills; reduce carbon emissions; deregulate transport networks efficiently; auction off radio spectrum. One measure of how good economists have become at these tasks is the £22 billion raised by the British government in selling spectrum to mobile telephone companies in 2002, through an auction process. Previously, officials had chosen which companies would receive earlier allocations of spectrum, raising no money for the government. Smith and other economists such as Charles Plott introduced the use of laboratories to test market designs before policy makers implemented reforms, and such experimental economics is now reasonably well accepted, although not used nearly as much as might be desirable.

This approach to experimental work is obviously completely different from the kind of psychological experiments described earlier. Whereas they uncovered the departures of human behavior from rational choice, Vernon Smith's type of experiment aims to find institutional structures which induce people to behave collectively as if they were making rational choices. The self-ordering of human interactions in the context of many types of institution or market structure does lead to the same outcome as the competitive equilibrium predicted by conventional economic theory. Hundreds of experiments confirm this, especially in auction markets. The reason is that markets economize on the information people need to reach the equilibrium outcome: the public aggregation

139

of prices and quantities captures a vast amount of private information which could not itself be known or comprehended. This is Adam Smith's invisible hand: an order emerges in somewhat mysterious ways from the vast complexity of individual motives and decisions. Chapter 7 will pick up this theme.

For now, the important point is that psychological realism does not necessarily spell doom for the powerful analytical tools of economics, but instead takes these tools into new territory. Accepting that people take most decisions fast and intuitively, rather than reasoning carefully and deliberately, the policy conclusion is not that experts must take some decisions for other people, or even steer those decisions by framing the choices appropriately. Rather, it suggests a policy of designing market institutions to accommodate normal decision making. This is still a form of framing, of course, but at one remove, which makes it perhaps more comfortable for the libertarians among us.

What both strands of research, both behavioral and experimental economics, lack is a unifying framework. Although the research has identified regular departures from rational choice, we're not able to offer a theory about when emotion overrides reason or vice versa. Nor about when trial and error will lead people to the rational equilibrium market outcome; that has to be tested in laboratory experiments. Some clues are emerging, however, from the most recent branch of this fruitful research, neuroeconomics.

APPLYING BRAIN SCIENCE

The task of applying the insights of psychology and behavioral economics is complicated by the fact that we lack self-awareness and rationalize our decisions retrospectively. Colin Camerer describes an experiment on patients with a severed corpus callosum (the link between the two hemispheres of the brain). Their left eye reads on a screen an instruction to wave, which is processed in the right half of the brain. When the patients are asked why they waved, the left half of the brain (the language area) has to think up an explanation: "I saw someone I knew." This is a demonstration of the so-called homunculus fallacy, the idea that we have a small being inside us, in charge of things. Camerer says:

> The human brain is like a monkey brain with a press secretary. The fact that an apparently self-aware explanation is so typically given by the press secretary suggests that much of our faith in self-awareness is

illusory and should be taken skeptically. As they say in neuroscience, "Don't ask the person, ask the brain."

Camerer (2003, p. 12)

The press secretary is the cortex, the distinctively human part of the brain, the only part that is capable of reasoning like a rational economic agent.

Camerer is a leading researcher applying brain science to economics using the evidence derived from fMRI scans of brain activity during decision making. Some robust conclusions are starting to emerge that shed a bit of light on when the outcomes of decisions which might be irrational nevertheless look like the result of a collective rational choice.

One widely accepted conclusion is that the rationality or irrationality of a decision depends on whether there is a greater level of activity in the prefrontal cortex or the insula (Cohen 2005). The former is, roughly speaking, the front and top of the brain, just behind the forehead, the most recent area to evolve. The latter is a small, older area in the middle of the brain. For example, images of brain activity taken when people play the ultimatum game indicate that when there is more activity in the second player's anterior insula (associated with negative emotions such as disgust or pain) than in the cortex, the first player's offer is significantly more likely to be rejected. The brain activity effect was more marked when the offer was made by another human than when made by a computer. Imaging evidence reveals that the insula and other parts of the brain's limbic system (the old bits, in evolutionary terms) govern emotional responses to immediate rewards or losses, while the prefrontal cortex is engaged with the evaluation of future rewards. The cortex is associated with self-control and reasoning. According to Princeton psychologist Jonathan Cohen: "Prefrontal cortex activity was associated with utilitarian decisions that were made in the face of aversive emotional responses, and in the economic decision making studies, prefrontal activity was associated with the choice of more remunerative options in the face of price or impatience." Rational Economic Man is all prefrontal cortex and no insula.

Further evidence that decision making in the cortex is the essence of economic reasoning comes from studies which demonstrate links between abstract cognitive reasoning and attitudes to the future (see Frederick 2005). Consider the following question:

A bat and a ball cost $1.10 in total. The bat costs $1 more than the ball. How much does the ball cost?

_____ cents.

The intuitive answer is ten cents (the correct answer is five cents). Ranking people by how many of this type of question they answer correctly (or intuitively but incorrectly), it is possible to separate them into high scorers on cognitive reasoning and low scorers. The high scorers are significantly more likely to choose a higher expected return in future over a lower, immediate gain. They are significantly less risk averse than low scorers but also less willing to take risks to avoid losses. In short, high cognitive scorers turn out to be significantly more like conventional rational utility maximizers than the average human beings revealed by the psychological experiments described earlier; prospect theory applies most closely to the low cognitive scorers.[7]

It's tempting for me to interpret these imaging and cognition results as evidence for the greater cognitive skills and perhaps even evolutionary development of economists. But let's resist that temptation and conclude that people fall into one group or other, either Vulcans or normal humans, either rational expected utility maximizers or prisoners of prospect theory. With individuals taking decisions in these two distinct ways, what, if anything, can we conclude about collective outcomes? When (if at all) will markets deliver results that look something like the efficient equilibrium predicted by conventional economic theory?

One possible answer is that market outcomes will conform to rational-choice theory, even if rational agents are in a minority, when a choice by one person creates an incentive for an offsetting or opposite reaction by another person (Fehr and Tyran 2005). This is described as "strategic substitutability." Many markets are indeed like this, so Economic Man dominates the outcome even when in a minority. If instead my action creates an incentive for you to do the same, that is "strategic complementarity." It inflates a small amount of individual irrationality into a large deviation from the rational outcome. The obvious example of this complementarity arises in asset markets, a fruitful area for the application of behavioral economics (see Shiller 2000). Even if Mr. Spock is the only rational investor and can calculate that there is a high expected loss from a particular investment, he will ignore the market fundamentals on which his calculation is based if all the irrational fools in the market think the price is going up. The reason is that the resale value of the asset is also part of the return, so the view of the irrational majority

---

[7]There is an intriguing sex difference. Men are much more likely than women to have a high cognitive score, so Economic *Man* might not be a sexist misnomer. Having a high score makes a man more likely to take risks. Women who do have a high score are still risk averse but are more likely to be patient, and willing to wait for a higher gain.

gives rational man (or Vulcan) an incentive to act irrationally too. Indeed, asset price bubbles only need a small minority of irrational traders for this kind of momentum to take over. Colin Camerer argues that strategic complementarity is more likely to prevail in markets where there is not a known future time at which the outcome will be clear—like financial markets, where today's asset price depends on all future prices (Camerer et al. 2005; Camerer and Fehr 2006).

If confirmed, this hypothesis does offer a means of distinguishing between circumstances when policy should assume that people left to their own devices will make irrational or non-utility-maximizing choices, calling for a bit of benign paternalism; and those in which an appropriately designed market will provide the right incentives for just a few high cognitive scorers to exercise their prefrontal cortex and ensure that rational outcomes prevail. Further than this, we're not yet able to go.

ECONOMICS VERSUS PSYCHOLOGY

The Scottish Enlightenment philosopher David Hume was well aware of the difficulty flawed human beings have in devising sensible public policies. In his *Treatise on Human Nature* he wrote:

> There is nothing which is not the subject of debate, and in which men of learning are not of contrary opinions. The most trivial question escapes not our controversy... Disputes are multiplied, as if everything was uncertain, and these disputes are managed with the greatest warmth, as if everything was certain. Amidst all this bustle, it is not reason which carries the prize, but eloquence.
>
> Hume (1978, Book I, p. 39)

What is this if not an argument about framing? Rational conclusions, according to Hume, "vanish, like phantoms of the night," whenever it comes to public debate. Equally, he wrote that reason had to be motivated by passion: we'd have scant concern for public policy at all if we didn't care about other human beings, or experience a sense of fairness or justice. Lack of rational cogitation has an important place in society. The fMRI experiments reveal at least one group of people to be delusionally optimistic: we call them entrepreneurs. Their role in human society is taking a risk on a completely unknowable future.

As we've seen, one area of the brain, the prefrontal cortex, does take decisions the way conventional economic theory postulates. Daniel Kahneman argues that economics is a model of the kind of reasoning people do actually engage in when they are operating in that cognitive system, involving calculation and thinking hard; but most of the time people are not reasoning at all but rather acting intuitively. The reasoning parts of the brain are rational, but other decisions arise in other parts of the brain, such as the insula, related to perceptions and emotions.

What these lessons from psychology, laboratory experiments, and brain science do not do is overturn all of conventional economics. On the contrary, as we'll see in the next chapter, there are many circumstances, some of them highly emotional, in which the applicability of rational maximizing behavior in markets is extended.

Of course, there are other contexts in which the fruits of psychology make it clear that we need to modify conventional economic reasoning. Behavioral finance is probably the single area of economics where this lesson has been taken most warmly to heart—after all, you only have to observe the financial markets casually for a little while to appreciate the relative importance of emotion and reason. There are other areas of economics where behavioral insights need to be applied too, especially consumer financial decisions.

However, one of the fundamental difficulties for economists sympathetic to incorporating psychological realism is that there is no single, unified theory of psychology. Having such a theory has been a source of great analytical strength in economics, and should not be sacrificed lightly. So while the models stemming from behavioral economics are useful and exciting, they are not yet building into a new overarching theory. Kahneman and Tversky summarized their description of actual human decision making as prospect theory, but it is an umbrella term for a series of descriptive regularities (people care about changes in wealth, not levels; the reference point for such changes is often the status quo but can be something else; people are loss averse; and they have a diminishing sensitivity to change in both directions) rather than a theory deduced from a logically consistent set of axioms. What is more, prospect theory doesn't apply to all of us anyway. Some of us, albeit perhaps a weird minority, act like conventional *homo economicus*. As Daniel Kahneman wrote in a recent overview: "It now appears likely that the gap between the views in the two disciplines [psychology and economics] has been permanently narrowed, but there are no immediate prospects of economics and psychology sharing a common theory of human behavior" (Kahneman 2003b, p. 166). Edward Glaeser has noted that this might be because psychology is only informative about individual choices whereas economics is a discipline concerned with the aggregate outcomes resulting from those choices (Glaeser 2005).

On this dilemma, I leave the last word to the brilliant mathematician Benoit Mandelbrot, who has turned his attention to understanding financial markets: "One hopes for regularity but one lives in roughness" (BBC radio interview with the author, *Analysis*, December 2, 2004). For now, we have to live with the small insights instead of the grand unified theory. This doesn't really matter. For as I emphasized in the introduction to the chapter, there are many more areas of decision making by consumers and businesses where greater psychological realism would add nothing to the explanatory or predictive power of the absolutely conventional economic approach. The grand unified theory of the economic mainstream offends those who find the assumption of rationality psychologically unrealistic, but it works extremely well, with just a bit of seasoning from the psychologists when it comes to how we predict the future.

Information and Markets

INTRODUCTION

Most normal people have a lot of trouble with the basic building block of neoclassical economics: the utility-maximizing, rationally calculating individual with full information. The previous two chapters looked at the maximization of utility and the rationality postulates: at which parts of these are fundamental to economics, and at where economists themselves have been moving away from the restrictions of the neoclassical model. This chapter looks at the third area, the information postulate. It explores the importance of information to economic analysis in several different contexts before drawing them together with some thoughts about what they say about the boundaries of markets as a mechanism for ordering society.

Like the debates on utility maximization and rationality, the information debate is an old one which was submerged by the postwar dominance of conventional neoclassical economics in universities. In a classic 1945 article called "The use of knowledge in society," Friedrich Hayek, usually caricatured as an ultra-free-market prophet, wrote:

> There is something fundamentally wrong with an approach which habitually disregards an essential part of the phenomena with which we have to deal: the unavoidable imperfection of man's knowledge and the consequent need for a process by which knowledge is constantly communicated and acquired. Any approach, such as that of much of mathematical economics with its simultaneous equations, which in effect starts from the assumption that people's *knowledge* corresponds with the objective *facts* of the situation, systematically leaves out what it is our main task to explain.
>
> Hayek (1945)

Many subsequent researchers have lifted up their heads from the neoclassical grindstone and agreed wholeheartedly, leading to the development by the 1980s of a rich literature on the economics of information.

There are many strands to this literature. On the face of it, there's little in common between Joseph Stiglitz and Admiral John Poindexter. Professor Stiglitz is an archetypal liberal intellectual, bearded, bespectacled, who's spent much of his career working on the alleviation of poverty. He was born in 1943 in Gary, Indiana, a steel town destined to become part of the Rust Belt. In his Nobel autobiography, he noted that many distinguished economists (including Paul Samuelson) had also grown up in Gary, and comments: "Certainly, the poverty, the discrimination, the episodic unemployment could not but strike an inquiring youngster: why did these exist, and what could we do about them." The childhood experience of badly functioning markets has, it seems, inspired many economists. Stiglitz describes his mother and father as, respectively, a New Deal and a Jeffersonian Democrat, and clearly honors and upholds the values he grew up with.[1] The young Stiglitz was an activist, campaigning for the abolition of fraternities at his liberal arts college, Amherst, and joining civil rights marches. A spell doing research in Kenya in 1969 cemented his interest in understanding public goods and market failures. He writes:

> The time I spent in Kenya was pivotal in the development of my ideas on the economics of information. I have often wondered why. I think in part the reason is that seeing an economy that is, in many ways, quite different from the one one grows up in, helps crystallize issues: in one's own environment, one takes too much for granted, without asking why things are the way they are. As I studied development, I was forced to think everything through from first principles. Had I grown up in a world in which everyone was a sharecropper, I probably would have accepted this as the way things are. As it was, sharecropping seemed like a peculiar institution, for it seemed to attenuate greatly the incentives workers had to work (since they typically had to give one out of two dollars that they earned to the landlord).
>
> http://nobelprize.org/economics/laureates/2001/stiglitz-autobio.html

Stiglitz has remained engaged with public policy. In the 1980s he acted as an expert witness in litigation on behalf of Seneca Indians in upstate New York and in litigation attempting to block Reagan Administration sales of offshore oil licenses. He joined Bill Clinton's Council of Economic Advisers in 1992. He went on to become an outspoken and therefore

---

[1] They have clearly served him well in many ways. Stiglitz notes that he, like his father, had always insisted on paying social security contributions for the household help and so unlike other appointees to the new Clinton Administration in 1993 he had no difficulties during the vetting process about nonpayment of these taxes.

controversial chief economist at the World Bank, clashing bitterly during the 1997–98 financial crisis with the Clinton Treasury in the shape of another outstanding economist, Larry Summers.

Admiral John Poindexter is another native of Indiana (in his case from Odon) but, that aside, couldn't be a greater contrast to Joe Stiglitz. The career officer graduated first in his class from the U.S. Naval Academy in 1958, and went on to a distinguished naval career, after picking up a PhD in nuclear physics from CalTech in 1964. In 1981 he joined the Reagan Administration, serving as National Security Adviser from 1985 to 1986. He earned lasting notoriety (and a six-month jail sentence, later overturned) for the role he played in the Iran–Contra affair during the Reagan years.[2]

Many people might have sought a quiet life in the background after that episode, but after a period in the private sector Admiral Poindexter resurfaced in the policy world as director of DARPA's Information Awareness Office.[3] The mission of this office is to explore the defense potential of information: it has contributed to the Orwellian lexicon the phrase "total information awareness." After 9/11, the office launched an experimental online market trading futures contracts on events such as terrorist attacks. The Policy Analysis Market aimed to get experts to reveal through their bids their assessment of the probability of an attack or other event such as the capture of Osama Bin Laden, and to use the prices which emerged in the market as a better collective source of information about likely developments. Inevitably, there was a political uproar about gambling on terror—perhaps terrorists themselves could profit from taking part on the basis of their inside knowledge? The experiment was swiftly discontinued, and Admiral Poindexter retired.

The link between the radical economics professor and the conservative military man lies, then, in their interest in the role of information in decision taking and especially in how markets convey information. Stiglitz is, in the wider world, the most famous of the trio of economists who won the 2001 Nobel memorial prize in economics. He, George Akerlof, and Michael Spence had pioneered the modeling role of information in

---

[2]Poindexter and Colonel Oliver North oversaw an operation which financed violent, right-wing Nicaraguan groups trying to overthrow the elected Sandinista government, using funds raised from undercover arms sales to Iran. They then covered up the clandestine arrangement. Poindexter was convicted over his role in 1990, with the conviction overturned on appeal in 1991.

[3]DARPA: The Defense Advanced Research Projects Agency, spiritual parent of the Internet, among many other technologies.

economic theory and practice during the 1970s. Looking at the availability of information, and how it shapes individual decisions, goes to the heart of whether and when markets deliver individually and socially desirable outcomes. People often have access to different information or are uncertain about its reliability—described as *information asymmetries*—so their decisions will be formed accordingly. Their behavior might be intended to share information, which is known as *signaling*. Or the asymmetry will affect their behavior in ways which lead to a less desirable outcome, giving rise to *adverse selection*. Asymmetric information likewise might give people incentives to behave in undesirable ways from the perspective of the wider market or society, causing the problem of *moral hazard*.

In addition, information is in many ways a public good. Its use by one person doesn't use it up at all (it is nonrival or infinitely expansible), and if known by one it readily spills over to others (it is to a large extent nonappropriable). These characteristics were most elegantly and famously expressed by Thomas Jefferson: "He who receives an idea from me receives [it] without lessening [me], as he who lights his [candle] at mine receives light without darkening me." Recall from chapter 3 the importance of knowledge spillovers in growth theory—knowledge is the word used for information in that particular context, trying to understand innovation. Even if it is possible to prevent others from acquiring information, it is likely to be socially inefficient to keep it private. Furthermore, the quality of a piece of information can't be assessed before it's acquired, so trust and reputation are likely to matter.

These considerations all suggest that the characteristics of information mean that markets don't work as well as neoclassical theory would have us believe. On the other hand, it's very clear that markets are good at aggregating information. The great historical experiment of communism proved that markets are better than central planners at allocating resources. Vernon Smith's experiments, as we saw in the last chapter, demonstrate how good (well-designed) markets are at combining individual buy and sell decisions into the market-clearing price and quantity. Markets economize on the information any individual needs because it's all summed up in the price.

That strand of research in experimental economics has given birth to a range of new literatures. One of these looks at the design of markets for use in arenas of public policy such as environmental protection or spectrum auctions. Another strand concerns "information markets," Internet-based markets in information which hold out the promise of being the best way to aggregate expert information in areas ranging from elections to, yes, the likelihood of terrorist attacks. Some enthusiasts for information markets believe they could improve decision making throughout public life, in effect making important public policy decisions less technocratic, less reliant on the opinions of a small number of politically selected experts. Needless to say, this suggestion that "decision markets" should replace conventional chains of political accountability is, like Admiral Poindexter's planned information market, highly controversial. Many people still find the merits of using market mechanisms in emissions trading or auctions of scarce resources such as the radio spectrum, touching on important areas of public policy, very uncomfortable or counterintuitive.

In short, information goes to the heart of the appropriate roles of markets and government in the economy. This chapter ends with a discussion of some of the issues raised by these debates, and what they say about both the technical and moral limits of markets.

The Information Problem

At least since Hayek some economists have been fretting that information is plainly not as readily and symmetrically available as it is assumed to be in traditional equilibrium theory. The desirable results of the theory—the existence, stability, and optimality of a competitive market equilibrium—rest on the assumption that everybody has the same, correct information. Some approaches to tackling the evident unreality of the assumption were firmly neoclassical in spirit. An early approach, published by Nobel laureate George Stigler in 1961, had introduced the notion that acquiring information was costly, requiring time and effort. People would have to decide how much to spend on information gathering, and would continue up to the point where the extra information was worth exactly the same to them as the extra effort, and no further (Stigler 1961). This approach introduced a new decision margin, again entirely in the neoclassical vein: there was a market for information with its own demand and supply.

A similar tack was taken during the 1980s by economists working on the basis of rational expectations, the assumption that while people would not hold information with certainty, they would have a forecast based on what they did know, and that forecast would be consistent with the underlying reality. Because if they proved to be systematically wrong, they would update their information base to correct their errors.

While this made the mathematical modeling more complicated, it could certainly be done and it too preserved the essence of equilibrium theory. The rational-expectations approach was extremely influential for a while. It gave a new theoretical impetus to the policy choices of the conservative governments in power in the United States and United Kingdom at the time, by revalidating the concept of the optimality of the competitive market equilibrium. What is more, a lot of economics graduate students just enjoyed the frisson of the highly technical mathematics involved: my Hamiltonian is bigger than yours!

Both the transactions-costs and rational-expectations approaches did in fact prove quite fruitful, but to Stiglitz and his fellow 2001 laureates, they were "Ptolemaic"—a reference to the bizarre complications Ptolemy had to introduce to the Earth-centered model of the Universe to keep it consistent with his astronomical observations of the Sun-centered reality (Stiglitz 2004). Both were seen by critics as brilliant but doomed attempts to preserve a false model. Akerlof, Stiglitz, and Spence drew inspiration instead from earlier work by James Mirrlees and William Vickrey. Mirrlees asked how a government should design the tax system. The ideal would be for everyone to be taxed according to his or her ability (and of course receive public services according to his or her needs); but the government doesn't know my ability, and if I'm a productive person I have every incentive to disguise this in order to minimize my tax bill. The tax system therefore has to use income as a proxy for ability (Mirrlees 1971).

All of these economists started by noting in their own field of interest an institution which was blatantly nonrational and even dysfunctional. They asked why people would accede to an institution which was so obviously flawed. For Stiglitz, the institution was sharecropping, where the tenant farmer pays the landowner a large share of the crop rather than a fixed rent, often half or two-thirds. It seems inefficient because it's equivalent to an enormous tax on labor, massively denting the farmer's incentive to produce as much as possible. However, for the worker it is a better arrangement than renting: even if he has the cash to pay rent, he doesn't know how good the harvest will be, so sharecropping splits the risk with the landowner. For the landowner it's better than paying a wage: he doesn't know how hard the farmer will work especially if being paid a wage unrelated to his effort or the output of the crop. There's uncertainty about the future and asymmetric information about the worker's skill and effort. In these circumstances, sharecropping is rational. Stiglitz went on to note that the same information structure characterizes the modern corporation, where owners must incentivize

151

managers to perform well without being able to observe how productive those managers actually are (see Stiglitz (2000) and Nalebuff and Stiglitz (1983) for overviews).

George Akerlof started with an entirely different observation, noting that only cars in terrible shape, or "lemons," seemed to get sold second hand. If you want to sell your reliable and well-maintained car, you're unlikely to get a good price for it. In his 1970 paper "The market for lemons" (rejected as trivial by editors of the first two journals it was submitted to), he pinpointed the problem as asymmetric information between buyer and seller (Akerlof 1970). Only the seller knows the true state of the vehicle; and he has every incentive to misrepresent it to the buyer, making it out to be in better shape than it really is in order to get a higher price. Suppose a second-hand price emerges which reflects the average quality of a used car. This will be less than the high-quality ones are worth but a higher price than the low-quality ones should get. Sellers of high-quality used cars won't bother to put them on the market. Sellers of lemons will pile in, or in other words there will be adverse selection as more and more of the second-hand cars for sale are lemons. In the end, the market might collapse altogether, with no price that can match buyers and sellers. Akerlof argued that problems like this arising from asymmetric information could perhaps explain all kinds of institutions which wouldn't be needed in a theoretical market equilibrium—in this case, guarantees offered by used-car dealers, or advertising paid for by a dealership to establish its credentials as a reliable business.

Michael Spence took another tack on asymmetric information, managing to do Nobel prize quality work in his PhD thesis on market signaling (Spence 1976). Spence asked how employers could figure out which potential employees were really more highly skilled than others and therefore worth employing at a high wage. The answer is that qualifications that are costly to acquire serve as signals of the underlying skills— and at the same time a candidate with a PhD is someone who found it less costly in terms of time and effort to acquire that degree than all the other candidates who left college two degrees earlier. The purpose of gaining the doctorate is not only (or perhaps even mainly) the love of knowledge for its own sake, but the message that qualification will send. Spence has had plenty of opportunity to watch students jumping over the qualifications hurdles during his distinguished academic career. He was chair of the economics department when I was at Harvard working on acquiring my PhD certificate. (A few years earlier he'd taught economic theory to two bright undergraduates who both got As, Bill

Gates and Steve Ballmer. If only Gates had graduated instead of dropping out, he'd have gained qualifications which would have signaled his skill to prospective employers (http://nobelprize.org/economics/laureates/2001/spence-autobio.html).) A signaling example in the context of developing countries is the vastly expensive investment poor villagers in India will make in paying for a wedding (often borrowing at crippling rates of interest to pay for the celebration), in order to signal their caste and social status and ensure better marriage and work prospects for their family in future. Having a fun day is not the point of spending the money (see Srinivas 1980, 2004).[4]

The three economists laid the foundations for a multitude of other research looking at the implications of asymmetric information in a huge range of contexts, including insurance contracts, labor markets, industrial organization, corporate finance, development economics, public services, and indeed virtually any market or nonmarket. There is scarcely an area of economic study where consideration of the available information and consequent incentives does not play a part. Asymmetric information is part of the human condition: as well as being nonrival and nonappropriable, a lot of information is nonverifiable too. So the assumption of information asymmetries is now part of the bread and butter of applied economics, even as the symmetric information assumption lives on in general equilibrium theory. (See Riley (2001) for a survey of the literature.)

From this rich proliferation of research premised on asymmetric information, common themes emerge. Here I summarize them under three headings. The first covers the effects of asymmetries in information: how does private information lead people to behave? The second concerns the responses to such effects: what kinds of institution emerge to order markets characterized by information asymmetries? The third question is the challenge of institutional design: what will naturally bring about an equilibrium or stable situation, and will it be the best that could be achieved?

ADVERSE SELECTION AND MORAL HAZARD

I know what I know. I don't know what you know, just that it's almost certainly different. But I also know that your behavior conveys information about your knowledge, and I'll adjust my behavior accordingly.

---

[4] One can argue that this phenomenon exists in many developed and developing countries.

Take an area where information is central to the economic decision, the market for insurance. You know that you smoke and I, an insurance company, don't know. This information is key to my pricing your life insurance policy correctly. You have an incentive to seek life insurance cover because your risk of death is increased, but also an incentive to lie in order to pay a lower premium. Knowing this in the abstract, I will assume that some of my customers are lying and will price the policy a bit higher than I'd need to if everyone told the truth. At this higher premium, some nonsmokers will decide not to take out a policy: the price is too high given their objective probability of fatal illness. The proportion of my customers who are lying smokers will increase, and I'll need to increase the premium again.

This is the dynamic of adverse selection. The essence of it is that one party to a transaction has an incentive not to disclose private information, leaving their willingness to transact (to buy insurance or sell a used car or work for a given wage) as the only information available to the other party. In the extreme, adverse selection can cause markets to collapse, so economies have devised many ways of addressing the problem. For example, insurers will require customers to fill out long questionnaires about their health, will cross-check databases, and will invalidate policies discovered to have been taken out on the basis of false information. But the market itself, the willingness of both parties to undertake a transaction at a certain price, does not provide incentives for the disclosure of private information.

Adverse selection arises when there is an asymmetry of information prior to a transaction—before you purchase your insurance policy. There is a mirror problem which arises with regard to behavior after the transaction. We might start out with the same information but afterwards there's an asymmetry arising from the fact that I can't monitor your behavior. This is known as moral hazard. Moral hazard describes a divergence in incentives between the two parties to a transaction. In the case of insurance, buying cover for your household goods might make you careless about taking care of them. Insurers respond by charging a lower premium for people willing to accept a larger "excess," the amount of loss they must cover for themselves before making a claim on the policy. Countries which know the IMF will bail them out of a financial crisis might be less careful about running stable macroeconomic policies. Moral hazard can also operate in employment relationships when an employer pays a worker or contractor an hourly wage but is unable to check how much effort they put into the task—for example, should new

Table 6.1. Responses to asymmetric information.

	Informed party	Uninformed party
Selection problem (pre-transaction)	Signaling	Screening
Incentive/moral hazard problem (post-transaction)	Commitments/ guarantees	Monitoring, targets, incentive pay

software take a contractor two weeks or two months or two years to write and instal? There's every incentive for the contractor to take life at an easy pace and spin the work out for as long as possible. By definition, what can't be observed or monitored can't be included in the terms of the contract. One way of getting around this is to choose what is covered by the contract carefully—a fixed fee for completing a task, for example, as opposed to a fixed fee per unit of time spent on it.

Moral hazard as it's normally discussed in the context of insurance is a special case of a more pervasive problem, the relationship between a *principal* and an *agent* when the agent has better information than the principal. This is at the center of two areas of economics, the theory of the firm, where knowledgable managers act as agents for shareholders who are much less well informed about the state of the business; and public services where officials or other public servants act as agents for politicians and voters. These information gaps can be simply enormous, as the agents have large amounts of highly detailed and technical knowledge. Just consider the chasm between the medical knowledge of a doctor and that of a voter considering how much extra tax she'd be willing to pay to finance improvements in health care; or between an investor holding many shares in different companies and the executives of a technology company asking shareholders to accept a low dividend in order to finance new investments. No wonder "transparency" has become such a mantra of our times.

SIGNALING, SCREENING, AND BUNDLING

What are the responses to the problems of adverse selection and moral hazard? In different contexts we see a wide range of institutions emerging to supplement the central market transaction. Many of these responses fall into a few common categories (summarized in table 6.1).

One is for the party to the transaction who has the superior private information to undertake some costly method of signaling what it is.

The method needs to be costly to be credible. Thus in Michael Spence's thesis, the effort was four years at graduate school and the signal was a PhD certificate. While the specific topic might be of no interest at all to the employer, the degree is a signal that its holder is a clever person, capable of learning and hard work. Other examples are the investment in expensive showrooms by used-car dealers to indicate that theirs is a responsible business, here to stay, or similarly the investment by banks in imposing buildings to prove that they are serious about money and won't fritter away their customers' deposits. Some forms of advertising are also a signal meant to confirm the reputation of a business.

Note that signaling is effective in correcting asymmetric information problems only when the cost of signaling isn't too high. This might not be so in some developing-country contexts, where the cost of acquiring a degree or similar signal-sending qualification is simply prohibitive. Signaling also only works when it is worthwhile to the holder of private information to reveal it rather than keeping it secret. It's an effective mechanism if I want to earn a higher rate of return on my superior brainpower, for example; but I wouldn't undertake any effort to signal my stupidity or laziness, nor would a heavy smoker ever want to signal that fact to an insurer.

In such situations an alternative to signaling by the party with the superior information is screening by the party without the private information—by the employer or the insurer, to weed out the low-skill or high-risk candidates. The "excess" in an insurance policy is one such screening device, sorting out the low-risk customers who are willing to meet the first $100 of a loss out of their own pocket. There's a multitude of other forms of screening. For example, employers might ask job applicants to take a specific test and provide referees, to screen out the idle or boastful. Another approach which is pervasive wherever there are principal–agent problems involves monitoring, verification, or the search for additional information. Thus governments set targets for public officials, and shareholders demand quarterly reports from the managers of corporations. Alternatively, the incentive problem can be addressed directly. The ill-informed party might link pay to performance or offer a share option (or sharecropping) scheme. The informed party might offer a guarantee or other commitment which would make it costly for them not to behave as promised. All these alternative responses to asymmetries of information are categorized in table 6.1.

It should be pretty obvious that none of the solutions to the selection and incentive problems is without drawbacks. For example, signaling is costly, an activity which would not otherwise be undertaken. Monitoring uses resources, and setting targets is a tricky business which might itself distort behavior: many are the tales of Soviet factories meeting targets set in terms of weight of factory output by making television sets with bricks inside.

An important point to take away from this discussion is that market prices often have two functions. One is to aggregate and convey information about supply and demand, or relative scarcity. This is what underpins the efficiency of market economies and why economists often tend to advocate free-market policies. The other function of prices is to convey information about unobservable characteristics such as quality or effort or risk. To the extent that prices are sending signals about these characteristics rather than the relative scarcity of resources, markets might not be efficient.

Given the wide extent of information asymmetries, and the wide array of responses people have developed to work around them, what can we conclude about how best to design markets? Are there better ways than the huge variety of work-arounds which have emerged in so many contexts? This can be subdivided into two questions. Which approaches would deliver the best possible outcomes (which are optimal)? And are these the same as the methods which will be stable and deliver an equilibrium?

Just as in the context of knowledge spillovers, taking account of information in other fields opens up the possibility of multiple equilibria and jumps from one to another. The path taken from point A can affect where point B is. It might be possible in many cases to think of social or government interventions that would make everyone better off, although it's hard to generalize about what such interventions should be. That will depend on the details of each specific context.

IMPLICATIONS OF IMPERFECT INFORMATION

In the two and a half decades since the pioneering work on the economics of imperfect information, there has been a huge amount of research on specific applications of the insights described above. Following on from the pioneering work by Michael Spence, the role of signaling in education and labor markets has been analyzed extensively. In development economics, imperfect information can account for many of the institutions which seem perverse from the perspective of developed economies, such as sharecropping, seemingly inefficient irrigation systems, or allocations of fishing rights, or the absence of any credit markets. There are many situations in developing countries where the costs of signaling are sufficiently high that markets can't exist. The insights of information economics have also been applied to understand peculiarities of advertising, which is used to send signals about advertisers (or even purchasers) far more than it is used to provide factual information about the products and services being advertised.

One field where information economics has been particularly influential is the study of the organization of corporations (see Macho-Stadler and Perez-Castrillo 2001; Williamson 1985, chapter 12). The modern public company has a principal–agent problem at its heart, as the firm's managers are acting on behalf of owners (the shareholders) who know far less than the managers about the condition and prospects of the business, and cannot monitor the effort of the managers or assess their contribution to profits. This explains why there is so much interest in contracts which pay executives according to results. How can managers be incentivised to maximize profits rather than their own salaries? The variable chosen needs to be one which can be verified by people outside the company and also one which does not distort incentives. Thus incentive reward schemes which depend on the share price, originally a favored approach, fell into disfavor when it became apparent that some executives manipulated short-term share prices at the expense of long-term profitability or even honesty. Many executive reward schemes now depend on a range of measurable variables including sales and accounting profits, and over medium-term as well as short timescales.

Information economics has also been applied in analysis of the structure of organizations. What are the best principles for outsourcing or delegating tasks? How can outsourcing contracts be written to ensure that the supplier has incentives to provide the desired combination of quality and cost (rather than either cutting costs and corners, or exaggerating costs without providing adequate quality)? This will depend on what aspects of the product or service being provided can be monitored. Quality is easier to monitor in auto parts production or payroll services than in health care or computer systems. Information asymmetries and imperfections are pervasive in some services, such as health and education—doctors and teachers know much more than patients and pupils, and the quality of health and education outcomes is difficult to assess, at least for many years. The problems are compounded by the fact that these services are paid for by either insurers or taxpayers in most countries, adding another link to the chain of principals and agents. There isn't an OECD country where further economic analysis of these issues is not considered an urgent public policy problem.

When it comes to business, too, information asymmetries turn out to be central to understanding the organization of companies and industries. Economists George Baker and Thomas Hubbard give a striking example of the effect of information on structures of ownership in a well-known paper on the U.S. trucking industry. They looked at the impact of the spread of onboard computers monitoring truck drivers more closely. The computers made it much easier for nondriver owners to see what effort the truck drivers were putting in and how well they drove. As a result, the truck industry started to consolidate into fewer and larger firms that employed drivers, moving away from the practice of contracting out to owner-drivers. The rationale for the contracting out had been the inability to monitor driver skill and effort, making it more sensible to rely on the incentives of owner-drivers to run their own trucks well (Baker and Hubbard 2000).

A related issue, which has arisen since the computer revolution started to cut information processing and communication costs so rapidly, is what degree of hierarchy and centralization of decision making are desirable in organizations. If information is expensive, a centralized hierarchy will be the best corporate structure, because, in an analogy with hub-and-spoke transportation systems, it minimizes communication costs. In an age of cheap information, it will be better to delegate more decision making and reduce the number of levels of hierarchy. It's encouraging to know that management theory fashions for "delayering" and "network organizations" are economically rational.

It isn't yet clear what the implications of reduced information costs and the IT revolution are for other types of institution, but it seems certain that the optimal form of public-sector and social institutions should change too (see Coyle 2003). Chapter 8 returns to the links between institutions and economic growth. The impact of computers on institutions is fallow territory compared with the study of the productivity implications of cheap processing power.

MARKETS AND INFORMATION MARKETS

So far this chapter has looked at how taking account of imperfections of information undermines our confidence in the ability of markets to deliver the best possible economic outcomes. Yet paradoxically, markets

159

are also superb mechanisms for delivering the information, as they can capture a huge array of private information and make it public in a single price. The hypothesis is not that markets always get it right, but that markets aggregate information better than other mechanisms such as asking experts or polling a sample of people; it's known as the efficient-markets hypothesis. The name is perhaps unfortunate as many people look at the stock market and scoff that something so obviously vulnerable to bubbles, fads, and fashions can be described as efficient. Yet there is some evidence that markets in many circumstances do trump other mechanisms for aggregating information.

The last chapter described Vernon Smith's experimental markets, in which the student participants surprisingly converged on the theoretical equilibrium price. The program of research borne out of his pioneering work has led to a flourishing field of experimental economics concerned with how best to design markets in order to achieve specific policy outcomes. One field where, perhaps surprisingly, these specially designed markets are becoming widely used is environmental policy. I say surprising because a typical environmentalist would probably be allergic to the way economists think about environmental problems. Where an economist might ask about the opportunity cost of implementing a particular policy, those who care passionately about the quality of the environment are more likely to see it as a question of moral absolutes with no place for calculation. The environmental researcher Bjorn Lomborg became a hate figure for many environmental campaigners when he published *The Skeptical Environmentalist* (Lomborg 2001), which discussed precisely these typical economists' questions concerning empirical evidence and opportunity costs. Other economists have courted controversy by challenging the received wisdom that the Kyoto Treaty's greenhouse gas targets are a good thing by suggesting that the opportunity cost of reducing emissions is too high and the resources would be better spent on either technological innovations or simply coping with climate change instead. Many environmentalists remain philosophically opposed to governments issuing "licenses to pollute." What is more, regulation has been the normal approach to environmental policy: governments know how to do regulation, campaigners like the idea of tough rules, and even industry lobbyists like the idea of knowing exactly where they stand and trying to shape the rules. Why, then, is the use of market-based incentives—economic instruments as they are known in this context—spreading in environmental policy? The answer sheds light on the role played by information.

Environmental Markets

Perhaps it is the urgency of the need to address the possible cataclysm of global warming and environmental disaster which has encouraged policy experimentation in this field. Whatever the reason, there are now several prominent government-led schemes and several private exchanges involved in trading permits to pollute or emit greenhouse gases. One of the most successful in achieving reductions has been the Acid Rain Program of the United States Environmental Protection Agency (EPA), mandatory since 1995. The United Kingdom launched a greenhouse gas emissions trading scheme in 2002, which has been overachieving its initial targets for reduction of tonnes of carbon dioxide equivalent. The European Union more recently launched a CO_2 trading scheme (in early 2005).

Schemes of this kind are an interesting combination of administered and market-based policy. One obvious point to make is that they were launched by governments, not by private enterprise. The existence of externalities—the fact that the emitter of carbon dioxide does not pay the full social cost of climate change—means there is a market failure. Although not due to an information asymmetry as such, the price of the fuel used by polluters does not contain all the relevant information about the resources used. So governments have created emissions trading markets. Governments also enforce the obligations accepted by the participants, both by carrot and stick: underpinning the contracts with appropriate legislation, requiring participation, or in voluntary schemes offering incentives such as tax breaks. Governments also negotiate and set the targets established by the schemes, such as the targets for CO_2 emissions arising from the Kyoto Treaty obligations in the British and European Union schemes.

However, these types of governmental framework characterize all markets, which are social institutions, not abstract entities. All markets operate in a given framework of law, taxation, and social obligation or expectation. The key distinction of the environmental markets is that they were conceived and introduced as instruments of public policy. The incentives created by the possibility of trade deliver a better outcome, even where there are large externalities. "Better" in this context means an improved environmental outcome. The prices on the emissions exchanges capture the value placed by participants on permission to emit CO_2, and thus sum up their private information about the costs and opportunity costs of their methods of production,

161

and the resources used. In a review of the EPA scheme, environmental economist Robert Stavins concluded that one reason trading schemes were becoming more widely adopted—as opposed to higher pollution taxes or tougher rules—was the prior uncertainty about the costs to business of pollution abatement and the inherent difficulty in quantifying the benefits to the environment and human health. Administered solutions cannot be effective in conditions of such dense information fog (Stavins 1998).

This discussion of environmental markets is a prelude to asking whether there are other areas of public policy where the introduction of a market mechanism might produce socially more desirable outcomes. The answer will depend on the capacity of markets to elicit privately held information, and through the market prices pool it and share it.

INFORMATION MARKETS

Economist Charles Plott of CalTech has conducted many experiments involving complicated markets allowing speculation on assets, and incorporating private or "inside" information about the true state of the world held by a few participants. He finds that many converge quickly to the theoretical outcome, and then converge quickly to a new equilibrium when the system is "shocked" or disrupted by a change in its structure. Even when there is inside information but most players don't know there are "insiders," the price quickly moves to the true equilibrium. "In other words, the market 'knew' the state with near certainty," he writes (Plott 2000). The market aggregates all the information, even private information as the insiders reveal it by their choices, and then conveys it to all participants.

If experimental results don't convince you, consider the comparison between opinion polls and a well-known information market, the Iowa Electronic Market (IEM). This was launched in 1988 (by the University of Iowa, with permission from the U.S. Commodity Futures Trading Commission; www.biz.uiowa.edu/iem/). Permission was needed because information markets are financial futures markets. Participants offer a price for specified contracts depending on their opinions about how the future will turn out. The IEM is best known for trade in contracts concerning election outcomes. Its original contracts paid 2.5 cents for each percentage point of the popular vote won by George Bush senior and Michael Dukakis in the 1988 presidential election. It has also offered a range of contracts in more recent elections and also on economic decisions such as Federal Reserve Board interest rate moves. The aggregate of the trades in contracts for each candidate reveals a market forecast or expectation of the election outcome. The prices for the IEM's contracts have not only predicted election outcomes very accurately, they have also proven better predictors than large-scale opinion polls. In the week before the election, the average absolute error in the one-week-ahead market prediction of the share of the vote received by candidates has been 1.5 percentage points for the IEM compared with an average error of 2.1 percentage points for the final pre-vote Gallup poll (Rhode and Strumpf 2004).

Following in the footsteps of the IEM, and attracting a growing number of participants, there are now online electronic markets for elections, for other political and current events, for economic data, for sports results, for developments in science and technology, and for entertainment. Table 6.2 lists the best known. Contracts traded can range from who will win the Oscars, to what the opening box office take of a new movie will be, or the size of the increase in employment in the next set of nonfarm payroll figures, and of course the likelihood of terrorist attacks. Some companies have trialed internal prediction markets. The best known is Hewlett-Packard, where HP researcher Kay-Yut Chen called in advice from Charles Plott to introduce an internal market to forecast printer sales. The market had about a dozen participants, whose reward for being right was just $1, but its prediction was more accurate than the forecast delivered by the usual internal expert assessment. Indeed, the evidence is persuasive that information market predictions are often very accurate, and almost always more accurate than alternative predictions based on expert opinion, a consensus of expert forecasts or opinion polling (see Wolfers and Zitzewitz (2006a) for a comprehensive summary of the evidence up to that point; see also Boyle and Videbeck (2005)).

The intuition for these results lies in the fact that markets are a collective institution and so reveal to us other people's choices. Imagine you're in a strange city looking for somewhere to eat. Most people will choose a restaurant that has other diners in it rather than one that's empty. We choose books on the recommendation of others. To gamble on a horse race few of us go to the course and inspect the animals, while most of us look at the odds and read the racing tips in the newspaper. Markets offer us the verdicts of a huge number of other people in making our own choices.

Table 6.2. Leading information markets.

Market	Description	Real or pretend money?
Iowa Electronic Markets (U.S.)	Election markets, University of Iowa (www.biz.iowa.edu/iem)	Real ($)
University of British Columbia (Canada)	Election markets (http://esm.ubc.ca/)	Real (C$)
Technical University of Vienna (Austria)	Election markets (www.tuwien.ac.at/)	Real ($)
Tradesports (for-profit company, Ireland)	Sports, politics, current events, finance, entertainment (www.tradesports.com)	Real ($$$)
Economic Derivatives (Goldman Sachs and Deutsche Bank)	Economics and finance (www.economicderivatives.com)	Real ($$$$$)
Newsfutures (for-profit company, U.S.)	Politics, current events, sport, finance, pharmaceutical and technology events (www.newsfutures.com)	Pretend, with monthly prizes
Hollywood Stock Exchange (Cantor Fitzgerald)	Movies and stars (www.hsx.com)	Pretend
Foresight Exchange (nonprofit research group)	Polits, finance, current events, science and technology events	Pretend

Source: adapted from Wolfers and Zitzewitz (2004).

WHAT CAN PREDICTION MARKETS TELL US?

The information conveyed by the markets depends on the form of the futures contracts it offers. There are three kinds.

- A "winner takes all" contract which pays (say) $1 if and only if a specified event occurs. The price paid for the contract is the market's expectation of the probability that the event will occur.[5] If the "Bush wins the election" contract which pays $1 if he does win is trading at 84 cents, the market puts an 84% probability on his victory.

---

[5] Assuming participants are risk neutral, which is reasonable for the typically small stakes in these markets.

- An index contract pays a variable amount depending on a variable outcome: for example, a Bush index would pay 54 cents if he wins 54% of the vote, 40 cents if he wins 40% of the vote, and so on. The market price of this contract is the average expected value of the outcome. If you believe he'll win 54% of the vote you wouldn't pay more than 54 cents for this one.

- "Spread betting" contracts are bids on cutoff points such as whether a candidate will win more than a certain percentage of the vote (or whether a football team will win by more than a certain number of points). These contracts all cost the same, say $1, and are typically combined with a bet where losers lose their $1 stake and winners receive double their money (an "even money" bet). As this bet will be taken up to the point where a payoff is just as likely to occur as not, this kind of contract reveals the market's expectation of the median outcome.

Contracts can be constructed to reveal a lot of information. For example, a whole family of winner-take-all election contracts paying $1 if the candidate wins 49%, 50%, 51%, 52%, and so on of the vote will reveal not only the average but also the range of uncertainty about the outcome. It must be added that these interpretations of market prices as probability estimates do rest on some simplifying assumptions, and their use as such should be interpreted with care.[6]

WHEN DO PREDICTION MARKETS WORK WELL?

The reason that information markets make good predictions is that they create incentives for people to reveal truthfully what they know and then aggregate this information. It goes without saying that the contracts offered need to be clear and easy to understand with no ambiguity. They also need to be straightforward to adjudicate. So, for example, there can never be a contract on an open-ended negative event such as "There are no weapons of mass destruction in Iraq," whereas "WMDs will not be found in Iraq by July 2004" was a tradable contract. Indeed, it can be harder than it seems to tie down the contract to be suitably specific. Contracts on election outcomes look straightforward enough, but consider the example of the 2000 Presidential election: opinions still differ

---

[6]Charles Manski sets out the conditions and precise interpretations formally (Manski 2005).

as to whether President George W. Bush "really" won. Economic statistics can be revised frequently so these contracts need to specify which published estimate they concern. The Tradesports website was offering a contract in 2004 on whether Yasser Arafat would depart the Palestinian state by the end of 2005, and there was a debate when he fell ill in late 2004 whether "departing the Palestinian state" included seeking medical treatment abroad and then dying. (Tradesports adjudicated that dying did count as "departing," but going to hospital elsewhere for treatment did not (see Wolfers and Zitzewitz 2006a).)

The incentive for people to reveal what they know by making certain trades is the chance of making money or, interestingly, making pretend money, or just enhancing their reputation. It seems many people simply like to be right even if there's no financial benefit, or enjoy expressing opinions about certain kinds of issues ranging from sport to politics. Contracts on events of great interest and entertainment value therefore seem to work very well.

Needless to say, the events covered need to generate differences of opinion. Trade will only take place at all if there is disagreement, and enough people are confident that they are right and others are wrong. At the same time, equally well-informed people must be able to disagree reasonably. Contracts on events where it is very likely that some participants would have correct "inside" information, such as the identity of the next pope, have typically not been popular: after all, chances are that members of the Catholic hierarchy would have been taking part enthusiastically, and few other people thought much of their own chances of doing better. Although information markets work in practice, it's not clear that they do in theory. For in theory people should be wary that anyone willing to trade with them knows more than they do, for they should use that willingness as a signal to modify their own beliefs. (It's an upside-down version of the winner's curse which says that the winner in an auction pays too much because all those unwilling to pay as much must have had a good reason for bidding lower. Groucho Marx was of course well aware of this theoretical problem.)

OPEN QUESTIONS

This leads neatly on to the concern that information markets could be vulnerable to manipulation by people with inside information. This was a key aspect of the controversy about DARPA's "terrorism futures": could members of Al Qaeda planning another attack have bet in the market using their inside information and made a profit? The then Senate Democratic Leader Tom Daschle said the market might even create a financial incentive to commit acts of terrorism. However, any large-scale participation in the market in itself conveys information, so profit opportunities would quickly be competed away. As Charles Plott's experiments revealed, even unknown unknowns—inside information whose existence is not known—are quickly revealed in market prices. Alternatively, could a manipulator willing to lose money manipulate the outcome of a market in order to mislead people basing decisions on their predictions? The counterargument is that trades intended to mislead the market increase the profits for other participants, which encourages their participation and thus restores the accuracy of the market outcome. Again, the same argument about the information content of the insider trades applies. While at present there probably isn't enough evidence to assess these countervailing possibilities definitively, researchers who have attempted to manipulate various information markets have failed. Likewise, when Pat Buchanan's supporters tried to use the IEM to increase the market probability of his victory, the impact lasted for less than twenty-four hours (see Wolfers and Zitzewitz 2006a).

Prediction markets, like other asset markets, also reveal certain biases. Although the markets are efficient in the sense that they offer at best small and fleeting opportunities to profit from publicly available information or from arbitrage opportunities, some have certainly developed bubbles. Often they will overprice events whose probability of occurring is very low. This is known as the "favorite–long-shot" bias, the tendency for gamblers to bet too much on a long-shot horse (albeit with great odds in the remote chance that it wins) and too little on the favorite (likely to win but unexciting odds). I must admit to being a victim to this bias myself. Like many other Britons I gamble just once a year, on the Grand National, and always select a horse with long odds whose jockey is wearing silks in colors that appeal to me. Even economists give rationality a rest from time to time. This bias, a tendency to overestimate the likelihood of low-probability events, or an inability to distinguish between small and tiny, is as we saw well-known to behavioral economics and the basis of Nassim Taleb's investment success, described in chapter 5. In information markets, the favorite–long-shot bias means people with extreme opinions have a disproportionate impact on the price.

A third issue, highlighted by prediction market experts Justin Wolfers and Eric Zitzewitz, is the need for caution in interpreting the inferences we make from market outcomes, especially the more complicated contracts. They give an example of an IEM contract in early 2004 which offered to pay a penny for each percentage point share of the vote won by the Democrats in the November 2004 presidential election if the trader had correctly predicted who the Democratic nominee would be. The prices of these contracts indicated that if John Edwards were selected as nominee, the market expected him to win a 54% share of the vote in November. The figures were 50% for John Kerry and 46% for Howard Dean. It's tempting to conclude that the Democrats should have paid attention to the IEM and selected Edwards instead of Kerry as his chance of winning was seen as much better. But Wolfers and Zitzewitz argue that this is an overinterpretation. Recall the contract: the trader had to get the candidate right first. A world in which the Democrats had selected Edwards might have been a world in which Edwards stood a 54% chance of beating the Republican nominee. But the more conservative world in which the Democrats chose Kerry was a world that favored the Republicans (see Wolfers and Zitzewitz 2006b). Correlation and causation should never be muddled. Interpreting the results of multistage or multiple contracts as probabilities or simple averages must be done with great care.

MARKETS AS A SOCIAL DECISION MECHANISM

Bearing in mind these cautions, can we use information markets for forecasting and decision making? That was the purpose of Admiral Poindexter's terrorism futures. Some scholars are enthusiasts for using information markets to make decisions on a wide range of policies. Robert Hahn and Paul Tetlock argue that combining a prediction market with pay-for-performance contracts could be widely used by governments to achieve their aims more efficiently, and at the same time increase the transparency of policy making (Hahn and Tetlock 2005; Tetlock et al. 2006). For example, a contract could be offered allowing people to "vote" on how many points test scores would increase by in the three years following the takeover of a district's schools by a private contractor. Using the market outcome, the government could offer private contractors a three-year contract paying so many millions of dollars for every point improvement in test scores. Hahn and Tetlock contend that the estimates from such a market are more likely to be accurate than the assessment of officials and education experts, and furthermore that the method would bring public policy decisions out from behind closed doors. They write: "All we really ask of readers is to contemplate the failure of government-as-usual and to suspend disbelief that radical fixes could make a difference."

This provocative suggestion raises a deeper question. What is the best mechanism for decision making in society? This is a live issue. In the Western democracies there has been increasing experimentation with alternatives to the traditional mechanism of voting combined with delegation to specialist bureaucrats. Many countries now have independent central banks, where decisions on interest rates are taken by a group of highly qualified technical experts on monetary policy, unswayed by voters' preferences. At the same time, many are increasingly turning away from experts in other areas to use markets in some policy areas such as auctions (Treasury bonds, radio spectrum) and emissions trading. Which is the best route, in which circumstances?

The growing importance of this question was flagged up many years ago by Daniel Bell (1974) in *The Coming of Post-Industrial Society*. Bell noted the increasing technical and social complexity of modern economies, bringing scientists and economists to the center of what had been purely political decisions. He wrote: "The relationship between technical and political decisions in the next decades will become ... one of the most crucial problems of public policy." Some decisions, or aspects of them, are technically right or wrong; how can this be combined with the requirement for participation and accountability in a democracy? Hahn and Tetlock suggest that our combination of periodic elections and expert decisions behind closed doors is not the best we can do. They are persuaded by the evidence that information markets often outperform experts in collecting, aggregating, and sharing private information. What is more, markets offer everyone the opportunity to participate.

There is in addition a good amount of evidence that decisions made by groups such as expert committees are often flawed. In principle, expert groups should do better than expert individuals. This might seem to be a sensible compromise between using markets on the one hand and knowledgeable individuals on the other hand to make policy decisions: less radical than the former but less vulnerable to one person's idiosyncrasies than the latter. The best members of a group of experts could persuade the others; the groups could aggregate information held by individuals; or the process of discussion could lead all members to a better conclusion.

What happens in practice? In general, the results of group decision making are disappointing. On matters with a definite answer, groups

169

perform about as well as their average member, not their best member. The process of discussion brings members closer to each other's views, and makes them more confident that they are correct, which is only a benefit when their initial opinions are close to the right answer. The social pressure of group working can furthermore silence dissenting correct views, especially those held by socially "inferior" members such as women—the low-status members of a group will be wary about emphasizing information that their superiors seem to lack. And groups are more, not less, likely than individuals to display all the psychological biases discussed in the previous chapter—framing effects, preference reversals, and overconfidence are amplified by group debate. As Cass Sunstein says, describing one study: "The majority played a substantial role in determining the group's answers. The truth played a role too, but a lesser one." On the other hand, some groups end up polarized, with the discussion leading members to hold their original views even more strongly than they did to start with. This is often the case when groups are divided politically, perhaps with supporters of different parties. They are unable to reach effective decisions.

Some of these problems can be overcome. Knowing that groups focus on shared information, so members can reinforce each other socially, it is possible to take care to ask individuals for the information that's not shared. One mechanism is to designate a "devil's advocate" in each group who will challenge the majority view. Anonymous votes can help. So can ensuring that the members of deliberating groups have very different backgrounds and expertise, and are therefore less likely to be socially competitive about their reputations. For example, inquiry groups assessing mergers for the United Kingdom's Competition Commission usually consist of professionally mixed groups: an economist, a lawyer, an accountant, a retired bureaucrat. Studies by the Diversity Group at the Los Alamos National Laboratory have found that diversity in the classic politically correct dimensions of sex, ethnicity, and age makes for better decisions than homogeneous groups.

Equally, some groups have been shown to perform much better than their individual members. One intriguing study tried to assess the decision-making structure of the Bank of England's Monetary Policy Committee (nine individuals voting each month on the level of interest rates which would keep inflation close to a long-term target). In a trial students at the London School of Economics used an econometric model to set interest rates, their choices being assessed by the inflation rate generated in the model. The groups performed better than even the best individual in keeping inflation close to target. It seems that the key lies in whether members of the group believe there *is* a correct answer, in which case they are more likely to share information and to base their decisions on evidence rather than opinion.

When the information being sought is the view of the entire population about some matter, opinion polls ought to do better in some sense than smaller groups because they collect the views of enough people to form a representative sample of the relevant population. What do voters think of the candidates? Asking a large enough number of voters who are sufficiently similar to the electorate as a whole will give a reasonable answer. Yet even in this case, as we saw, information markets tend to outperform opinion polls as predictors of election outcomes because voters don't always tell the truth to pollsters. One might find it less embarrassing or intrusive to admit to voting for a particular political party anonymously to an Internet site than face-to-face or on the telephone to a nice young employee of an opinion research company.

What is more, polls of large groups (or "statistical groups" as they're sometimes referred to) can be hopeless at assessing matters of fact. It can be established in principle that groups (that is, their majority or average answer) do better than individuals, and large groups do better than small ones, only if each individual is more likely than not to be correct.[7] But if this condition does not hold, even large groups go wildly astray. For example, a study at the University of Chicago Law School asked faculty members to estimate the weight in pounds of the fuel used by a space shuttle, a matter about which they were untroubled by any knowledge. The median answer was 200,000 pounds, the mean was 55.8 million pounds, and the correct answer is 4 million pounds (see Sunstein 2004).

Information markets are therefore highly effective in circumstances where there is an objectively correct answer which will be known at a finite fixed date. Yet there is an important lesson in the latest of Admiral Poindexter's political fiascos, a lesson about the moral limits of markets. Many of the many critics of the DARPA Policy Analysis Market said it was immoral to bet on death and destruction. In the aftermath, Caltech's Charles Plott commented: "These markets will eventually prove their worth but you have to be very careful taking the idea outside the

---

[7]This is the Condorcet Jury theorem, which assumes that people will be unaffected by whether their vote will be decisive, that they will not be affected by one another's votes, and that the probabilities that individual members are right are statistically independent. That is, independent thinking and no tactical voting.

laboratory" (Harford 2003). The "right" solution to policy problems, in the sense of the solution which is technically the best, or which meets in some sense the aim of increasing social welfare, needs to be reached in a politically acceptable manner. While the technology of the Internet makes it possible to improve the technical quality of economic and social policy decisions, economists also need to pay due attention to the political quality of the decisions. This point will feature heavily in chapter 8, which looks at the importance of political and market institutions.

Joseph Stiglitz delights in the fact that the economics of information torpedoes mainstream economic theory, and the notion that there is a competitive general equilibrium which is optimal (in the formal sense of Pareto optimality, nobody can be made better off without someone else being made worse off). As soon as information asymmetries are admitted, economists cannot assert with confidence that in competitive markets all the information needed for maximum social welfare is efficiently decentralized through the price mechanism. As a liberal intellectual he is clearly delighted to have put the case for government intervention on a respectable, indeed Nobel prize quality, footing. But the Stiglitz case doesn't have obvious implications for what kinds of intervention will be best. To give an extreme example, neither nationalizing nor banning insurance markets would be a good solution to the problem of moral hazard. Indeed, the fact that a competitive market in insurance doesn't have the neat efficiency properties claimed by conventional economic theory does not imply that some other arrangement is optimal. There probably isn't a right answer to this problem: excesses on policies or no-claims bonuses might be the best we can do.

At the same time, markets still look like a more efficient vehicle than any other for distributing information. It's possible therefore that the reach of markets should be extended into areas which have traditionally been reserved for social or government action. While information markets are still very much at the experimental stage, and not a widely accepted tool for decision making, one area where the potential to use markets to get better outcomes is increasingly accepted is environmental policy. By no means all environmentalists would accept that it is either morally acceptable or beneficial to trade in permits to pollute or log forests, but a growing number do take the pragmatic view that markets will lead to better environmental outcomes, and the evidence so far is on their side.

The paradox of information economics is that pervasive asymmetries of information mean that markets are flawed, and yet markets in many circumstances remain better mechanisms for sharing and diffusing information than any alternative social institution we've yet devised. The next chapter looks first at the sources of this characteristic of markets in human nature and evolutionary history, and the subsequent chapter at what an economics grounded in those realities looks like. Recent developments in evolutionary biology and anthropology have taken economics back to the future with a revival of interest among economists in what always used to be called political economy, or the institutional and cultural framework which aggregates individual choices into social or collective decisions.

Prologue to Part 3

The first three chapters of this book looked at the central questions of economics—What makes economies grow? How can we end poverty?—through the lens of recent historical research, economic geography, and growth theory. This work has placed economies firmly in time and place, and makes it clear that growth is a collective or social process which depends on how people's decisions affect each other. Spillovers from one person's choices to another's, shaped by social and political institutions, affect growth rates for better or worse. The previous few chapters have all explored the reintroduction of human nature into economics through the relaxation of or challenge to specific assumptions made by the old-fashioned neoclassical orthodoxy. These assumptions were the maximization of utility where utility is usually proxied by output, rational calculation, and perfect and symmetric information. Together, the economics of happiness, behavioral economics, and information economics add up to a challenge to the notion of human nature that has come to be adopted (often implicitly) by economists, drawing to a large degree on psychology. Economic Man is becoming extinct.

The next two chapters bring together the social nature of the economy and the human nature of the individuals making up society. The next chapter discusses evolutionary economic theories, which focus on how an economy made up of individuals changes as they respond to each other and their environment; and complexity theory, which portrays economic outcomes as an order emerging, undirected, from the mass of individual decisions. Both are alternatives to the neoclassical general equilibrium model as a formalization of Adam Smith's metaphor of the invisible hand. They draw heavily on the biological sciences and anthropology. Both emphasize differences between individuals, and interactions between them, in contrast to many conventional economic models which assume identical individuals making independent decisions. The following chapter aggregates up from these biological microfoundations,

175

discussing how networks, social capital, and institutions affect economic growth. These are areas where economics overlaps with sociology and political science. This will have brought the book full circle, to the central question of growth, and to the intellectual tradition of the founding fathers of economics, Enlightenment philosophers such as Smith and Hume.

PART 3
Nature, Markets, and Society

Murderous Apes and Entrepreneurs

INTRODUCTION

Professors of economics are hardly notorious for their violence and savagery, unless it be the verbal kind. The ivory tower is generally free from the murders and beatings which sadly characterize so many parts of the world, and economists are probably gentler and more herbivorous than many other academics, although I have no data to prove this. Toulouse is not only home to one of the great universities of the world, but is also a spectacularly civilized city, with all the benefits and few of the drawbacks of French provincial life. It has a vibrant culture, exquisite restaurants, elegant shops (including possibly the best ice-cream shop in the world). Why then has Paul Seabright, a notably civilized and distinguished economist who lives in this calm and ordered university town, spent so much time thinking about the violent nature of humanity? His wonderful book, *The Company of Strangers* (Seabright 2004), opens by noting that *homo sapiens sapiens*, the "shy, murderous ape," violent, suspicious of strangers, habituated to hunting in small, mobile bands of relatives, has in just the past 10,000 years come to live in communities of millions, engaging in an extremely detailed and elaborate division of labor which ensures that we depend utterly on strangers for the satisfaction of our daily needs. "Nature knows no other examples of such complex mutual dependence among strangers," Seabright writes.

How can this be? In evolutionary terms, next to no time at all has elapsed since the "most aggressive and elusive bandit species in the entire animal kingdom" (i.e., you and me) switched from a life of hunting for meat in groups of kin, inclined to murder a stranger first and ask questions later, to a life of queuing for the bus each morning, listening to Tchaikovsky on the way to work, waiting obediently for the signal to cross the road, and spending the next eight hours tapping at a small keyboard before going home to eat an organic pizza. Indeed, in many places,

179

daily life is still horribly similar to the murderous pattern familiar to our ancestors tens of thousands of years ago. Yet the very speed of the transition from Cro-Magnon Man to iPod Person means that our analysis of modern society, in all its economic complexity, must be consistent with our evolutionary biology. As Seabright writes: "Some time in the last two hundred thousand years or so ... a series of changes, minuscule to geneticists, vast in the space of cultural potential, occurred to make human beings capable of abstract, symbolic thought and communication." These changes were the basis for the accumulation of knowledge in a shared reservoir of skills which has made possible large and complex societies.

Professor Seabright's question—Why aren't we still murderously suspicious of strangers?—focuses our attention on why we should think about economies in the light of our biological evolution. He uses recent research in biology and anthropology to try to understand why the complex, global economy can exist at all, and how we might try to ensure its stability given our suspicious, violent nature. This question extends a long and honorable tradition of evolutionary-type thinking among economists. As Vernon Smith puts it, an economic order is:

> An undesigned ecological system that emerges out of cultural and biological evolutionary processes.... People follow rules without being able to articulate them, but they can be discovered. This is the intellectual heritage of the Scottish philosophers, who described and interpreted the social and economic order they observed.
>
> Smith (2003)

Adam Smith and David Hume and other Enlightenment thinkers considered their study of economic order as one part of the broad scientific inquiry into the natural order. The same general principles would apply to human society as to the whole of the natural world, of which humankind is a part. Hume saw little difference in the methodology for thinking about how we see the refraction of light through a glass of water and for thinking about the flow of currency from one country to another. His price-specie-flow mechanism was as much a part of nature as the principles of perception.

Evolutionary economics per se had to wait for the intellectual discovery of evolution by natural selection with the publication of *The Origin of Species* by Charles Darwin in 1859 (see Darwin 1982). Some economists were swift to draw on scientific evolutionary theory. Engels, delivering the eulogy at the graveside of Karl Marx, claimed for his old friend the mantle of Charles Darwin's massive celebrity: "Just as Darwin discovered the law of evolution in organic nature, so Marx discovered the law of evolution in human society," he said (quoted in Bowles (2004, p. 400)). As it turned out, Marx got his laws wrong, but it was many years before that became clear. Meanwhile, others also sought evolutionary social laws. One of the best known of the late-nineteenth-century wannabe evolutionary theorists was Thorstein Veblen. Biographies all describe Veblen as unkempt, strange, and rude or gruff. He certainly looked odd, with lank hair falling from either side of a center parting, and too much moustache. The child of Norwegian immigrants living in rural Wisconsin and then Minnesota, he didn't learn English until his teens. This makes his books read rather strangely, and his publishers forced him to rewrite the famous *Theory of the Leisure Class* several times. (I find it still almost unreadable.) He was a skeptic about religion in a pious age, and thus viewed with some suspicion. He fell out with most of his academic advisers, who included the famous pragmatist philosopher Charles Sanders Peirce. Peirce, along with William James and John Dewey, was influential in introducing Darwinian thought to the United States (Menand 2002). James even prefigured the concept of memes in an essay on the natural selection of ideas in the minds of individuals (James 1880). Despite Veblen's illustrious advisers and an excellent academic record as a student, he couldn't get a job when he graduated with a PhD in philosophy from Yale in 1884; for years he lived off his wife's family. Finally, in 1892 he was employed as a teaching assistant at the new University of Chicago. His famous books, published during his years at Chicago, were initially not well-received—they were highly critical of conventional economics, their tone sarcastic—and Veblen was, unsurprisingly, chippy about other academic economists. Chicago eventually offered him (in 1906) an assistant professorship but quickly forced him to leave: not only was he bad tempered, hostile, and unattractive, it seems he was also a flagrant womanizer. Veblen moved to California, and was duly expelled from a job at Stanford for similar reasons. New York came next, and Veblen was briefly involved in the founding of the New School. He died in obscurity in 1929 (see chapter 8 of *The Worldly Philosophers* for more fascinating detail).

At the height of his brief contemporary academic fame, Veblen (1898) posed the question, "Why is economics not an evolutionary science?" It is apparent before the end of the first paragraph of the article why he was unpopular with colleagues: "Economics is helplessly behind the times, and unable to handle its subject matter in a way to entitle it to standing as a modern science," he wrote. The essence of his criticism is that economics is too preoccupied with static analysis of equilibrium and has no theory of the process of change. In a passage that seems prescient, given modern growth theory, he says: "All economic change is a change in the economic community—a change in the community's methods of turning material things to account. The change is always in the last resort a change in the habits of thought." It was many years, though, before Veblen's work regained prominence, and then more for his sarcastic analysis of the idle rich and their "conspicuous consumption," a habit which he explained by reference to anthropological theories of status.

In the twentieth century, economics grew less concerned with dynamic questions, although with prominent exceptions. Among the exceptions were the Austrians Joseph Schumpeter and Friedrich Hayek. Schumpeter coined the phrase "creative destruction" to describe the constant dynamism of capitalism, the process of birth and death of new businesses and technologies (Schumpeter 1962). Born in the old Austro-Hungarian empire, a bourgeois longing to be an aristocrat, and a brilliant student at the University of Vienna, Schumpeter was one of the many brilliant intellectuals who left central Europe in the 1930s. He pitched up at Harvard via a brief marriage in England and a spell in Cairo as financial adviser to an Egyptian princess. He was clearly a very irritating man. He used to wear riding clothes around the university, and boasted about his brilliance as an economist and as a lover. Even more irritating, he was indeed academically brilliant (little seems to be recorded about his prowess in bed). Schumpeter admired the intellectual edifice of the emerging mathematical, neoclassical economics, but disagreed with its focus on the concept of equilibrium. He said that he "felt very strongly that this was wrong, and that there was a source of energy within the economic system which would of itself disrupt any equilibrium that might be attained. . . . It is such a theory that I have tried to build and I believe now, as I believed then, that it contributes something to the understanding of the struggles and vicissitudes of the capitalist world" (quoted in Andersen (1996); the quotation is from *Capitalism, Socialism and Democracy*). His theory, which he conceived as a corrective to Marx's analysis, focused on the role of the entrepreneur in the formation of new businesses and development of new technologies. *Capitalism, Socialism and Democracy*, published in 1942, was an account of endogenous growth via technological innovation. It was utterly out of tune with the times, an era of central planning and Keynesian demand management, and for decades after World War II nobody was interested in a theory of destruction, even creative destruction.

Despite disagreeing strongly with Marx, Schumpeter too felt capitalism was doomed. He foresaw the emergence of bureaucracies stifling entrepreneurial initiative, delivering a kind of de facto socialism everywhere, and the growing internal opposition to capitalist forces:

> Capitalism creates a critical frame of mind which, after having destroyed the moral authority of so many other institutions, in the end turns against its own; the bourgeois finds to his amazement that the rationalist attitude does not stop at the credentials of kings and popes but goes on to attack private property and the whole scheme of bourgeois values.
>
> Quoted in Heilbroner (2000, p. 302)

One feels, looking at mass demonstrations in France in 2006 against a modest deregulation of employment law, that Schumpeter might have been right after all.

Schumpeter's critique of capitalism was sociological. His work is influential with evolutionary economists now—although Schumpter himself rejected an explicit evolutionary framework—for its analysis of the process of the birth and death of new firms. Friedrich Hayek, by contrast, was interested in the development of economic institutions, in the specific context of arguing against socialism and central planning; and he did see this as fitting into the general framework of evolution. Hayek was another brilliant student at the University of Vienna. He left in 1931, first for the London School of Economics, moving in 1950 to the University of Chicago. He was firmly antitotalitarian and anticommunist (socialism was *The Road to Serfdom*, to quote the title of his best-known book); more than Schumpeter, Hayek (who won the Nobel memorial prize in 1974, in perfect time to inspire the policy wonks working to elect Ronald Reagan and Margaret Thatcher) is claimed as a forefather by today's right-wing free-market economists.

Hayek was interested in the emergence of spontaneous order—"that which is the result of human action but not of human design"—in a market economy. His argument was that the institutions of a modern economy, whether large businesses or markets consisting of many competitors, were so complex and so information heavy that they could not have been intentionally planned. They had emerged or evolved through a mechanism of group selection, coordinated by the price mechanism, and while the existing institutions of the market economy were by no means ideal, it would be dangerous to try to supersede them with deliberate planning. Hayek saw the modern capitalist economy as an "extended order," an interconnected system of complex links between strangers, made possible by institutions and laws which replaced the personal trust underpinning transactions in a traditional society. The relevance to today's "natural history" of economics set out by Paul Seabright is clear.

However, like other strands of the subject, evolutionary economics was pushed to the fringes by the dominance of the neoclassical mainstream in the years after World War II. The mainstream favored a "comparative static" approach to analyzing models, which could be solved mathematically for two separate points in time and compared, and which ignored the details of the dynamic process of moving from one stable equilibrium to another. From the 1950s to perhaps ten years ago, formal evolutionary modeling has been a minority sport, although one with some interesting and rigorous work by economists including Richard Nelson and Sidney Winter in the United States and Geoffrey Hodgson and Stan Metcalfe in the United Kingdom (see Hodgson 1998, 2005; Metcalfe 1998; Nelson and Winter 1982). These economists acknowledge the prominence in particular of Schumpeter, and have concentrated on innovation and growth. Will Baumol has also emphasized the vital role of entrepreneurship and innovation, integrating it into the formal theory of the firm in microeconomics (Baumol forthcoming).

The more recent revival of evolutionary theorizing in economics has grown from a number of newer roots. One of the most influential is the impact of developments in biological research, developments which have tried to apply the arguments of biology on a broader canvas, in evolutionary psychology and sociobiology. Some evolutionists indeed argue that evolutionary thinking has a wide range of applicability, going well beyond genetics and biology. Richard Dawkins, the passionately Darwinian scientist, coined for this the term Universal Darwinism. Although controversial, this has inspired social scientists to try to build a bridge from their own subjects toward the biologists. A second new root is the development of techniques which have helped overcome economists' reluctance to sacrifice the analytical muscularity of their conventional models. In particular, evolutionary game theory has a clear appeal to economists, as the tool is their own, and has been adopted by biologists. In addition, the mathematics of nonlinear dynamic systems used by biologists, and the ability of today's computers to simulate complex dynamic systems when analytical solutions do not exist, are also nudging economists toward trying approaches from biological science. These approaches seem to offer fruitful insights into aggregate economic behavior.

The next section sets the scene with the question of the wider applicability of evolutionary theory, before going on to evolutionary approaches to growth, evolutionary game theory, and complexity.

UNIVERSAL DARWINISM

Charles Darwin didn't discover evolution. His own grandfather Erasmus Darwin was an early evolutionary theorist, publishing (posthumously) *The Temple of Nature*, a long and popular poem setting out the theory:

> Organic life beneath the shoreless waves
> Was born and nurs'd in ocean's pearly caves;
> First forms minute, unseen by spheric glass,
> Move on the mud, or pierce the watery mass;
> These, as successive generations bloom,
> New powers acquire and larger limbs assume;
> Whence countless groups of vegetation spring,
> And breathing realms of fin and feet and wing.

The popularity of the poem seems to have stemmed more from its lascivious tone than its literary quality—in 1802, a long poem on the sex life of plants was about as risqué as publications could get (see Uglow 2002).

Of course, before and since the two Darwins, Erasmus and his more famous grandson Charles, the concept of evolution (the word derived from the Latin for "unrolling") has a longstanding general meaning: unfurling, development, changing over time. We often use the word in this general sense, and often imply in doing so that the change is an improvement over what went before. In biology, the word has a much more specific meaning, one originating in Charles Darwin's great works *The Origin of Species* and *The Descent of Man*. Darwin theorized—and supported his theory with a lifetime of empirical observation and experimentation—that evolution in animals consisted of a process of variation in individuals in an animal population, selection for successful variations whereby those individuals were more likely to survive and reproduce; and reproduction which passed on the successful characteristics to the next generation, gradually increasing the proportion of the population with the selected-for characteristics. Some Victorian clergymen found it impossible to believe they had evolved from hairy apes. Even today some people disbelieve in biological evolution despite the overwhelming amount of evidence in its favor; indeed we've evolved not only from apes but from a kind of primeval fish with short front legs, which crawled onto land.[1] One can only conclude that evolution hasn't moved some of us quite so far on from the primeval fish stage. Since Darwin's time, biologists have worked out the exact mechanisms through which evolution operates: sexual selection for advantageous genes and the expression of the genes, as they interact with the environment, in phenotypes, the observable physical characteristics of a species or individual (see Ridley (2000) or Dawkins (2004, 2006) for an overview).[2]

It is very unlikely that these biological mechanisms can help us directly in thinking about the economy in evolutionary terms, amusing as it might be to ponder the scope for applying sexual selection to the theory of the firm. Yet the general evolutionary principles—variation, selection, replication—might be useful in other contexts. We might expect them to be especially useful in economics, which is, after all, a study of how scarce resources are allocated in a society. The contest for resources is exactly the driving force of natural selection. Darwin himself famously drew inspiration from an economist, the gloomy Malthus, whom we met in chapter 2. In September 1838 he began to read ("for amusement," he later said) Malthus's *Essay on the Principle of Population*. Years later in an autobiographical note Darwin explained:

> It at once struck me that under these circumstances [i.e., lack of food] favorable variations would tend to be preserved and unfavorable ones destroyed. The result of this would be the formation of new species. Here, then, I had at last got a theory by which to work.
>
> Browne (2001, p. 431; see also p. 385ff)

From the economist's grim vision of humanity's sentence of inevitable cycles of growth and starvation evolved the theory of natural selection.

---

[1]A fossil of *Tiktaalik roseae* was discovered in the Canadian Arctic (reported in *Nature*, April 2006; available at http://news.nationalgeographic.com/news/2006/04/0405_060405_fish.html).

[2]Note that it was not until genes were discovered that it was possible to rule out Lamarck's hypothesis that children could inherit characteristics acquired or learned by their parents, perhaps in response to changes in the environment. Instead, natural selection favors genes which are successful in their specific environment; individuals with favored genes are more likely to enjoy reproductive success.

It's hardly surprising then that other Victorian intellectuals in turn applied Darwinian principles to human society. One of the most famous was Herbert Spencer, who contributed the phrase "the survival of the fittest" to the language. Spencer applied evolutionary principles to human society before Darwin published *The Origin of Species* in 1859, but his "social Darwinism" was greatly boosted by the success of Darwin's work. Spencer thought all aspects of life could be explained by evolutionary principles, and gave evolution the gloss of progress, the improvement of species culminating in the flower of perfection which was Victorian manhood, and the improvement of society. It was an upbeat philosophy, one which was taken up by Oliver Wendell Holmes and Charles Peirce across the Atlantic. In time, however, the survival of the fittest came to be seen as an uncaring approach to the weak. Social applications of evolution were further tarnished by Darwin's distant cousin Francis Galton, another grandson of Erasmus. Galton was inspired by the publication of his cousin's book *The Origin of Species* to apply the concept of selection to humans. He studied twins to try to distinguish the roles of nature and nurture, and in 1883 coined the phrase eugenics to describe the breeding of humans to be fitter and cleverer. The subsequent embrace of eugenics by the Nazis, among others, meant that the application of evolutionary thought to social science was thoroughly discredited for decades.

The revival of the evolutionary analysis of human society in the shape of sociobiology after the publication in 1975 of Edward O. Wilson's *Sociobiology: The New Synthesis* (see Wilson 2000) was hugely controversial, in large part because of these antecedents. Sociobiology is the discipline which looks at the evolutionary context of the interactions between individual members of a species, and the resulting patterns of behavior. It gives genes a starring role in explaining how we behave, as does evolutionary psychology, and prompted the long and ultimately pointless "nature versus nurture" wars (see Pinker (2002, pp. 105–20) for a discussion of this episode). Sociobiology extends mechanisms of selection to the group rather than just the individual, acting on the distribution of characteristics in a population. A social group is shaped by its "gene pool." Sociobiology has strongly influenced some other social sciences, notably linguistics and anthropology. Evolutionary thinkers have made a further land grab to try to explain swathes of human culture. Richard Dawkins, for example, has posited the meme as a cultural equivalent of the gene, a basic unit of culture subject to the mechanisms of variation, natural selection, and replication. Examples of memes are tunes, phrases, fashions, techniques for making things, customs, and scientific ideas (see Blackmore (1999) for a general introduction). Dawkins described them as parasites infecting one brain after another, a concept memorably used by novelist Neal Stephenson in *Snow Crash*.

This, then, is the flourishing, if controversial, intellectual context in which evolutionary ideas have reemerged in economics. There are disagreements among Universal Darwinists, some of whom see evolution and natural selection as a grand unifying theory of natural life, while others see it as a fruitful way of understanding phenomena we observe in society. The attraction of evolutionary theory is the absence of a plan, a designer, a central organizing intelligence—the invisible hand, the emergent, self-organizing economic order. Some techniques of modern evolutionary biology have had a direct impact on the methods used by economists and will be discussed a little later in the chapter. But most work in evolutionary economics is not closely tied to the universal gene-based biological theories, but more descriptive and empirical. For example, Richard Nelson, one of the foremost evolutionary economists, argues that memes or similar conceptions are just too simple to be useful in analyzing the complexities of modern economic life, such as multinationals, the technologies of semiconductor manufacture, or patent law: "None of these analyses attempts to come to grips with the paths of cumulative evolution taken by cultural structures like science, technology, the law, standard forms of business organization and the like" (Nelson 1995).

How Does the Economy Evolve?

Nelson nevertheless writes: "The proposal is that human culture has been shaped by forces of variation and selection that, while different from those of biological evolution, have some general things in common" (Nelson 2006, p. 3). But the mechanisms are clearly different. An evolutionary model of the economy will need to specify the processes of variation, selection, and replication which will apply in an economic context. What are the sources of change? What are the criteria for a variation to succeed in a given economic environment—how is "fitness" specified and what are the mechanisms for selection? How are successes passed on to other units? Indeed, what "units" should we be analyzing? What types of variation are of interest? Further questions concern the economic environment which shapes and constrains the behavior of these units. How does it evolve, and how do the units interact with each other and the environment?

So many questions. Let's start with the most common, and convincing, application of a formal evolutionary model of the economy, which addresses technological innovation and the evolution of industry structure. Competition between firms in a struggle for profits, or even survival, seems a natural candidate for the evolutionary framework. Firms engage in rivalry, seeking to distinguish themselves from each other in a competitive market through innovations either in their products and services, or in their processes. Innovation is the source of economic variation. Competitive advantage is reflected in higher profits or larger market share or both, the selection mechanism. Rivals then seek to imitate the successful innovations, the replication mechanism. This is clearly not like biological evolution—for example, learned characteristics can be "inherited" by successor firms—but equally clearly, it falls into the general pattern of variation, selection, replication.

This seems straightforward enough. Even in this obvious context for the application of evolutionary theory in economics, however, the modeling involves some tricky questions. The immediate one is what is the correct unit of selection? In biology it is the gene. In economics it has been the firm, or the business unit within a firm, or an "organizational/technological complex." But why not the individual manager within a firm? And what about the clusters of networked organizations operating across international boundaries which have become more common forms of business organization—should we think of these as basic evolutionary units, or rather as analogous to shoals of fish? While it obviously makes sense to talk about rivalry between firms, there are some interesting issues to explore here, which could lead us toward ecology rather than evolutionary biology.

A related question is how we should combine different firms into a relevant population. The obvious answer is those which are subject to the same competitive environment, but there's an inevitably circular flavor to this, especially as businesses frequently try to influence the competitive environment to favor themselves and harm potential rivals, through lobbying for lighter regulation or tax breaks for example. In competition inquiries, one of the key areas of analysis is market definition, as a company which has a 50% share of one market might have only a 20% share of a more widely defined market. The boundaries are set by the possibility of substitution, by consumers and by competitors. If consumers cannot find a ready substitute, and/or if competitors cannot expand their output to serve customers, you've hit the boundary of the market. But there is a real art to the empirical analysis as in reality these borders are not crisp but fuzzy. Still, this is true in nature as well as economies. Species aren't as sharply distinct from each other as one might imagine.

Then we have the question of what defines fitness in business. Profitability would be an obvious measure. It is closely linked to the survival of the firm, as those losing money tend to be closed or taken over. Evolutionary economists prefer to use market share or relative rate of expansion of sales, presumably because of the analogy with population dynamics in biology. Scale is certainly what motivates many real-life business executives. Using the relative scale of activity also links to what it is that is replicated in business, namely the capability to imitate a certain set of business activities, usually called "routines" in the literature. Routines are therefore analogous to genes, firms are their phenotypes or organisms. Routines can consist of everything from the idea of what is being produced down to the day-to-day procedures involved: for example, the idea of a mortgage, the buildings and people and equipment and software needed to produce a mortgage, all the business processes involved including regulatory approval, all the way to the scripts followed by call-center operatives responding to a query from a potential customer. If one firm is gaining mortgage market share, others will try to imitate the reason for their success, while at the same time seeking to differentiate themselves in the eyes of customers.

If firms try to copy the reasons for another's success, they will tend to become more like each other. What, then, is the source of variation? The answer is innovation. Firms also deliberately set out to introduce variety themselves. Innovation plays a key role in evolutionary economics, and in contrast to variation in nature, it is a purposive activity. While the operation of markets is similar in evolutionary theory and conventional economic theory, intentional innovation rules out in the former case the possibility of a state of rest or stationary equilibrium. The target is always moving, some less successful firms will always engage in activities to make them more successful.

Richard Nelson and Sidney Winter were early developers of formal evolutionary growth models, publishing their first papers in the late 1960s and 1970s, and a number of others have followed. The models have in common a process whereby firms both innovate and allocate investment to the more profitable existing technologies. Technological advance consists of both improvement in successive generations of technologies and the expansion of the use of more productive technologies relative to less productive ones. The latter component will be stronger the more variation there is in the productivity of the technologies in use by different firms. This pattern fits very comfortably with Will Baumol's observation that small firms tend to develop radical innovations, whereas large firms focus their R&D on incremental improvements in existing technologies. Aggregate productivity growth will depend on both kinds of activity.

It would be hard to deny, for even the most died-in-the-wool orthodox neoclassical economist, that the framework of evolutionary competition offers a much richer and realistic account of innovation. In many industries, there is a pattern of a large array of small competitors at an early stage of the life of a new technology, with many new entrants, and many closures, followed by a process of consolidation to a small number of large competitors producing dominant variants of the technology. For example, fourteen firms entered the fledgling U.S. auto industry between 1885 and 1898, nineteen in 1899, thirty-seven in 1900, twenty-seven in 1901, and then forty-eight a year on average from 1902 to 1910. The number of start-ups diminished from that level until there were almost no new entrants by the 1920s. Meanwhile, the number leaving the industry showed a similar pattern of increase and decrease and from the 1920s the industry consolidated quickly. By the late 1950s there were seven carmakers in the United States, down from a peak of 275 in 1907 (Geroski 2003, pp. 63, 64). While the numbers and dates vary, many industries display this characteristic pattern.

What explains the failure of the many who exit the industry and the success of the few and increasingly large survivors? Dominance of an industry is not necessarily established by technical superiority. Chance plays a part. So do lobbying, regulations, and standard setting. Network externalities can turn an early lead into runaway success, as the benefit to each successive customer of choosing one variant is greater the larger the number of other users. Indeed, any early lead can snowball because customers need to learn how to use a new technology, so the QWERTY keyboard is here to stay because everyone is used to it (David 1985). Furthermore, new technologies often need a lot of complementary infrastructure and products or services, so a switch from the internal combustion engine to hydrogen-fuel-cell-powered vehicles is proving costly and difficult as we already have a vast network of gas stations, mechanics, carmakers, and suppliers producing and servicing internal combustion engines. Not to mention the vast lobbying power of the auto makers and oil companies. When an industry has reached the established stage of a small number of large firms, new entry is hard because there are high hurdles posed by the know-how and scale of the incumbents, and the most likely source of change is the next cycle of innovation, with the introduction of a disruptive new technology.[3]

Part of the appeal of the evolutionary approach is that this model does capture empirically robust regularities about the process of competition. It is not only the history of technology which confirms this, but the vast literature on business economics (see, for example, Geroski (2003) and Geroski and Markides (2005); there are very many other examples). The consequences of the emergence of a dominant design for the profitability and market share of the firm which owns the technology are very large. Rivals are indeed forced by the competitive environment to innovate either by improving their business processes to offer the dominant technology better or cheaper, differentiating it as best they can in the eyes of customers, or by developing radical new technologies which can displace the current dominant version. This pattern of competition is pervasive. However, the pattern can be described and analyzed without recourse to any formal evolutionary theorizing. Many economists, especially those interested in technology and business, could be described as evolutionary thinkers in this more general sense, returning to the heritage of thinkers like Smith and Hume, Veblen, Schumpeter, and Hayek. Numerous orthodox neoclassical economists, who might or might not have any overt sympathy with the evolutionary tendency, have described and analyzed the life cycle of industries without tying their work to the Darwinian stake (see, for example, Geroski 2003; Baumol 2002).

Evolutionary thinking in the sense of formal models of variation, selection, and replication remain a minority interest in economics. Yet any economist who studies industrial organization and technical change clearly has a strong intuition that it is an evolutionary process. What is more, the influence of biology on economics has become much more extensive since the 1980s. This is partly because of sociobiology and the claims of the Universal Darwinists. It is also due to the utility of certain modeling techniques which are widely used in evolutionary biology and ecology. One is game theory—a loan from economics, just as the concept of evolution was borrowed by Charles Darwin from an economist and taken up again by social scientists. The other is the mathematics of nonlinear dynamic systems in which order at the aggregate level emerges from chaotic individual behavior.

---

[3]There is a large literature on the history of technology and these path dependencies (see, for example, Arthur 1989; Arthur et al. 1997; David 1985).

There are many economists who work on innovation and growth, and who might even automatically reach for evolutionary metaphors or develop the same kind of narrative as the evolutionary economists, without buying into an explicitly evolutionary framework. For all the similarities between the evolutionary models and endogenous growth theory with its emphasis on innovation, the two approaches have not yet joined up. The biggest attraction of the evolutionary growth models lies in their consonance with the mass of examples we have from business histories and management studies that firms do behave and industries do evolve in the ways that are captured in the evolutionary models. But I suspect most conventional growth theorists would be content to regard evolutionary thinking as the narrative embroidery on a more robust underlying model. After all, evolution is, if you'll forgive the pun, the natural metaphor to use. But the precise specification of the building blocks of the analysis is not as apparent in economics as it is in biology. Can the analogy between a gene and a "routine" be any more than metaphor? Even if it can, we're still a very long way from the precision biology has reached. Another key difference is the fact that in business, survival is rarely at stake; and in culture in general, selection involves discussion, argumentation, conscious choice, and decision making. We lack good theories or empirical studies of these mechanisms.

THE ACTION IN THE INTERACTIONS

Evolutionary thinking has made a bigger splash in its contribution to modeling the interactions between individuals and between firms. As just noted, in contrast to orthodox theory, evolutionary thinking emphasizes differences between firms rather than analyzing "representative" identical firms. This gives the evolutionary model its appealing realism. In addition, it sees the selection environment as the market in which a firm is operating, which makes the interactions with consumers and with everything else that goes into the formation of market institutions—governments, regulators, lobbyists from other firms, international trade agreements, and so on—part of the selection mechanism (Metcalfe 1998). Interactions between firms and their environments shape the evolutionary outcome. Market institutions can promote—or inhibit—change, and if they promote change it will be in some sense change toward a "better" outcome because it involves selection pressures. Innovation and structural change in the economy, brought about through the interaction of individuals or firms in the operation of competitive markets, is at the heart of the process of growth.

In the earlier discussion of competition between firms I noted that the definition of the competitive environment felt somewhat circular. The reason is that firms contribute to shaping their own competitive environment (as indeed humans do in nature more generally). They act with a sense of purpose to advance their own prospects. Others will be trying to shape the market for their own purposes too. In other words, in human society, evolution is a goal-oriented, purposive process. We consciously try to affect evolutionary outcomes.

This means that in the economy, firms and market institutions *coevolve*, and the interactions between them are important. (Veblen actually wrote about "the natural selection of institutions," seeing institutions too as evolutionary units.) In fact, when you start to think about the rich array of firms, markets, and institutions in the economy, it seems clear that the economy is a whole system which is coevolving (in either a formal or metaphorical sense), a whole ecology. To the original evolutionary principles of variation, selection, and replication, we need to add interaction.

Darwin was well aware of the importance of interactions between organisms. He wrote:

> The plants and animals of the Galapagos differ radically among islands that have the same geological nature, the same height, climate etc.... This long appeared to me a great difficulty but it arises in chief part from the deeply seated error of considering the physical conditions of a country as the most important for its inhabitants; whereas it cannot, I think, be disputed that the nature of the other inhabitants, with which each has to compete, is at least as important, and generally a far more important element of success.
>
> *The Origin of Species*, p. 388

Nature abounds with examples of mutual dependencies as well as competition between species. Interaction has therefore become an important principle in evolutionary biology.

In the economy, what this means is that the selection environment is itself constantly evolving, and in such a way that what today's environment is like depends on how it got to be the way it is, what interactions occurred along the way. As a new technology becomes established, economic relations and social relations develop together. This is part of the process of the industry becoming self-conscious and aims to mould its own selection environment. The firms in an industry shape their own environment through trade associations, lobbying, standard-setting, links with universities, lawsuits, and so on. Political action and the legal framework are vital to the environment. The law of tort and the limited-liability company played a vital role in nineteenth-century industrialization, for instance. Cars and airplanes needed governments to build roads and airports, to set the rules of the road and run air traffic control. The shaping of the competitive environment is also cumulative in important ways: the invention of computers gave birth to computer science, and computer scientists develop the new innovations in the computer industry.

This coevolution of firms and their environments explains why many industrial economists conceive of the process of innovation as a system of institutions, shaped in important ways by the existing state of technology. For example, Michael Piore and Charles Sabel have explained the dominance of vertically integrated and hierarchical mass-production companies in the United States in the late twentieth century as the product of interactions between the technologies and the U.S. institutional context of the time (Piore and Sabel 1984). Michael Best has surveyed the systems prevalent at different times, including the flatter and less-integrated "just-in-time" production processes of Japanese manufacturers, and the horizontal network organizations which have become more prevalent in the United States and Europe with the introduction of the latest information and communication technologies (Best 2001). Chris Freeman uses the term "techno-economic paradigm" for the same concept (Freeman and Louca 2001). (All can be seen as extensions of the idea common to both Karl Marx and Joseph Schumpeter that different economic eras are defined by different fundamental technologies.)

Organisms can't change their genes but firms can change their routines according to the competitive environment—or they can try to change their environment. In fact, they aren't very successful: firms do die more often than might be expected. Of new businesses started in the United Kingdom, four-fifths are defunct within five years. The average life of a listed company in the United States is estimated at about fifteen years before the firm goes out of business or is, more commonly, taken over. It seems surprisingly hard for firms to change their routines in response to a change in demand or costs or technologies. Not only do individuals not like to change what they do from day to day, it is very difficult to change the whole package of jobs and processes and skills which would allow a company to respond to a changed environment (Milgrom and

195

Roberts 1990). It is very obvious that many think it would be easier to change the environment back, and so they put huge amounts of effort into lobbying for protection from overseas competition or tax breaks to offset higher costs or regulations to restrict entry, or whatever might be needed. Many management theorists, prominent among them Clayton Christensen, have written on the organizational difficulty of adapting to disruptive technologies (Christensen 1997). Nelson writes: "Organizations may be more like organisms than many economists are wont to believe, and significant economic change may involve large elements of creative destruction" (Nelson 1995).

EVOLUTIONARY GAME THEORY

However, the real buzz in evolutionary economics arises not from all this fascinating descriptive work, but from two specific modeling techniques. In a talk he gave to evolutionary economists at the dawn of this recent renaissance, Paul Krugman pointed out that both evolutionary biology and conventional economics are concerned with aggregate outcomes deriving from the behavior of self-interested individuals:

> At a deep level, they share the same method: explain behavior in terms of an equilibrium among maximizing individuals....The fact is that maximization and equilibrium are astonishingly powerful ways to cut through what might otherwise be forbidding complexity.
>
> Krugman (1994c)

One particular approach, game theory, is so good as a method of understanding nature that evolutionary biologists borrowed it from economics.

I would not be able to do justice here to the incredibly colorful and exciting history of game theory. One good starting point is Sylvia Nasar's (1998) biography of John Nash, *A Beautiful Mind*. Nash is well-known thanks to the movie of the book, but the field of game theory dates back earlier, to *The Theory of Games and Economic Behavior*, a 1944 classic by John von Neumann and Oskar Morgenstern. John von Neumann was a child prodigy, a refugee from Hungary in the 1930s whose mathematical brilliance helped the United States develop atomic weapons. Morgenstern was German-born and was working at the University of Vienna when the Nazis occupied Austria; he fled when the occupiers described him as "politically unbearable" and also found himself, like von Neumann, at Princeton. The technique they presented, a mathematical tool for studying interactions, was quickly developed further in research at RAND, as the strategic uses of game theory were immediately obvious. One well-known example of this application is Thomas Schelling's classic book *The Strategy of Conflict.*

The lead in biology was taken by John Maynard Smith, who published a hugely influential book, *Evolution and the Theory of Games*, in 1982. It applied game theory to population genetics, using "replicator equations" derived from equilibrium strategies to predict the behavior of attributes of a population over time. His concept of the "evolutionarily stable strategy" is the same as the stable (Nash) equilibrium in conventional economic theory. It is the best strategy for an individual in a population, given everyone else's strategy. One well-known example is the tit-for-tat strategy, which says (in a repeated game): do what the other player did to you last time. Cooperate if you experienced cooperation, retaliate if you experienced retaliation. Suppose some bad types enter the population with the strategy of always cheating. They will find that they're always cheated in return by the tit-for-tatting population, who are on average doing much better because at least some of them are cooperating with each other. Tit-for-tat is a better strategy, an evolutionarily stable strategy. This game is seen as a persuasive model for explaining how cooperation can evolve in a population of self-interested individuals, and is consequently popular with economists (Axelrod 1984).

Biologists do seem to be more self-aware than economists in their use of these modeling devices, however, more alert to the fact that nature is not really in equilibrium, whereas some economists do seem to regard game-theoretic equilibrium as a realistic way to characterize an actual economy. Still, game theory is a wonderfully flexible tool for modeling the intricacies of economic organization. It formalizes the role of interactions, and the coevolution of different entities and their environment and has given economists a mathematical approach to an area which was formerly almost entirely descriptive. In the game theorist's view, an institution is the equilibrium of a game: that is, the self-enforcing outcome of a game involving many players.

One classic example in game theory is the "prisoner's dilemma," whereby there is a best strategy for each individual which, if chosen, will make each of them worse off than if they had cooperated to choose an alternative strategy. This is a fruitful way of thinking about externalities and public goods—Sam Bowles gives the example of the tragedy of the commons. Each fisherman will do best by fishing as much as he likes in the ocean, but if all do so they will be worse off than if they had coordinated to set limits which would prevent overfishing (Bowles 2004, pp. 27–29). Economists have been using game theory with huge enthusiasm for years. Thomas Schelling (cowinner of the 2005 Nobel memorial prize) gets the credit for making the technique so popular, thanks to his wonderful books. *The Strategy of Conflict*, about the application of game theory to the Cold War, was published in 1960 and seems to have had a significant impact on U.S. geopolitical strategy. His 1978 *Micromotives and Macrobehavior* summarized his application of game theory to many social contexts.

One of Schelling's most influential articles looked at how racially mixed neighborhoods can suddenly become segregated: the process doesn't even require any antipathy to members of another racial group, but simply a modest preference not to be in the minority group in the neighborhood. Even this mild preference means that the proportion of members of one group can decline in response to small events until, at a critical level, it drops to zero. (This is the "tipping point" popularized by Malcolm Gladwell in his book of that name.)

Schelling's vision of game theory as a unifying framework for thinking about social phenomena won him the Nobel memorial prize (along with Robert Aumann of the Hebrew University of Jerusalem, who extended game theory to situations of long-term repeated relationships). Game theory is an incredibly powerful and flexible modeling tool for application in situations where individuals react to each other's choices, and has for years now been part of the basic toolkit used by economists day-to-day. So why do economists look to other evolutionary models as well? For game-theoretic approaches have been applied alongside other mathematical techniques borrowed from biology, which also emphasize the interactions between individuals.

POPULATIONS, COMPLEXITY, AND EMERGENCE

Modeling techniques used in biology and other natural sciences to analyze the behavior of crowds of interacting creatures, or particles of one kind or another, are exciting interest in social science because of evidence that social networks follow the same laws as biological networks. Mark Granovetter was a graduate student in sociology at Harvard in the heady days of the late 1960s, but he managed to avoid the distractions of campus politics and concentrate on his doctoral thesis. For this he looked at how managerial and professional workers in a nearby neighborhood of Boston found their jobs. Contrary to his expectation that most would have found their jobs through friends, significantly more in fact were helped by a mere acquaintance, a friend of a friend or someone even further removed. He called the subsequent paper "The strength of weak ties," and although in canonical fashion it was rejected by the first journal he submitted it to, the paper has profoundly influenced the way scholars have subsequently thought about our social links (Granovetter 1973). We have two types of social connections: strong ties to our family and closest friends and immediate neighbors; and weak links to more distant contacts. The two types of relationship serve different purposes. The strong ties offer us emotional and moral support, reinforcement, love, and warmth. The weak ties bring us a flow of fresh information and links to the wider world beyond our immediate circle. In the world of work, and many other economic transactions, the weak ties are the important ones.

We all typically have many more weak ties than strong ones. And some individuals, more sociable than most people, stand out as hubs in their social networks with a much greater number than the average of such ties.[4] What is more, the number of people who have a given number of social links seems to follow—where it has been counted—a particular pattern. In social networks such as communities of researchers in science who coauthor with each other, or Hollywood actors, or websites linking to each other, the pattern follows a power law, best known in the wider world as the 80:20 rule. In other words, the best-connected 20% of individuals have 80% of the social connections, and vice versa.[5] This is remarkable enough in itself: an empirical regularity so consistent begs for a theoretical explanation, especially as it mirrors power laws that economists have spotted in other areas, such as the size distribution of American cities or the size distribution of companies (see, for example, Krugman 1993; Axtell 1999). What is more, the same pattern holds in many natural phenomena as well. For example, power laws apply to the behavior of molecules in the transition from liquid to gas, and they apply in populations of other animals and insects, as well as human society. The work on social networks has converged with research in biology and physics. In each case, the mathematics of self-organizing complex systems apply because the underlying structure is identical: a

---

[4]This is one of the key observations in Malcolm Gladwell's *The Tipping Point*, as these social "hubs" play a key role in setting new trends alight.

[5]The number of people N with K links is given by $N = K^{-y}$, where y is the degree exponent of the power law and usually lies between 2 and 3 in social networks; hence the 80:20 regularity.

growing network of relationships or links, with the growth occurring in a way which is not random but favors some of the individuals over others (perhaps just because they were there first). As Albert-Laslo Barabasi, one of the gurus of this field, puts it: "Some feature of complex networks bridges the micro- and macro-worlds" (Barabasi 2002, p. 102).

Well, economists love this set of mathematical tools, a toolkit which allows them to study human society in the same way that other scientists study the natural world. There have been many applications. In a well-known paper, "Ants, rationality and recruitment," economist Alan Kirman (1993) noted that the behavior of ants choosing between food sources provided a very good match for certain kinds of economic behavior. Given a choice between two identical food sources, rather than half the ants choosing one and half the other, or all the ants exhausting one source then switching to the other—or any other logical system—in fact the patterns are much more random. A majority of ants will choose one supply, but will switch unpredictably, in seemingly random proportions. Kirman noted that people do the same when choosing restaurants. A popular restaurant will have long lines when a neighboring one is empty, and then the fashion will change and a different restaurant will be popular. Financial markets likewise display unpredictable patterns when investors herd toward one stock or another, for not very obvious reasons. Kirman shows that the same simple model involving "recruitment" of one ant or trader by another can explain a range of social and economic phenomena.

The vital difference here from conventional economic modeling is once again the fact that people are allowed to influence one another in their decisions. Introducing interaction leads to fundamental changes in the kinds of prediction a model makes. "The behavior of the group as a whole cannot be inferred from analyzing one of the identical individuals in isolation," Kirman writes. In particular, if there is "positive feedback," trends and behaviors are amplified—just as we saw in the endogenous growth models of chapter 2. But it's not just economic growth; there are many parts of economics where positive feedback seems to apply. For example, participants in the financial markets seeking returns on investment look very much like the ants of the experiment hunting for food. The British economist Paul Ormerod, a specialist in this kind of modeling, describes similar dynamic processes occurring in the business-cycle swings of the economy as a whole, and the size of firms in the economy. He makes a strong case for ditching conventional macroeconomic forecasting and instead regarding the economy as a complex system composed of millions of interactions by individuals who tend to reinforce each other. Despite the uncoordinated and apparently random nature of individual choices, an aggregate pattern nevertheless often emerges. At the edge of chaos there is order. The ups and downs of the business cycle or herding and bubbles in financial markets are readily explained as self-reinforcing interactions in this approach. However, in contrast to the kind of order predicted by a conventional economic model, the outcomes in this world are not predictable and not amenable to manipulation by the government. This advanced mathematics has delivered a rigorous version of Hayek's world of spontaneous social order in which the government should do less rather than more.

The mathematical modeling and computer simulation required in complexity theory is, well, pretty complex. Nevertheless—or actually, perhaps *because* there's macho mathematics involved—the techniques of complexity theory and emergence have had a big impact in economics, and have clearly also touched a nerve in the popular imagination.[6] Many people seem to have a strong intuition that models of this kind do capture the essence of how social structures like markets and the economy actually operate. In the financial markets in particular, models of nonlinear dynamics have really caught on. The hero here is mathematician Benoit Mandelbrot, creator of the beautiful Mandelbrot set, which almost everybody will recognize from computer-graphics applications.[7] A discussion of what conclusions we might be able to make about policy from modeling the world like this is postponed until the next chapter.

CONCLUSIONS

Outside the formalities of game theory, there is no clear understanding of how the multitude of economic and political interests, professional expertise, legal practice, social norms, cultural habits, and so on coevolve to create the set of market institutions which form the competitive environment. Somehow, the leading Western economies have

---

[6]Recent popularizations of the techniques described in this section can be found in *Critical Mass* by Philip Ball (2004), *The Tipping Point* by Malcolm Gladwell (2000), *Emergence* by Steven Johnson (2004), and *The Wisdom of Crowds* by James Surowiecki (2004). A slightly more technical introduction can be found in *Linked: The New Science of Networks* by Albert-Laslo Barabasi. *Butterfly Economics* by Paul Ormerod (1998) is an accessible application of complexity theory to economics. More technical references can be found in all of these.

[7]For a readable overview of the application of this kind of mathematics to finance, and further references, see Bass (1999).

enjoyed a coevolution of technology, industrial organization, and economic and political institutions which has encouraged economic growth (and benefits such as health, longevity, comfort, and fun which go with prosperity). Individual activities, perhaps "self-organized" into a felicitous order, and collective actions mediated through a variety of institutions including formal politics have combined to favor growth. But how? I'll leave the last word to Sam Bowles, a prominent critic of the economic orthodoxy: "The Walrasian paradigm provides the only fully worked out, economy-wide model of the way that the actions of large numbers of autonomous actors support aggregate social outcomes" (Bowles 2004, p. 478).

But alternatives to the conventional (or Walrasian) approach have gone some way toward this worked-out, economy-wide nirvana. The next chapter concludes our canter around the frontiers of economics by turning to society, and the importance of the ways in which individuals interact for those aggregate social and economic outcomes.

Economy versus Society

INTRODUCTION

James M. Buchanan, winner of the 1986 Nobel memorial prize in economics, liked to spend as much time as possible away from the ivory tower, preferring his log cabin in the Virginia mountains, he said in a 1995 interview. There he has a few cattle, grows vegetables, picks berries, uses a wood stove for heat. He said: "I found out something about my utility function." (Spoken like a true economist.) "I found out that every step I took toward genuine self-sufficiency really gives me a big charge."[1] It's a little ironic that these sentiments should be expressed by a scholar who revolutionized how we think about government and politics. Or perhaps not: that he finds self-sufficiency appealing might not come as such a big a surprise to critics of the type of analysis for which he won his Nobel prize. Buchanan introduced the principles of rational choice, maximization, and individualism to the study of the collective organization of society. He unleashed the tools of economics on politics and government, and this "public choice" approach has been both controversial and influential. Buchanan is a darling of the libertarian, ultra-free-market conservatives, a prominent advocate of limited government and balanced budgets. Yet even those who reject his political affiliations have to recognize the influence and importance of the systematic analysis of politics introduced by the public choice school. When we look at our elected representatives, can we honestly say that their own self-interest plays no part in the decisions they take?

Buchanan was born in Murfreeboro in Tennessee in 1919. Although his grandfather had been governor of the state, it was a tough upbringing. Money was scarce. He studied in local schools and returned home each

---

[1] Federal Reserve Bank of Minneapolis, *The Region*, September 1995 (available at www. minneapolisfed.org/pubs/region/95-09/int959.cfm, accessed August 25, 2006).

day to milk cows and carry out other chores on the family farm. His autobiography is called *Better than Plowing*, and no wonder. Eventually, he went to the University of Chicago to study for his PhD, and since graduating in 1948 he has lived and taught in Virginia. It's clear from Buchanan's comments on winning the Nobel that his southern, rural background has strongly colored his approach. He wrote:

> I am perceived, and widely so, as the only Nobel prize representative of the "great unwashed" in American academia, those thousands of faculty members and students who spend their lives in the public and private colleges and universities of our land without the prestige value of intellectual-scientific, and social, ranking.... [H]ow many farm boys from Middle Tennessee, educated in tiny, poor, and rural public schools, and at a struggling state-financed teachers college, have received Nobel prizes? How many scholars who have worked almost exclusively at southern universities have done so, in any scientific discipline?

The essay links the development of public choice theory, which puts the insider structures of politics under the scientific microscope, to his outsider status. To indulge in a little pop psychology, perhaps there's something about feeling on the outside of the elite that puts people off the idea of government. Another notorious critic of big government was Margaret Thatcher, daughter of a small-town shopkeeper. Despite—or because of—her deep distrust of the political elite (especially in her own party), she made it to the top of politics, thus achieving her ambition to influence the lives of all her fellow citizens. In a famous interview, Prime Minister Thatcher criticized people who always expected the government to set right social problems:

> You know, there's no such thing as society. There are individual men and women and there are families. And no government can do anything except through people, and people must look after themselves first. It is our duty to look after ourselves and then, also, to look after our neighbours.
>
> *Woman's Own* magazine, October 31, 1987

Was Mrs. Thatcher right? Is "society" irrelevant to economic outcomes? This chapter looks at the role of collective institutions, especially government, in economics. The starting point is the public choice approach, which is fully in the spirit of neoclassical economics. While public choice theory remains influential, economists have subsequently taken two paths in their study of institutions. One, known as the "New Institutional

Economics," analyzes institutions as optimizing responses in the presence of transactions costs and real-world frictions. The rationality here may be bounded, but this is very much a world of individual maximizers.

More recently, however, economists have turned toward sociology and grown interested in social networks, social norms, and social capital. This wider perspective from sociology and anthropology, giving social interactions a role in the allocation of resources, has two roots. One is evolutionary theory, and the toolkit available from game theory and the study of complex systems. The other is the growing body of econometric evidence indicating that woolly (to an economist) sociological and cultural variables are positively linked to economic performance. Institutions, norms, or culture, or all of these, clearly favor or inhibit economic development and now stand at the center of development economics. "Good governance" dominates current proposals for enhancing growth in poor countries.

PUBLIC CHOICE THEORY

The public choice revolution—for it was revolutionary—started with the publication in 1962 of *The Calculus of Consent* by James Buchanan and Gordon Tullock. In it they say: "Our purpose in this book is to derive a preliminary theory of collective choice that is in some respects analogous to the orthodox economic theory of markets ... to extend the assumptions of the economist to the behavior of the individual as he participates in the political process" (Buchanan and Tullock 1962, pp. 17, 298). With some exceptions (such as Schumpeter, who saw politicians as entrepreneurs motivated by seeking votes), economists had previously treated government as a benign outside force, motivated by social welfare, and had disregarded the political process. Public choice theory instead treats politicians as vote-maximizers, with their ideologies forms of product differentiation rather than (or as well as) matters of principle.

The book had a massive impact, which was soon reinforced by the 1965 publication of *The Logic of Collective Action* by Mancur Olson. Olson, the child of Norwegian immigrants, saw himself as left-of-center, in contrast to his friend James Buchanan. But he too claimed the territory of political science for the tools of economics. Olson argued that policy decisions could be explained by looking at politics as a competition between the private interests of specific groups, rather than a process for delivering the public interest. He went on to explain the lack of economic development as the result of special interests distorting economic policy. The larger the group, the harder it is for it to further the common interests of all its members, which is hardest of all for a society as a whole. There are all too many economies which are run in the interests of a very small group of people indeed, namely a dictator and his family and friends. The only thing worse than competition between special interests is a special-interest monopoly.[2]

Buchanan has since described public choice theory and Olson's extension of it as systematic ways of looking at political decisions, in contrast to the "romantic" or idealistic view which he sees as the alternative. The two economists were founder members of the Committee for the Study of Non-Market Decision-Making (subsequently the Public Choice Society), set up in 1963. For some time, most economists ignored public choice theory, having no interest in nonmarket decisions, while most political scientists detested it. Yet by the mid 1970s, when the postwar record of economic growth in the Western democracies started to turn sour, there was a substantial body of research which lent itself to the presumption that governments had overreached themselves.

Public choice theory has become less closely identified with conservative politics with the passage of time, as more and more scholars have used it as an interesting tool of analysis. The theory's approach has nurtured a large literature on voting behavior. Each individual is rational to pay little attention to his or her vote, as it will make no difference to the outcome of the election; indeed, abstention would be the rational choice. A vote-maximizing politician will seek to give the majority of voters what they want. This leads opposing politicians to fight bitterly over the middle ground—the "median" voter is decisive—and this insight has led to the spectacle of "triangulation" practiced so avidly in American and British elections, or in other words staking out a terrain of policy midway between the opposite party and the weight of public opinion. This in turn helps keep voters at home on election day, as there is in reality less and less to choose between the candidates.

At the same time, Olson's contribution has led to the study of the influence of lobby groups which have a strong incentive to campaign on particular public policies affecting their special interests, in contrast to the very small incentive each individual voter will have to vote against the

---

[2]Olson did also argue that once a bandit had monopolized his territory he might become less predatory, seeing a greater benefit in maximizing revenues over time rather than snatching everything available in one go. It appears that most bandit rulers are too impatient for this to be true, however.

special-interest group. Olson argued vehemently that inefficient policies resulting from special-interest lobbies such as business groups operated against the public interest.

The influence of public choice theory extended to empirical studies of what in fact affects people's votes. How far could economic explanations account for political decisions? (See Olters (2001) for a literature survey and plentiful further references.) One strand of research has looked at how much economic performance affects election results: to sum up a vast amount of work in different countries in half a sentence, growth and unemployment seem to have very little influence on election outcomes, while inflation has somewhat more, but not much and not always (Olters 2001). Another perspective turns the research question the other way round and asks how voting affects economic outcomes. Specifically, the requirement to hold elections in a democracy leads politicians to engineer short-term economic booms in the period before the election through lower interest rates or lower taxes, which the winner has to reverse to correct monetary and fiscal policy after the election. There is good evidence of the existence of a "political business cycle" in many countries. Its discovery explains the institutional development of independent central banks and mechanisms such as inflation targeting. An independent central bank is a means to prevent manipulation of the economy in the interests of politicians, and contrary to the public interest. Many public choice theorists advocate a similar mechanism for fiscal policy, such as a balanced-budget amendment.

The analysis of the political business cycle is an important result stemming ultimately from public choice theory. A similar approach to the systematic study of political outcomes lies behind an active area of current research, which looks at the many ways in which political institutions and structures affect the economy. One question which is extremely relevant now, a time when income inequality in some countries including the United States has been increasing for the first time since the early twentieth century, is whether and how politics affects the distribution of incomes and the interests of different groups of citizens. For example, a fascinating book by Alberto Alesina and Edward Glaeser explores the different social choices made in the United States and much of Europe (Alesina and Glaeser 2004). In the United States, voters accept growing income inequality, whereas in Europe there is a strong voter preference for higher taxes and welfare spending to limit inequality. Alesina and Glaeser suggest that the contrast reflects the fact that voters in European countries are more alike than voters in the United States, that there is a demographic basis for "social cohesion." In general, the question of the "right" level of taxation and government spending for the health of the economy and public well-being, and the related question of where to draw the boundary between the state and the private sector, are live issues, to say the least.

So too is the question of how to improve the quality of government decisions. Joseph Stiglitz, drawing on his own experience in public administration, asked why so many government decisions were so bad, a troubling issue to someone like him who advocates government activism. Specifically, he asked why it was so often difficult for politicians to introduce policies which ought to be uncontroversial, because they would make some people better off and very few people worse off (nearly a Pareto improvement, in the professional jargon). Examples include deregulating milk prices (price supports penalize poor families and children) and making U.S. hydroelectric markets operate more efficiently. The traditional public choice analysis would draw on Olson's theory of interest groups. Stiglitz argues instead that the problem is the government's inability to commit future governments to similar policies. Even if milk producers were compensated for price deregulation with a production subsidy, for example, they might believe their subsidy to be more vulnerable to future budget cuts, whereas price arrangements, because they are harder to understand and change, might be less vulnerable to cuts. Stiglitz's solution is to rely more on transparency, explanation, and consensus building in policy making (Stiglitz 1998).

The research into these questions, and the agenda for the reform of public services, have their roots in public choice theory. It opened up for debate the motivation of politicians and officials, the importance of incentives in public life as well as private choice, the influence of special-interest groups, and ultimately the broad question of how our collective political institutions shape economic outcomes.

New Institutional Economics

The public choice approach was swiftly extended to study nonpolitical organizations. The obvious extension was to public bureaucracy and government regulation, and early contributions came from economists such as George Stigler and William Niskanen. Gary Becker is sometimes counted as a public choice theorist; although his work has not been concerned with political institutions, since his PhD thesis in 1955 he has applied rational choice to countless social institutions, including the family and the firm.[3] His 1992 Nobel Lecture was entitled "The economic way of looking at life" (available at http://nobelprize.org/economics/laureates/1992/becker-lecture.html). Becker's argument is that the model of rational choice is a powerful tool for understanding any aspect of society or social behavior as well as individual choices in a conventional market. He emphasizes that he is not making any assumption about our motives, but rather using the rational-choice approach as a methodological tool.

Becker, along with the public choice economists, helped lever open a huge new terrain of study for economists. Previously, economics had more or less been confined to the study of markets. But the allocation of resources in society is clearly not determined by markets alone. Political and private institutions, including families and firms, play an important part. Herbert Simon expressed this in a graphic image: if market transactions are visualized as red lines, and institutions as green dots, a visitor from outer space would see the economy as a large collection of green splodges with a few short red lines connecting them. Conventional neoclassical price theory doesn't apply to child care in the home or the arrangement of work in the office, for instance (Simon 1991).

So even to its many practitioners and admirers, one of the shortcomings of economics as it was typically practiced in the 1960s or 1970s was its failure to account for the prevalence and importance of institutions. While the classical economists had been acute observers of institutional detail, the models of neoclassical economics abstracted from institutions, and simply added up individual decisions to reach aggregate outcomes. Institutions clearly matter for an explanation of economic outcomes at the level of the group rather than the individual. Even if it were reasonable to ignore institutions if your interest lies in macroeconomic variables such as inflation and growth (and that turns out not to be reasonable anyway), an economist interested in what happens within an industry simply can't overlook the existence of big firms or unions. But how could organizations like these be given a toehold in a theory which built up individual choices from individual preferences and available technology. Where could a multinational company fit in?

Public choice theory and the related work by Gary Becker and other labor economists who turned their attention to the family, offered one approach. Another vital key was provided by Ronald Coase (see Coase

---

[3]He coauthors a blog with eminent judge and legal scholar Richard Posner, available at www.becker-posner-blog.com/.

(1960) and also www.econlib.org/library/Enc/bios/coase.html). Back in 1937 he published "The nature of the firm," the first of the two articles which won him the 1991 Nobel memorial prize (Coase 1937). A socialist in his youth, the story goes that he fell to wondering why, if General Motors worked so well, Lenin couldn't run the Soviet economy like a big firm? The answer he proposed was that the big firms came into being because there were transactions costs involved in using markets, so it was more efficient to bring certain transactions within an organization rather than conducting them in a market. The boundary of the firm was drawn by these costs, which arise because it is sometimes too difficult or expensive to monitor and assess deals between independent parties. Transactions costs often relate to information gaps of the kind explored in chapter 6. Coase's second world-changing paper was published in 1960, and looked at the problem of the best way to tackle problems arising from externalities such as pollution. The presumption is that, as the price mechanism misallocates resources when there is an externality, a solution administered by the government is always better. Coase argued that transactions costs mean administered solutions don't always work well either: there are government failures as well as market failures. The choice between markets and institutions should depend on a detailed study of the opportunity costs in each specific case.

The transactions-costs approach explained both why institutions matter for market outcomes, and why institutions are flawed. To put it in the language of economic theory, transactions costs mean there cannot be a complete set of contracts covering every possible turn of events. Including transactions costs adds real-world detail to the rational-choice methodology. It has been applied, broadly speaking, in two contexts. One involves looking at how the fundamental rules of the economy emerge—the development of the legal framework, the status of property, the political process. The second concerns the operation of a given framework, how organizations are structured (especially firms), and what kinds of transaction take place; it is often known as the "New Institutional Economics."

The economist most prominently associated with the former is historian and Nobel laureate Douglass North. Here's how he describes the framework:

> Throughout history, institutions have been devised by human beings to create order and reduce uncertainty in exchange. Together with the standard constraints of economics, they define the choice set and

therefore determine transaction and production costs, and hence the profitability and feasibility of engaging in economic activity.

North (1991)

Institutions can take the form of informal constraints such as social norms and customs, or formal constraints such as constitutions, laws, and property rights. In either case, they shape the incentives facing individuals in the economy. The name most prominently associated with the analysis of the structure of organizations such as firms is Oliver Williamson. North and Williamson, with Ronald Coase, founded the International Society for the New Institutional Economics in 1997.

North was a Marxist radical in his student days at Berkeley—in the late 1930s and early 1940s. One summer he worked with Dorothea Lange, head of the photographic division of the Farm Security Association, traveling with migrants in central California. North spent World War II in the merchant marine, and became engrossed in the economics books he had plenty of time to read. On returning to the United States he had to decide whether to become a professional photographer, encouraged by Lange, or a professional economist, encouraged by Lange's economist husband Paul Taylor. It is clear in his work that he's long been driven by a passion to understand the causes of poverty and the reasons for the presence or absence of development.

North's research in American then European economic history led him to focus on the importance of institutions. The transition from a simple economy to a complex one, where people specialize more and more, and engage in transactions with many others, requires the development of suitable institutions. In North's summary, the minimum requirements are impersonal enforcement of contracts, the effective guarantee of property rights, and markets for products and the factors of production (labor and capital). The state plays a major part in shaping these institutions as the scale of a modern economy is too large for private organizations to be able to enforce rules. But constraints on the state are important too, to prevent expropriation. Impersonal rules and anonymous transactions are crucial to protect individuals from imbalances of power. North sees many examples in economic history of positive feedbacks between economic growth and institutions: an increase in trade gave merchants the incentive to devise mechanisms for enforcing contracts with other traders; and the existence of these mechanisms reduced the cost of transacting, increased the profitability of trade, and extended its scale. Every so often, merchants called on their ruler to safeguard

211

their trade deals, while rulers called on merchants to finance their wars. However, as North notes, economic history is overwhelmingly a story of failed institutions. Many poor countries lack the institutional incentive structures which would encourage growth (http://nobelprize.org/economics/laureates/1993/north-lecture.html).

North went on to become more interested in the psychological and behavioral foundations of economic institutions. As he put it in his Nobel autobiography:

> The development of a political-economic framework to explore long-run institutional change occupied me during all of the 1980s and led to the publication of *Institutions, Institutional Change and Economic Performance* in 1990. In that book I began to puzzle seriously about the rationality postulate. It is clear that we had to have an explanation for why people make the choices they do; why ideologies such as communism or Muslim fundamentalism can shape the choices people make and direct the way economies evolve through long periods of time. One simply cannot get at ideologies without digging deeply into cognitive science in attempting to understand the way in which the mind acquires learning and makes choices.
>
> http://nobelprize.org/economics/laureates/1993/north-autobio.html

Oliver Williamson's research on the institutions arising from the existence of transactions costs also raises questions about psychology and behavior. He combines the rational-choice methodology—the assumption that people act in their own interests—with an assumption of bounded rationality, which is, as we saw in chapter 5, a stepping stone on the way to the extensive program of research in behavioral economics. As Williamson put it in his book *The Economic Institutions of Capitalism*, "an economizing orientation" arises from the fact that people intend to act in their self-interest, but institutions emerge because they can't quite manage to be consistently rational. Bounded rationality is what gives rise to decision and governance structures as alternatives to rational choice in the marketplace.

Much of Williamson's work has concerned business corporations and unions, the most prominent of the institutions between which market transactions in a modern economy take place. When will a firm be vertically integrated or when will it instead buy components from suppliers? What explains the kinds of contract that unions seek to negotiate for their members—why are conditions other than wages important? Why are some companies more hierarchical than others? What form should corporate governance take in order to protect shareholders or employees or customers? And so on. Williamson argues that these types of private institutional arrangement are just as important as formal politics and governments for determining whether an economy is orderly or lawless (Williamson 2005). All can be brought under the umbrella heading of "governance," which in all its manifestations asks whether the institutions in the economy function well.

This type of institutional analysis is central to the current approach of economists working in the development business, and has been strongly advocated by the World Bank, for example (see, for example, Burki and Perry 1998). "Good governance" has become the new motherhood and apple pie of the development business. In the approach of the new institutional economics, the prevailing institutions are seen as a solution to problems caused by various social constraints or frictions—given the constraints, they are in fact an efficient solution. What appear to be nonrational choices by individuals (bartering goods rather than selling produce for cash in the market) are interpreted as rational, given the constraints of the social situation (excessive inflation due to excessive government debt).

But not everyone is convinced that the institutionalist adaptation of the conventional economic approach is the whole story. While it takes a giant leap from the assumption that there are no frictions in the economy, its methodology is still based on individuals exercising rational choice, given their own preferences. Sociologist Mark Granovetter has argued that this is all a bit circular, because observed institutions are defined to be an efficient outcome given the existence of transactions costs and frictions, and what is more it still ignores the fact that the individuals making up an economy have social relations. These social structures aren't allowed to impinge on their rational, self-interested choices. That this is a serious gap is suggested by the fact that institutional structures vary so much from one society to another: some factors other than rational choice in the face of transactions costs must be coming into play.

Granovetter also criticizes the opposite tendency in sociology and anthropology to see behavior as entirely constrained by social relations—except for economic behavior: "This view sees the economy as an increasingly separate, differentiated sphere in modern society, with economic transactions defined no longer by the social or kinship obligations of those transacting, but by rational calculations of economic gain" (Granovetter 1985). As a result, there is little sociological or anthropological research into large swathes of modern life, such as behavior

213

inside the corporation. This permits economists to continue to ignore the social relations inside institutions. At the same time in the rest of life, rational choice is excluded, with choices made according to social rules and behavior patterns, which allows sociologists to ignore the important role that is played by self-interest (Granovetter 1985).

You don't need to spend a lot of time socializing around the water cooler in the office, chatting about last night's television shows, to realize that the truth lies somewhere in between these two alternatives. Both rational self-interest and social obligations play some part in the decisions which make up economic life and social life alike. Granovetter's own research has explored the way the two decision modes combine, in one of the most frequently cited social science papers of all time. In reply to the intrusion of economic models into the study of institutions and social relationships through public choice theory, Granovetter took sociology into the heart of economics.

NETWORKS

We saw some of this in the previous chapter: the tools of networks allow us to model economic "contagions" or cascades, such as stock market booms, bank crises, or recessions, as if we were ants marching in step toward a new food source. Here I want to focus on just one aspect of social networks: the part which concerns how we run our societies and economies as a whole. Knowing that human networks appear to follow some natural laws, what does this tell us about the overall structure of society? How do the institutions by which we run our affairs take shape? Why do societies and economies then end up being so different from each other? If we all form interpersonal networks according to the laws of complex nonrandom systems, why are some countries rich and some poor? What difference does understanding that there is a natural, presumably biological or evolutionary, basis of social networks make to economic policy prescriptions? It seems, contrary to Mrs. Thatcher's notorious assertion, that individuals are the same everywhere, and the differences are all down to society.

SOCIAL NORMS

The answers to these questions about the explanation for the differences between economies lie somewhere in the formation of social structures. But where? Economists have a problem in turning to sociology and anthropology to give them a handle on this because the concepts commonly used in other social sciences—such as "culture" or "social capital"—have competing definitions and are usually rather abstract and not readily measurable quantities. So we'll come on to those later but let's start with a potentially more narrowly defined concept, that of social norms. We saw in the last chapter that a recession can emerge, like a tornado on the plains, out of the mutually reinforcing choices of individuals, each reacting to the others. It is a self-fulfilling prophesy. Suppose that instead of recession—the coincident decisions to cut investment or fire workers in the expectation of a downturn, because others are doing the same thing—we think of another type of behavior, such as the decision to drop litter because others do so, or to give up smoking because others are quitting. The same mechanisms, in other words, can explain the prevalence of "social norms," the acceptable patterns of behavior in a society.

Intriguingly, norms clearly do change over time, periods as short as a decade or two. Smoking (in Western countries) is a good example. The advertising of cigarettes has been progressively restricted. Smoking is no longer permitted on most flights and many train and bus journeys. Several governments have recently banned smoking in public places, including bars, or have mandated the creation of separate smoking rooms in restaurants. This has occurred within the space of twenty years, which means that people of my generation have made the mental transition from regarding smoking as normal, possibly even cool, to disliking the smallest whiff of smoke. Although health concerns have obviously triggered the social transition, there can be no doubt that the social norm has changed. To light up now is to be regarded as a social leper.

There are countless examples of social norms, but one that has particularly intrigued economists is crime. Crime is an activity where it ought to be possible to apply a straightforward economic analysis: is it profitable for a rational, utility-maximizing individual? The answer will depend on factors such as the availability of legal jobs, prevailing wage rate in the legal job market, the likelihood of being caught, and the severity of the penalty if punished. While these will vary from country to country, the crime rate (in total and by offence) varies much more between jurisdictions than these potential explanatory variables might lead you to expect. For example, in the 1990s the murder rate ranged from 75.3 deaths per 100,000 people in South Africa (1995) and 28.2 in Estonia (Estonia?!) through 5.7 in the United States (1999)

215

down to 1.4 in England and Wales (1997) and 0.62 in Japan (1994). So for example, almost equally prosperous Japan and America have very different murder rates. One controversial interpretation was offered by Steven Levitt, who argued that the decline in the U.S. murder rate during the 1990s was the result of a higher rate of abortions starting in the late 1970s, which he argues reduced the size of the pool of potential criminals by cutting the rate of teenage pregnancy and birth (see Levitt 2005). I don't want to address that argument here, as it involves other issues such as changes in abortion laws in different countries.

What interests me is that there also seem to be social norms in operation in explaining crime—one might call them fashions. In a 1996 study, Edward Glaeser, Bruce Sacerdote, and Jose Scheinkman (Glaeser et al. 1996) looked at the serious crime rate in different localities in the United States. The figure (in 1990) ranged from 0.008 serious crimes per person committed in Ridgewood Village, NJ, to 0.384 in Atlantic City. Within New York, the range went from 0.022 in the 123rd precinct to 0.21 in the 1st precinct. They could attribute less than a third of the variation between locations to local economic influences such as the unemployment rate or local incomes. A greater contribution came from "positive covariance across agents' decisions about crime," or, in other words, peer pressure or social interactions. The role of social influence was weak for very violent crimes, where you might expect individual psychology to be all-important, but very strong for crimes such as larceny and car theft, and moderately strong for crimes such as assault and burglary, a ranking which makes intuitive sense. There are evidently some communities where joyriding in a stolen car is regarded as a normal way to spend the evening, and not therefore liable to expose the perpetrators to strong social sanctions from their acquaintances.

Edward Glaeser has gone on, with other coauthors, to document the existence of a range of social norms, interactions between people which affect, for example, the prevalence of obesity (see Glaeser et al. 2000, 2002, 2004). Most interestingly, for us, he has also looked at the importance of social interactions in determining the economic performance of cities, which takes us well on our way to looking at the social underpinnings of the development of a whole economy (see Glaeser and Scheinkman 2000). At this higher level of aggregation, the literature does not refer to norms, the expected patterns of behavior, but rather to the concept of social capital.

Social Capital

The new interest in the economy as more than the mere sum of individuals' rational self-interested choices has been fueled by one of the hottest areas in sociology: the study of social capital. I wish I could offer a neat, capsule definition of social capital, but unfortunately there are many alternatives. Try this one: "Features of social life—networks, norms and trust—that enable participants to act together more effectively to pursue shared objectives" (Putnam 2000). Or perhaps: "An instantiated informal norm that promotes co-operation between two or more individuals" (Fukuyama 1996). We'll come back to the precise definition in a moment, but for now it's enough to accept it as a concept claiming to speak to the aggregate outcome of individual decisions. Both the name and these definitions also suggest that social capital—whatever it is—is a good thing, enhancing effective cooperation.

The term "social capital" was first used in 1916, but the concept took flight following the 1993 publication of a study of the Italian regions. The author, Robert Putnam, found links between economic performance and income levels of each region and their political and social traditions. The south of Italy was poor not because of a lack of financial or physical capital, but because of its civic shortcomings. Southerners were less likely to trust the institutions of the state, less likely to transact with strangers, more likely to depend on patronage for personal advancement, more inclined to reserve favors for family and friends. Putnam started the research in 1970, when a change in the Italian constitution decentralized many political decisions. At that time the south already lagged behind the north—Putnam observes that many families in Pietrapertosa, one southern village he studied, lived in one- or two-room stone hovels and threshed grain in the fields by hand. Would the devolution of power help the economy catch up with the industrial and prosperous north? It did not. After twenty years, the south still lagged behind. Putnam concluded:

> Collective life in the less civic regions of Italy has been blighted for a thousand years and more. Why? It can hardly be that the inhabitants prefer solitary and submissive squalor. Foreign oppression might once have been part of the explanation for their plight, but the regional experiment suggests that self-government is no panacea.
>
> Putnam (1993, p. 163)

He proposed social capital, an indicator of civic mindedness, as the means by which groups can achieve cooperation for their mutual benefit.

217

Putnam's research stimulated others, including many economists, to explore the links between social capital and economic outcomes. Several studies confirm a positive link (see, for example, Bowles and Gintis 2002; Dasgupta and Serageldin 1988). In this research, social capital is often measured by positive responses to questions in surveys, often the World Values Survey. Covering many countries every five years, this asks respondents: "Generally speaking, would you say that most people can be trusted or that you can't be too careful in dealing with people?" The complicated definitions are thus typically reduced to one broad-brush question. Nevertheless, the regression results are impressive. One early and influential paper found that trust had a statistically significant and large explanatory power for various measures of performance by large organizations. The authors concluded: "Putnam's results for Italy appear to be confirmed worldwide" (La Porta et al. 1997). In the same year, other empirical research also found that "Trust and civic co-operation are associated with stronger economic performance" (Knack and Keefer 1997b; see also Knack and Keefer 1997a).

This empirical work shows that there are certainly social indicators positively associated with good economic results. But to put this finding into practice by deriving policy recommendations, we need to be clear about precisely what aspect of social relationships is important for the economy. For while the studies mentioned above regress economic outcomes on a measure of social capital, there are many others reporting positive results for alternative social indicators such as cultural beliefs, institutional indicators, or political variables such as the presence of democracy. We also need to be clear about the direction of cause and effect. Are we sure that we're not observing strong economies creating harmonious social relationships?

So we have to go back to the definitions. What is social capital exactly? How is it related to norms of behavior? Is there a useful concept of culture which is distinct from social capital? What is the relationship between social capital and the institutions and political processes by which we govern our economies and societies? How can we usefully model all these concepts to incorporate the feedbacks which undoubtedly exist between them, and to tease out the direction of cause and effect? I think it is fair to say there is absolutely no consensus either among economists or between economists and other social scientists about the right framework for addressing these questions. Nor is there any agreement about the empirical evidence available so far, for instance about whether "culture" is more important than "institutions" or "social capital" as an ultimate cause of economic outcomes—and this matters for policy analysis, as there is a big difference between trying to reform institutions and trying to adapt traditional social relations or cultural beliefs when it comes to improving economic performance.

Some economists are thoroughly skeptical about the usefulness of broad concepts such as social capital, or culture. For example, Charles Manski has highlighted the inconclusive state of the empirical evidence due to unclear conceptualization of what is being tested. He proposes three specific channels of social interaction:

- other people's choices constrain yours;
- you act on the basis of your expectations about others' choices;
- your preferences (and hence choices) depend on others' preferences.

Manski suggests that the idea of "social capital" adds nothing beyond these three channels (Manski 2000). Given the lack of an agreed and tight definition, what follows is my own take on how to think about these related social concepts, and what we can draw from the empirical research to date, after reading a moderately large part of a voluminous and rapidly growing literature.[4]

One of the fundamental explanations for cooperation between individuals must lie in our evolutionary past. It's widely thought that reciprocal altruism stems from the early cooperation of humans to kill animals for food: survival chances are much improved by cooperating in hunting, and it's clear why this should have caused a "do as you would be done by" morality to take shape (see Bowles and Gintis 1999). Some researchers also argue that we have an inherited propensity to acquire social norms, parallel to our wiring to learn language, although as with language the exact variant we learn will depend on our upbringing (see Ostrom (2000) for discussion and also Ostrom (1990)). The degree of reciprocity and cooperation, although having an evolutionary basis, varies widely across time and space. Experimental evidence suggests some common patterns, however (Bowles 1998; Fehr and Gächter 2000). There are different types of individual. Some are selfish, some are born cooperators, and some can be either depending on circumstances. For a cooperative outcome, there have to be enough reciprocators but not necessarily a majority. The reason seems to be that we are sufficiently willing to punish the

---

[4]I am particularly indebted to a paper by Partha Dasgupta (2005b) for clarifying my thoughts.

selfish very heavily, even at some cost to ourselves, which discourages noncooperation. The threat of punishment makes social norms stick even if selfish individuals are in the majority. Our beliefs about others' beliefs play a part too: selfish as I am, I'll still cooperate if I think everyone else is going to do so. Interestingly, face-to-face communication strongly enhances cooperative behavior. So social sanctions, communications, mutual expectations, and also how people's choices are framed all affect the extent to which we cooperate with each other as opposed to making self-interested, (boundedly) rational choices.

The basic question is therefore the one posed by Paul Seabright: What stops us from murdering each other, as we used to not very long ago in evolutionary time and still do in some countries? What makes us instead trust each other, in increasingly large, dispersed, but interdependent societies, to do what we say we will? Trusting each other is fundamental to economic development. (Indeed, some authors use "trust" and "social capital" essentially synonymously.) We trust our very closest family members because of mutual affection. We also appear to have an evolutionary disposition to reciprocate favors in small groups, such that I will share my mammoth with you because you helped me kill it, and in return I'll help you kill your mammoth and will expect a share in its meat. Otherwise, trust depends on the existence of an *institution* that ensures that it's in everyone's interest to keep their promises. To an economist, an institution is an equilibrium strategy in a game. Institutions coordinate individuals' behavior such that all the expectations about how everyone else will behave are satisfied.

The most beautiful example was offered by Thomas Schelling (1978): the traffic light. It is in everyone's interest to stop at a red light because they have an incentive to avoid a crash; and each person can be confident that (pretty much) everyone else will stop at red lights too, as they have the same incentive. This is in a sense an ideal institution because it needs very little monitoring and enforcement. Others may need policing, when private incentives and social imperatives do not coincide so neatly. Still others can police themselves in the sense that, even if an individual has no immediate incentive to behave in a certain way, they have invested in a reputation for being a community-minded person in order to benefit themselves in future.

In this framework, the mutually reinforcing rules of behavior which it is in everyone's interest to adhere to are the *social norms*. It is the norm to drive on the left-hand side of the road and to stop at a red light in my own country, the United Kingdom. In India, for a formative period a British colony, the formal rule is the same, but the social norm is to drive in the middle of the road and often to drive straight across an intersection, because as everybody else does the same obeying the formal rule would make your journey impossibly slow. Social norms, and the corresponding institutions, which encompass the norms, are self-fulfilling. This means that there can be multiple equilibria—some much better or worse than others in terms of social and individual well-being.

What determines which equilibrium will prevail? The possibility of many outcomes means that the one which actually prevails now will be very strongly determined by the past—this is another case of *path dependence*, which we met in chapter 2. Decisions taken at any point in time have a large and lasting influence on outcomes forever into the future. But even acknowledging the importance of history, there are two types of answer, and it's not clear which is correct or even whether they're mutually exclusive.

Social Capital Matters

The first is that social norms and institutions are shaped by the relationships between individuals, by the interpersonal networks of communication, and by the number and prevalence of strong and weak ties. Partha Dasgupta interprets "social capital" to mean precisely the social networks in the economy. This has the appeal of clarity, and it contrasts with the many definitions which include all kinds of disparate abstractions such as rules and beliefs as well. We know that networks are an important phenomenon empirically, and social networks are similar to other networks in the natural world. So this definition means that we can also use the toolkit available for analyzing networks to understand the patterns and effects of social capital. A focus on social networks also helps us understand the dynamics we see in social behavior and attitudes. The network toolkit permits the analysis of contagion effects; of changes in social norms of behavior (sometimes occurring at a critical moment to give a "tipping point" phenomenon); of the importance of especially well-connected individuals; of 80:20 patterns in social and economic indicators such as income distribution; even of "first mover" effects.

In this case, the correlation between social capital and the economy will stem from the interaction of social networks and markets. In many cases, social networks complement markets in increasing economic activity. One example is the case of the industrial cluster. It's long been appreciated that economic activity is geographically clustered, and there's a lot more of it in towns and cities than in the countryside. Many of the clusters are specialized, with many companies in one industry locating close to each other. Sometimes the reason stems from physical geography, such as the presence of a natural resource or a favorable climate. Often, however, the explanation is a combination of historical chance and the presence of mutually reinforcing spillovers of the kind which are so important in endogenous growth theory. An industrial cluster will quickly build up a pool of skilled labor and suppliers. Firms like to be there because they have a plentiful choice of workers and contractors. Workers like to be there because there are plenty of employers demanding their skills. In the phrase of the economist Alfred Marshall, there is specialist know-how "in the air." Social networks are clearly very important for these clusters of industry. People exchange ideas and tips about how to do the work, or find jobs, or whether a particular supplier is up to scratch.

In other instances, however, social networks can prevent markets from functioning properly. There are many examples from developing countries, where traditional relationships might prevent people from seeking a job in another part of the country or from selling their produce to a different wholesaler. But there are plenty in developed countries too. Children are still sometimes expected to choose the same profession as their father. Villagers in Sicily are still suspicious of strangers and strongly advised to pay their "tax" to the local godfather. And, as Mancur Olson pointed out, some groups are very good at furthering the interests of their members at the expense of the interests of any broader group. His view of civic associations would be very much more negative than Robert Putnam's take on them. One of the empirical studies cited earlier found that "trust" was good for the economy but strong family ties had an adverse effect (La Porta et al. 1997).

This should make it plain that social capital (as defined here) is *not* always a good thing. It has its dark side. Networks exclude people as well as including them. Networks can also incorporate hierarchical relations, where some people exploit others. Many developing economies are characterized by this kind of social relationship—the relationship between a sharecropper and landowner is one example often given. Depending on your perspective, social obligations can look like corruption, and civic associations can look like special-interest groups. A good example of this is provided by the 1997–98 global financial crisis, which started in Asia when some big companies defaulted on their bank loans. Prior to the crisis many commentators had praised the so-called "Asian values," which were supposed to contrast with Western individualism, selfishness, and lack of solidarity; after the crisis, they suddenly looked like corruption and conformism. Asian values became "crony capitalism" overnight. In fact there are many examples of networks that are too close-knit. The Mafia is one, and Putnam's findings suggest that in southern Italy people are, generally speaking, too closely tied to their family and village networks, and insufficiently trusting of people outside those networks, for their own well-being and the good of the economy as a whole. Exchange in a market is certainly more anonymous, but anonymity has its merits. (See Bowles and Gintis (1993) for further discussion on this topic, although they are skeptical about the merits of markets. McLaren (2000), on the other hand, argues that markets can better protect individuals from exploitation than more-personal relationships.)

The interplay between networks and markets is one of the key debates in social science, and one which tends to divide economists from other social scientists. Networks are personal—each individual's identity and reputation matter. Markets are anonymous. To many social scientists, it is a matter of regret that the domain of the market seems to be growing and the domain of the network diminishing—and this has been a theme virtually since the dawn of capitalism. In nineteenth-century Britain the Romantic poets hated the effect of market transactions on social relations. John Ruskin, better known as an art critic, wrote a huge best seller, *Unto This Last*, criticizing the "soi disant science of political economy" for its "idea that an advantageous code of social action may be determined irrespective of the influence of social affection" (Ruskin 2000, p. 1). Another well-known trumpet blast against market relations is Karl Polanyi's 1957 book *The Great Transformation*, which argued that markets should properly be minor adjuncts to economic life, with the principle of social reciprocity rightly ordering economic decisions. The market view which, he complained, had come to dominate modern life was damaging society. In fact, he blamed liberal capitalism for the social disaffections which paved the way for fascism and the war. A look around the bookstore today will reveal a huge number of "anticapitalist" titles, many of them best sellers too, ranging from almost incoherent tracts against globalization to serious sociological works, by scholars such as Richard Sennett (see Sennett 1998) or Mike Davis (see Davis 2006), regretting the impact of markets on society.

Yet while markets can inhibit or damage traditional social networks, networks can prevent markets functioning. They can prevent resources from moving to more efficient uses, and keep incomes and living standards lower than they would otherwise be. For the people at the wrong end of traditional social relations—the poor, those of low caste, members of minority groups—the anonymity of markets is a big improvement on those personal relationships. As Partha Dasgupta puts it: "When social networks within each community block the growth of markets, their presence inhibits economic progress."

This is much more complicated than the "social capital is good" argument presented above. In the empirical research cited earlier, social capital was found to be positively linked to good economic outcomes; in that research, social capital was measured by a proxy, usually a survey-based indicator of the general level of trust in each society. A tighter analysis of the definition of social capital as the aggregate of interpersonal networks suggests that it can be either good or bad for the economy. Dasgupta concludes: "Determining the right interplay between personal networks and impersonal public institutions remains the central problem of the social sciences." But however defined, others see social capital and/or institutions and economic outcomes as jointly resulting from a deeper cause: culture.

Culture Matters

Culture is another term which it's hard to define in such a way that you can measure it. A variety of metrics have been used in social science. Max Weber famously used religion as an indicator of a set of attitudes and beliefs which were favorable to the development of capitalism. Culture can manifest itself either as individual values and preferences or as social norms. And there are many types of belief or norm which might be of interest to us. One widely used categorization defines culture along three axes: individualism versus collectivism (or autonomy versus embeddedness); egalitarianism versus hierarchy; and mastery of the natural world versus harmony with the natural world (see Licht et al. 2004). Where on each of these scales does a culture lie?

The usefulness of a concept of culture is that it can potentially help explain why a society will settle in one of the multiple possible equilibria rather than another. In game theory, Thomas Schelling introduced the concept of the "focal point," something from outside that nevertheless directs the outcome in one direction rather than another (Schelling 1960). Culture plays the part of the focal point, and channels societies along different historical paths. The argument that culture plays the causal part in determining how well an economy does rests on the observation that the same formal institutions seem to operate differently in different economic and social environments. Just as in making the case for a role for social capital, we could point to the example of Italy, which has been unified under a national government for more than a century and a half without the prosperity gap between the north and the south narrowing.

It seems to me unimportant whether one labels the "something" that is the root cause of development or its lack "social capital" or "culture." Social capital is an abstract term which I narrowed down to define as social networks. In practice for econometric work it is usually measured as a generalized indicator of the level of trust (i.e., outside the family) in the society of interest. Culture is another abstract term whose definition might include that general level of trust but also other indicators. The following are all measured by questions in the same World Values Survey that measures trust.

Control: do people have confidence that their individual efforts will pay off, or are they fatalistic?

Respect for others: are other people (outside the family) regarded as being important and worthy of consideration?

Conformity: are the younger expected to obey their elders, inferiors their superiors, or is there more individualism?

Whether such indicators are used or a narrower indicator of social capital or trust, the central empirical question is whether or not culture/ trust/social capital determines both the shape of the institutions in the economy and therefore economic outcomes or whether the institutions themselves determine economic outcomes with the side effect of altering levels of trust or cultural attitudes. This is difficult to answer because there are clearly feedbacks. A modernizing economy does, slowly perhaps, affect social and cultural attitudes. That is exactly the complaint of Ruskin, Polanyi, Sennett, and others. Was it economic growth which made the West individualistic and trusting of strangers as well as family? Or did having these cultural characteristics at least since the Middle Ages explain the economic dynamism of the West?

The most common strategy for addressing this question empirically is to try to find variables which are closely linked to culture but not to economic outcomes. The first step is to run a regression of culture on these other variables—language, perhaps, or religious origin. The second stage is to use the output of these first-stage regressions, the part of culture

225

explained by the independent variables, as "instruments" for culture in a second regression, with income or growth as the variable to be explained. Guido Tabellini, for example, uses pre-1850 literacy levels and political institutions in different regions of Europe as instruments for culture, taking advantage of the fact that the regions within the present national borders of Europe (within Italy, or within Belgium, for example) have diverse political origins thanks to the centuries-worth of wars fought on European soil (Tabellini 2006). Amir Licht and his coauthors use a linguistic trait, the ability in some languages to omit personal pronouns, as an indicator of culture (Licht et al. 2004). In each case the assumption is that the culture indicator used as an instrument is not itself related to current economic development, and in each study the authors find that culture makes an independent contribution to both forms of governance (or institutions) and economic development. So does a recent survey of empirical work on the economic impact of culture (Giuso et al. 2006)

The econometric approach isn't the only one. Many economic historians have traced the divergent stories of economies which started out at a similar stage of development using an account based on culture. One wonderful example is *The Wealth and Poverty of Nations* by David Landes (1998). Another specific case study is presented by Avner Greif, who focuses on the contrast between the "collectivist" and "individualist" cultures of the Maghribi traders of North Africa, the southern Mediterranean, and traders from Genoa, in the northern Mediterranean, in the eleventh and twelfth centuries (Greif 1994).

CULTURE OR INSTITUTIONS?

Arguments about the importance of culture are quite persuasive. I think we are very prone to thinking in cultural stereotypes, finding it a useful shorthand for mentally categorizing and reacting to people. But is culture more important than institutional structures, as described above, as a fundamental explanation of economic performance? They obviously affect each other. Is it possible to determine the direction of causality? Just as there is an empirical literature testing historical versus geographical explanations for growth, so there is one weighing up the importance of culture versus institutions. Guido Tabellini's paper is a recent example, and his verdict was that culture is what matters; it shapes institutions. However, many others find institutions to be key. One paper, for instance, looks at the "reversal of fortune" in the relative economic ranking of countries during the nineteenth century, finding that institutions

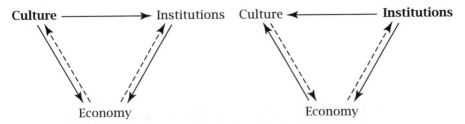

Figure 8.1. The alternative proposed directions of causation; bold indicates causal variable.

were vital to how well countries were able to take advantage of industrialization (Acemoglu et al. 2002). This echoes the recent findings, described in chapter 2, that organization is important in productivity growth resulting from information and communication technologies in the 1990s. A number of other results also emphasize the primacy of institutions (these are surveyed in chapter 7 of Helpman (2004)).

I don't think that anyone has got to the bottom of this yet. The reason it's so difficult is clear in figure 8.1, which show the alternative proposed directions of causation, the dashed lines showing feedbacks. The differences are extremely subtle. Using a variety of indicators as proxies for the abstract concepts, with correlated explanatory variables, and using historical data as well, it simply isn't possible to draw firm conclusions yet about such a nuanced question.

A TAXONOMY

To get to this rather inconclusive point, this chapter has covered an enormous amount of ground in terms of the range of potential links between the economy and society. One helpful way to think about where the pieces of the debate slot in is the taxonomy shown in table 8.1, adapted from one presented by Oliver Williamson (2000).

We've come full circle, back to the big question about why economies differ, why some grow and others don't. This chapter has approached it from the perspective of how individuals interact and how their decisions aggregate. I want to end by noting the link back to the chapters in part 2, about the aims people have in mind, about the psychology of decision making, and about the importance of the information they have in making their choices. In the past, questions about the best way to run economic policy for the benefit of "society" have often been posed in markets-versus-governments terms. I hope both parts 2 and 3 have made it obvious why this is far too simplistic. Both governments and

227

Table 8.1. A taxonomy of the social basis of economic theory.

Level	What is it?	How long to change (years)?	Origin/policy aim	Type of economic theory (authors mentioned here)
0	Evolutionary biology and psychology	Evolutionary time	Pressure of natural selection	Reciprocity, underpinnings of social behavior and institutions (Seabright, Ostrom, Fehr, and Gächter)
1	"Informal institutions": norms, culture, traditions, religion, etc.	1,000–10,000	Spontaneous/emergent; social relationships	Analysis of social capital, culture, norms, networks (North, Dasgupta, Ostrom, Putnam, Granovetter, etc.)
2	Institutional environment, formal rules of the game: politics, rule of law, property rights, etc.	10–1,000	Institutional and political reform	Public choice theory (Buchanan, Coase, Olson, Alesina); social norms and networks (above authors and Glaeser)
3	Governance, play of the game, transactions	1–10	Quality of governance	New Institutional Economics (Coase, Williamson); networks (Granovetter)
4	Resource allocation and employment	Continuous adjustment	Incentives and allocation at the margin; market design	Price theory, agency theory (see earlier chapters)

markets are specific forms of institution, taking different shapes in different times and places. There's a kaleidoscopic array of institutions we humans have developed for managing our interactions with each other. Partha Dasgupta writes:

> When they have needed to, and have been able to, people have developed what are often crisscrossing institutions, such as extended-family and kinship networks; civic, commercial and religious associations; charities; production units; and various layers of what is known as government. Each serves functions the others are not so good at serving.... Their elucidation, in particular our increased understanding of their strengths and weaknesses, has been the most compelling achievement of economics over the past 25 years or so.
>
> Dasgupta (1998)

Networks, norms, culture, social capital, institutions, markets, governments, all words for mechanisms which turn individual choices into collective actions. One of the aims of the continuing research in this area must be further evidence about which form of collective arrangement delivers desirable outcomes, for there isn't yet a comprehensive taxonomy. Each can fail in certain circumstances, each has its strengths and weaknesses. In the case of markets, anonymity can be a benefit in some circumstances and a burden in others. The close traditional ties of the village can be either supporting or stifling. Social capital can be positive or negative. Trust reduces transactions costs, making it more likely that markets will function efficiently, but the wider the extent of markets, the harder it might become to sustain trust. No framework for collective action stands still, as today's institutions shape tomorrow's economic performance, which in turn feeds back to the evolution of institutions. There remains an enormous research task in trying to understand these feedbacks, in one of the most exhilarating areas of economics today.

Why Economics Has Soul

John Kenneth Galbraith cared enough about the teaching of graduate students in economics to establish a prize for the best teacher in the department at Harvard University, where he was a professor for fifty-seven years. A committee of five students selected the winner each year, and both the winner and the selection committee were treated to a dinner at Galbraith's Cambridge, MA, home. One year, I was a member of that selection committee. I missed the opportunity to have a conversation with the great man, mainly because I felt too short to talk to him. My fellow students, strapping young North American males well over six feet tall themselves, only came up to Galbraith's shoulder, and as I didn't even reach *their* shoulders, it seemed unlikely the great professor and I would manage any meaningful discussion.

Besides, the student committee decision that year had been a some-what bitter three–two split, and I was in the losing minority.[1] Let me explain the context. This was 1982. Ronald Reagan had recently been elected as U.S. president. Both he and Margaret Thatcher, across the Atlantic Ocean, justified their policies by reference to free-market economic theory. In economics it was the height of the rational-expectations mania, when an ultra-rational-choice, perfect-foresight approach to business cycles and macroeconomic management dressed itself up in dauntingly difficult mathematics. Some students loved this stuff; it appealed to the macho element who wanted to show how well they could do calculus. I found it intriguing because it took the foundational assumptions of economics to an extreme and thereby made the contrast between the simple model and the "real world" potentially illuminating. My thesis was about testing the specific *ways* in which the theory failed to explain the levels of employment and wages in U.S. industries. I didn't think you

---

[1] This is written from memory as I don't have notes. It's possible I was in a minority of one, and was even crosser at the dinner than I remember.

had to be a conservative to do this kind of economics. But needless to say, people's political views were refracted in their attitude to what had become the cutting edge of macroeconomics.

Back to our student committee. The majority opted for Steve Marglin, a tenured professor who taught us economic history. Marglin had been a conventional neoclassical economist when appointed by Harvard, and turned Marxist after the tenure decision. I though he was a perfectly good teacher but not as good as Olivier Blanchard, the other candidate, a gifted economist (now at MIT) who turned what was for us a dauntingly technical introduction to grown-up macroeconomics into an exciting challenge. I felt my colleagues voting for Professor Marglin were doing so for ideological reasons, demonstrating their radicalism and losing sight of the purpose of the award, namely to reward the quality of the instruction we received.

I tell you this story to illustrate the way political or ideological views influence the frequent critiques of neoclassical economics, and also because Galbraith himself is a good example of what other people think economists should be like. I'll return to the point about politics later. Galbraith is, of course, one of the few economists widely known and read by the general public. His many books were best sellers, and deservedly so. They're well-written, thought provoking, and even contributed new phrases to the language ("conventional wisdom" was one of his, and "private affluence and public squalor"). Yet, despite his Harvard professorship and public acclaim, many economists don't think Galbraith counted as an economist himself. Sour grapes? Certainly academics in any field are often disdainful about their colleagues who enjoy commercial and popular success.

But, looking back through *The Affluent Society* (Galbraith 1991), after Galbraith's death in April 2006, I think there's more to it. The reason many economists think Galbraith wasn't really one of us lies in his methodology. His work covers the terrain of economics—the operation of business, growth and wealth, running public services, inflation, and so on—but it uses the methods of sociology and history. The point isn't just that Galbraith's books are literary and contain no equations; Paul Krugman is another wonderful writer and popularizer, in the same part of the political spectrum as Galbraith, but we in the profession count Krugman as a *bona fide* economist. By contrast many of us spurn Galbraith because he wasn't a modeler. Models don't have to be expressed in mathematical equations, but the thought process a modeler brings to trying to understand the world involves trying to select a small number of variables and relationships which can perhaps, with elegance and economy, explain the phenomena we observe. So we modelers can read *The Affluent Society*, and even agree with it, without finding it persuasive. It gives us no grip on how to confront its hypotheses and claims with empirical evidence. Economics isn't defined by its subject matter but by its way of thinking.

Well, many noneconomists would conclude from this that Galbraith good, economists bad. For there is a vast and ever-growing critique of economics, much of which I've masochistically read and filed away. What I want to set out in this conclusion, having spent the past couple of hundred pages describing what economists do these days, is address the critique directly. My argument in short is that some criticism of the orthodoxy is justified—well, of course it is—but most of the critics attack a caricature of economics, for reasons related to their personal ideological beliefs. I believe that many of the critics outside the subject are simply unaware of the content of economic research during the past twenty years. In fact, actually existing economics, as it's practiced in universities and government today, is experiencing, virtually unnoticed by the wider world, a golden age of discovery. This is not an exaggeration. Empirical economists are charting the economy and society with a wealth of detailed applied results that truly bear comparison with other epochs of discovery in other sciences.

Is Economics "Autistic"?

The faculty of economics at the University of Notre Dame split into two in 2003. It consists now of a Department of Economics and Econometrics and a Department of Economics and Policy Studies. From the outside, this seems bizarre, for there's nothing mutually exclusive about econometrics and policy studies. What happened was that the economists working in the previously united department no longer had enough in common, intellectually, to carry on working together. A committee of university administrators and academics from other departments was formed to resolve the intellectual (and no-doubt personal) tensions and they concluded: "We regard the differences between the heterodox and orthodox economists to be so great that reconciliation within a single cohesive department is wholly unrealistic" (quoted in Monaghan (2003)). So they split the department in two.

The new "heterodox" department (that is, Economics and Policy Studies) includes some of the luminaries of the post-autistic economics movement. This movement traces its origins to the late 1980s, and the growing demand for a variety of alternatives to mainstream economic theory. Criticism of mainstream economics dates back many, many years, at least to Thomas Carlyle's famous dismissal of "the dismal science," and comes from both outside the economics profession and inside. In my personal collection of attacks on economics is a 1985 *Atlantic Monthly* article by Robert Kuttner, which accuses universities of turning out economics students who are *idiots savants*, "brilliant at esoteric mathematics yet innocent of actual economic life" (Kuttner 1985). Much of his article criticizes not only the use of mathematics in economics but the use of modeling as an approach at all. He ends with a plea for a "new paradigm" (in Thomas Kuhn's sense) but despairs: "No dissenting paradigm seems able to gain a foothold within economics. Thus the economic orthodoxy is reinforced by ideology, by the sociology of the profession, by the politics of who gets published or promoted and whose research gets funded."

There is a long list of books criticizing the mainstream of economics, including works by economists such as George Brockway (1995, 2001), Robert Heilbroner (1993; see also Heilbroner and Milberg 1995), Tony Lawson (1997), Deirdre McCloskey (1998, 2000), Philip Mirowski (2002), and Paul Ormerod (1994, 1998, 2000). There's even a strange novel (Legendre 2006) in this company, drawing on the obscure work of Nicholas Georgescu-Roegen (2006).[2] All of these books are gleefully reviewed in literary journals, newspapers, and magazines: review editors simply adore a chance to insult economists in print. To cap it all, a *Financial Times* journalist, of all people, concludes:

> If the profession is misunderstood, it has nobody but itself to blame. It worships mathematical technique, but pays little attention to the behavioural and institutional forces at play in the real world—which is too messy to model with tidy equations. It has lost relevance by trying to pretend economics is a "hard science" totally divorced from such related subjects as politics, psychology and sociology. It has lost its ability to communicate with the laity.
>
> M. Prowse, "A wake-up call from Laura Tyson," January 18, 1993

The same journalist a year earlier had praised "the extraordinary diversity of modern economics," but as I used to be a journalist, I'll forbear from criticizing that profession.

---

[2] Georgescu-Roegen, too, argues that economics is too mechanistic, but he means it literally, saying economic theory overlooks the second law of thermodynamics.

The spirit of dissent has now taken institutional shape within the profession. The *American Economic Review*, the leading mainstream journal, published an article in 1992 calling for "a new spirit of pluralism in economics." In 1993 one of its authors, Geoffrey Hodgson, helped found the International Confederation of Associations for the Reform of Economics (now renamed ICAPE, the "P" standing for "pluralism"). In 2000 and 2001 economics students and some academics founded post-autistic economics movements in France, Italy, the United Kingdom, and the United States. The post-autistic critics are astute in their use of language: they are pluralist, intellectually tolerant, they seek critical debate, and they are open-minded. By implication, the orthodoxy is the opposite. Actually, they are so pluralist that there are some strong disagreements within the heterodox world—a cynic with experience of left-wing student politics might wonder how long it is before the movement splinters into bitterly warring factions. Nevertheless, it is clear from the numbers of supporters and subscribers to the online journal that there are plenty of economists who think mainstream economics is "autistic," never mind noneconomists.

There are several statements explaining why economics is autistic and what a post-autistic version could look like. Those I've read argue that neoclassical economics, as still taught in most universities today, is a creature of the Cold War (see Fullbrook 2002; Garnett 2005; Mirowski 2002). There's no doubt that there's some institutional truth in this: U.S. military budgets did contribute to the development of game theory and linear programming in U.S. universities in the 1950s. Those receiving the military funding, mainly in the northeastern United States along with some in California, did go on to dominate the economics profession and remain at its pinnacle. A second and related influence shaping the neoclassical orthodoxy was its mathematization, starting with Paul Samuelson's *Foundations of Economic Analysis*, under the powerful influence of one school of mathematics (see Mirowski 2002; Weintraub 2002).[3] These universities and the analytical approach they embraced have been the overwhelmingly dominant influence shaping modern economics. I don't think anybody in the profession disputes the broad outlines of this history. The issue is how much weight to put on it and what it means for current practice.

---

[3] The school was a group of mainly French mathematicians of the 1930s writing under the collective name Nicolas Bourbaki. Strange but true. There is a decent Wikipedia summary.

According to the post-autists, the mainstream view has a monopoly in the classroom. It ignores the world's economic problems ("globalization, inequalities, environment, technical progress, etc.," according to Edward Fullbrook (2005)) although this claim seems simply bizarre, as such subjects are frequently discussed in the classrooms and lecture halls. The mainstream prohibits "critical thinking" and "has brainwashed successive generations of students into viewing economic reality exclusively through its concepts." The post-autists specifically criticize the rational-choice methodology and the assumption that individuals behave independently of each other, the assumption of utility maximization, and the emphasis on growth instead of well-being. Finally, the mainstream ignores the environment and the sustainability of growth. Anybody who has read so far through this book will realize that mainstream economics has in fact been testing and exploring these various assumptions for at least two decades. Many of the critics don't refer to much of the work published during the past fifteen or twenty years. So if the mainstream is post-autistic, what are the post-autistic economists complaining about? Have they simply failed to notice that the monolithic old enemy has ceased to exist?

WHY THE CRITICISMS STICK

Mechanistic, mathematical, removed from the "real world," reductionist, autistic—why do so many people, even so many economists, insist that these descriptions characterize the subject, which they portray as unchanged in more than a generation? Why do the critics, numerous as they are and almost never confronted with a reply from a mainstream economist, always present themselves as beleaguered mavericks battling a monolithic and reactionary establishment? Having thought about this for many years, I think there are several mutually reinforcing reasons.

The Public Face of Economics

What the nonspecialist sees of economics is largely the kind of macroeconomic debate covered in the news programs and newspapers, the forecasts about how much the economy will grow, what will happen to inflation or the dollar, whether the financial markets will go up or down. Most of this economics is

(a) of poor quality and spuriously precise, as it's not possible to forecast these things in any detail, and shame on economists for still pretending it is;

235

(b) jargon-ridden and possibly not understood even by the person spouting the jargon on television; and

(c) being used for a purpose such as advancing one political party or gaining an investment bank some good PR.

No matter that this isn't what most economists do, it's what most people mostly see of us. That the public face of economics is usually a dull but pompous, middle-aged, white man makes matters even worse.[4] When a critic charges economists with only caring about money, it's easy to believe, as that's all we're seen to talk about in public.

The Use of Mathematics

There has been a lengthy debate about the proper use of mathematics in economics. Most economists agree with the often-quoted advice of Alfred Marshall:

> I had a growing feeling in the later years of my work at the subject that a good mathematical theorem dealing with economic hypotheses was very unlikely to be good economics: and I went more and more on the rules—(1) Use mathematics as a short-hand language, rather than as an engine of inquiry. (2) Keep to them till you have done. (3) Translate into English. (4) Then illustrate by examples that are important in real life. (5) Burn the mathematics. (6) If you can't succeed in (4), burn (3). This last I did often.
>
> Quoted in Pigou (1966, pp. 427, 428)

I also like Edgeworth's comparison of mathematical modeling to scaffolding: a building can't be put up without scaffolding but isn't complete until it's taken down. Many economists think that people who criticize our overreliance on equations just can't do the mathematics. This might well be true in some cases, but I don't believe it's an important reason for their critique, and anyway it always sounds a patronizing response. It is probably true that the extensive use of equations in models misleads noneconomists into thinking that economics is more formalistic than it is in reality.[5] We use the mathematics for clarity and to ensure logical consistency. But anyway I think the real problem, in the minds of the

---

[4]Beards are heavily overrepresented and female glamour heavily underrepresented in the subject.

[5]As Robert Solow puts it in his inimitable style, "It is not surprising ... that outsiders think that there is a lot of formalism in economics, just as half a cup of blood spread around a bathroom can make it look like a scene from *Psycho*" (Solow 1997, p. 40).

critics, isn't so much mathematics as modeling, or in other words the strategic simplification of complicated reality (see Dasgupta 2005c).

The Scientific Method and Literary Culture

The 1995 Nobel memorial prize winner Robert Lucas has described how one of his key insights followed from a note his colleague Ed Prescott left in his mailbox, a note containing just a single equation representing the labor market. Lucas wrote:

> The normal response to such a note, I suppose, would have been to go upstairs to Ed's office and ask for some kind of explanation, but theoretical economists are not normal, and we do not ask for words to "explain" what equations mean. We ask for equations that explain what words mean.
>
> Breit and Hirsch (2005)

The value of mathematical modeling, Lucas argues, lies in the struggle to capture the essence of behavior. A tractable model which conforms to empirical evidence is the source of new insights in economics.

This for me is the heart of the matter. Economics is a science not because it mimics the same specific techniques or equations as natural scientists, nor because it consists of falsifiable statements which would keep Karl Popper happy, but because it tries to model human behavior in general statements (or equations) with relatively few variables, and seeks to bring the models face to face with empirical evidence. Its scientific method is similar to the approach taken in other largely non-experimental sciences such as evolutionary biology or geology. I believe that many of the critics of economics, especially those working in the humanities, simply do not accept that it is appropriate to study human culture and society with this methodology, that is, using models, at all.[6] Of course, economics is not alone in coming under attack for its alleged reductionism. Another prominent victim of the same kind of charge is neo-Darwinism. Advocates of so-called "intelligent design" see modern genetic science and biology as reductionist and deterministic in character. I'm firmly with the Darwinians.

---

[6] The centrality of models was the subject of a charming parody by Axel Leijonhufvud: "In explaining to a stranger ... why he holds the Sociologs or the Polscis in such low regard, the Econ will say that 'they do not make modls'" (Leijonhufvud 1973, p. 330). He saw elaborate "modls" as a sign of decadence in the Econ tribe.

The Politics of the Critique

Finally, many if not most of the legion of critics of economics are left of center in their politics, and I think they see economics as a powerful weapon used mainly by those whose politics are right of center. It's certainly true that the heyday of Reaganism and Thatcherism put the free-market version of neoclassical economics at center stage. Economic "realism" was used to justify policies such as privatization and the deregulation of many markets. This sense that economics is innately right wing lives on in the hugely popular attacks on globalization which dominate today's best-seller lists, nearly thirty years after Mrs. Thatcher first came to power. But this is an incorrect conclusion to draw from the use of economics by some conservatives during a specific period. After all, the free-market economists celebrated in the 1980s had been out in the intellectual wilderness in the 1950s and 1960s, when Keynesian views were triumphant in academic economics and were used by centrist and left-wing governments to justify intervention in markets. Today's critics of what they suppose mainstream economics says should wise up and explore the lessons of economic research for people of all political beliefs. As I discuss below, the growing wealth of empirical findings is likely to cut across conventional political orthodoxies.

Is There a Bias in Mainstream Economics?

For what it's worth, the available evidence (based on surveys) suggests that economists lean to the left. In surveys of American economics graduate students in 2001–3, David Colander found that they classified themselves in the following way: 47% liberal, 24% moderate, 16% conservative, 6% radical, 6% nonpolitical. However, the proportion describing themselves as conservative increased with the number of years of study (Colander 2005). A survey of American academics in the social sciences in 2003 showed the following breakdown of political allegiances (Klein and Stern 2005, www.sofi.su.se/wp/WP05-8.pdf):

	Ratio of Democrats to Republicans
Anthropologists and sociologists	21.1:1
Political and legal philosophers	9.1:1
Historians	8.5:1
Political scientists	5.6:1
Economists	2.9:1

While economists were substantially less likely than other social scientists to be left of center, Democrats still outnumber Republicans at least among academic economists by nearly three to one. Controlling for their party allegiances, economists' beliefs (about matters such as free trade and the effectiveness of free markets) differ systematically from the beliefs of like-voting members of the general public, however (Caplan 2002). The disagreements between economists and their critics are not about party politics. According to an analysis of a 1996 survey of the views of 1,510 members of the public and 250 holders of PhDs in economics:

> There is a kernel of truth to ideological stereotypes about the economics profession: views typical of extreme right-wing ideologues in the general public are often economists' conventional wisdom. But this is primarily a reflection of economists' willingness to endorse immoderate conclusions, not their political leanings, which are in fact mildly left wing.

This economist, Bryan Caplan, finds his colleagues guilty not of political bias but rather of holding (as a group) views at either extreme of the political spectrum. I think we economists might have to plead guilty to the charge of arrogance.

WHAT CHANGED ECONOMICS?

My years as a graduate student, 1981–85, saw the high-water mark of neoclassical economics of the kind which is still the target of the critics. Although I hope I've given credit throughout this book to the pioneers of the kind of economics widely practiced by academics now, they were often lonely pioneers—until the 1980s. One of the reasons the tide turned is that the kind of models which became popular (especially among impressionable graduate students) in the late 1970s and early 1980s acted as a kind of *reductio ad absurdum*. The attempt to explain business-cycle fluctuations in growth and inflation as the equilibrium outcome of a model with identical, perfectly informed rational agents was, on just a little reflection, pretty silly. As a modeling exercise it might bring some insight but it wasn't a good tool for empirical explanation. And, say what you like about economists, we love data. One of the oddest bits of the critique is that economics is divorced from the "real world." Partha Dasgupta (a mainstream economics professor at the University of Cambridge who studies poverty, social organization, and the environment) was so irritated by this often-repeated accusation that he counted

239

the number of articles of different types carried in the *American Economic Review* in the five years to 1995. There were 156 describing empirical or experimental research, 100 trying to find a theoretical explanation for observed facts, and just 25 pure theory articles (see Dasgupta 1998). Robert Solow describes us as "obsessed with data" (Solow 1997, p. 37).

Still, there was, up until the early 1980s, a relatively narrow orthodoxy or mainstream, albeit never as extreme as the usual caricature. But, as I hope I've demonstrated in this book, that picture has changed dramatically. David Colander's survey, referred to above, followed up an earlier one conducted in 1985 (Colander and Klamer 1987). The differences between the two confirm that many of the changes described in this book have taken root in the professional training. Between the two surveys, mathematical and problem-solving skills have declined in importance while skill in empirical research and thorough knowledge of the economy have increased. Colander writes: "Students believe their ability to do good empirical work separates them from other social scientists.... The perception of a rigid neoclassical economics has been replaced by an eclectic mainstream" (Colander 2005, pp. 181, 193). Mainstream economics is no longer monolithic. It is more empirical than ever. Many of the assumptions made for analytical simplicity (and then out of habit) are now frequently relaxed in our models, so imperfect information, nonidentical agents, bounded rationality, and spillovers from one individual to another, for example, pop up all over modern economics. What explains the change?

Computers

The most fundamental answer is the availability of cheap computer power. The increased capacity to do more empirical research in turn facilitated some theoretical developments, which I discuss below. But the bottom line is that computers transformed economics, just as they transformed biology and geology and other sciences whose theoretical underpinnings were previously, as it turns out, limited by the amount of computation that was feasible. In my student days we had a limited budget for the empirical work we could do to support our thesis research, and had to work on a time-share mainframe, writing our own regression programs for the most part as there was little prepackaged software. And, as I point out to my children, I'm not even all that old! Computer processing which used to cost us hundreds of real dollars is essentially free now.

There has been a cost to the availability of cheap and powerful computers, which is an explosion of really, really bad econometrics. I'm afraid this is the real scandal about the economics profession—not that we think econometrics is a valid tool for analyzing society, but that there are so many economists spilling such rubbish out of their computers. As early as 1983 Ed Leamer warned about the abuse of statistical techniques, and Deirdre McCloskey has conducted a vigorous campaign against the abuse of econometrics (Leamer 1983; McCloskey 1998). A simple litmus test a would-be critic of economics can apply to empirical work is to ask the economist to explain the *units* of the regression he or she is trumpeting. A good econometrician knows what the results *mean*, and are testing one clear hypothesis against another, so they can explain themselves.

It's hard to overstate the importance of the computer revolution for economics. Just as the sequencing of the genome wouldn't have been possible without the vast amount of number crunching by applied biologists, the body of applied knowledge that economists are building up has fundamentally depended on computers, and the related development of rich new data sets and computational and simulation techniques. It is hard to appreciate from outside the profession just how much empirical evidence we are collecting, as much of it remains to be synthesized. The leading journals don't publish many more articles than they used to, so while the character is becoming more applied, you don't get a sense from their contents about the quantity of applied results. The specialist email newsletters which are widely circulated among economists give a better idea. For example, I subscribe to one in industrial and competition economics which sends me abstracts and links for perhaps twenty new papers a week, almost all applied, covering industrial structure and specific markets and businesses from all over the United States and Europe. The National Bureau of Economic Research, in Cambridge, MA, is the largest and most prestigious publisher of working papers by academic economists in the United States. It published 583 of them in 1999, 618 in 2000, 635 in 2001, 732 in 2002, 775 in 2003, 814 in 2004, and 903 in 2005.

Data Sets

Of course, empirical discovery depends on data, so extra computer power would be of little use without additional data. Luckily, the collection and publication of data has itself been facilitated by computers.

241

Chapter 1 described two important data sets: the historical GDP and population data developed by economic historians like Angus Maddison; and the cross-country GDP data in the Penn World Tables. Chapter 2 went on to describe the impact the evidence had on growth theory. Many national statistical offices and other collectors of data now make their figures available easily and often free or very cheaply online. As well as macroeconomic aggregates it is often now possible to find statistics on industries, on groups of households, and on subnational geographic areas.

There has also been substantial growth in the number of panel data sets and surveys, which follow a cross section of specific individuals over time—usually people or households, but increasingly individual firms. Countries like the United States and the United Kingdom are blessed with a growing number of these which collect a great deal of detailed information about specific individuals or households over time. The pathbreaking survey is the Panel Study of Income Dynamics set up at the University of Michigan in the 1960s, but for a long time it was the only such example. Within the past ten years the number of surveys in the United States and Europe has mushroomed. The British Household Panel Survey, for instance, started in 1991 and tracks the same representative panel of 10,300 individuals, with every member of 5,500 households interviewed. The Millennium Cohort Study is following nearly 19,000 children born in 2000–1, collecting information on their health and education as well as their families' income, geographical and social context; it over-samples children from poor and ethnic-minority backgrounds, and includes detailed information about their mothers including her health and living conditions during pregnancy. Surveys such as these are proliferating in all the rich countries, and there is also a growing amount of survey work being carried out in poor countries.

The earliest of these newer surveys are therefore now reaching maturity, with ten to twenty years' worth of data. They are allowing for the first time a wealth of rigorous empirical research on social and economic questions. The reason I started this book with a chapter on historical data reflects the importance I think the collection of masses of data will hold for economics. The statisticians building these data sets are our fossil hunters.

Econometric Techniques

Alongside the availability of the data has come the development of better econometric techniques. The 2000 Nobel memorial prize was awarded to

James Heckman and Daniel McFadden for their fundamental contributions to microeconometrics, the development of statistical techniques now used throughout the social sciences, to be applied in answering questions about individuals' choices and life chances. The techniques they developed deal with the structure of the typical panel data set. For example, choices are discrete (not continuous) because people face a limited set of choices, such as going to college or not, or living in one of half a dozen neighborhoods. Samples are often not random, and might have characteristics which aren't observable or for which there are no data. So, for instance, if you want to test hypotheses about the impact of wages on how many hours people work, there will only be data on wages for those actually working, and you won't have information on what wages were on offer to those who are not working.

In his Nobel autobiographical essay Daniel McFadden (like James Buchanan, a child of the rural south who used to have to milk cows, and now runs his own small farm) explains that the origin of his work lies in his interest in psychology and how individuals make choices (available at http://nobelprize.org/economics/laureates/2000/mcfadden-autobio.html). This led him to develop the "multinomial logit" model now widely used in applied microeconomics. He writes:

> A common theme of my research has been an emphasis on tightly binding economic theory and the problem of economic measurement and analysis, and on developing theoretical and statistical tools that expand the options available to applied economists. I have a strong appreciation for elegant and innovative mathematics and statistics, but as a matter of scientific priority try to keep my research focused on concrete applications, and provide templates for applied economists to follow.

What's particularly beautiful about the microeconometric work is precisely the way it weaves together the economic analysis and the statistical methodology. The model and the empirical evaluation fit seamlessly together, and today's microeconometricians are familiar with the nooks and crannies of their vast data sets in a way which impresses us old-timers no end. In the old days, we'd develop a theoretical model and have to scrabble around to find some data to test it against, making do with whatever data we could find. Now, an applied microeconomist will be aware of both the implications of the theoretical approach and the characteristics of the data, and the modeling and testing will go hand in hand.

It isn't just in microeconometrics, though, that there has been tremendous technical advance. In 2003 Robert Engle and Clive Granger won the

Nobel for their contributions to macroeconometrics, the statistical analysis of time series such as GDP, inflation, stock prices, and so on. Previously, macroeconomists had been unable to correct for common characteristics of time series data, such as periods of turbulence followed by periods of calm in stock prices (volatility which varies over time) or the fact that many aggregate variables such as GDP do not fluctuate around a fixed average but have a strong time trend. This meant that econometric estimates well into the 1980s were invalid, a problem that most macroeconomists were simply unaware of. Engle and Granger changed that, and within a few years the problem was understood, and the techniques they had developed were widely used. Having started my career as a time series econometrician excited by these innovations, I've become steadily more skeptical about the usefulness of macroeconometrics—more sympathetic to the idea that nonlinear relationships and spillovers make it a mug's game to try to estimate stable aggregate models or produce macroeconomic forecasts. When I see how much weight economists place on linear regressions using poor-quality, short time series from developing countries, say, I worry a lot. I'm not alone, either. Econometricians such as David Hendry address exactly these concerns in their careful treatment of time series data, and some economists such as Paul Ormerod go much further, not using times series econometrics at all (see, for example, Clements and Hendry 2002; Ormerod 2000).

I'm not at all sure that the best-practice techniques are used yet by all macroeconomists over the age of forty-five working outside academia. Equally, not all microeconometricians have caught up with best practice. The availability of cheap computer power and easy-to-use software does still encourage sloppy applied work. But there's no excuse for it now.

Simulations

Another technical development enabled by computers is the use of simulations. As discussed earlier in this book, one of the appeals of the textbook model (rational, identical agents, linear equations, and so forth) was its analytical tractability. This kind of model can be solved and estimated econometrically. More recent theoretical approaches, whether in behavioral economics or drawing on network theory or introducing nonlinearities and spillovers in a model of endogenous growth or increasing returns to scale in industry, is not so neat analytically. But it doesn't matter: it's now possible to simulate the results of the new types of model. For example, Thomas Schelling's model of neighborhood segregation can easily be set up on a computer.[7] The simulations make it easy to see, visibly on screen, the emergent properties of a nonlinear model with nonidentical individuals. It is easy to see how much difference a change in particular parameters will make, or to work backwards and calibrate the kinds of outcome from the simulations to observed data to see the implications for the parameters of the model.

Paul Ormerod, of the consultancy Volterra Economics, specializes in this kind of work. He describes one project as follows:

> When we were looking at how a market in permits to pollute might evolve, we could not examine any actual markets, for the simple reason that they do not exist. We were obliged to create artificial economies on the computer, populating them with agents following specified rules of behavior. Our focus of interest was in a *macro* phenomenon of this system—the evolution of the price of permits. This *emerged* from the decisions and interactions of the individual, *micro* agents in the model.

I heartily agree with Paul—who, by the way, as the author of *The Death of Economics* (Ormerod 1994), sees himself as one of those beleaguered "heterodox" economists attacking the citadel of conventional mainstream—when he says that students should be taught this technique in their macroeconomics courses.

Experiments

Another innovation of the past decade or so is the increasing use of experimental laboratories, especially in policy areas such as auction design or market design, or in areas of research such as consumer theory. While this approach has permeated less widely in universities than the new microeconometric and macroeconometric techniques, the behavioral economics on which the experiments draw is firmly established within research centers in several major American and European universities. I suspect the extent to which experimental economics spreads will depend on the future of relations between behavioral and conventional economics. Behavioral economics is clearly incredibly fruitful and poses important challenges to the conventional approach. Its practical applications will ensure it becomes an increasingly vigorous area of research

---

[7] Examples can be found on the web, for example at www.brookings.edu/es/dynamics/models/default.htm. See also an excellent article on these computer simulation models by Jonathan Rauch in the *Atlantic Monthly*: www.theatlantic.com/issues/2002/04/rauch.htm.

(after all it netted £22 billion for the British government from one auction; it's the kind of result that buys a lot of intellectual credibility). But it will remain a thriving island until economists work out how to integrate it with existing approaches.

Game Theory

Moving on to the theoretical innovations of the past twenty years, game theory would be at the top of many economists' league table. It's been so important that Hollywood made a movie about it, *A Beautiful Mind*, based on the life of Nobel laureate John Nash.[8] And Hollywood probably chose exactly the right innovation in economics to single out (much as we might hope for a whole string of films with economists as heros). Here's one appraisal from inside the profession: "The formulation of Nash equilibrium has had a fundamental and pervasive impact in economics and the social sciences which is comparable to the discovery of the DNA double helix in the biological sciences" (Myerson 1999).

There's no doubt that the concept of the Nash equilibrium, when no individual can do better for themselves given the strategies of all the other players, is incredibly powerful. It's so powerful that evolutionary biologists adopted it as their preferred technique. Almost any situation can be understood as a game with an equilibrium of this kind. For this reason the use of game theory has without question extended the reach of economics, into the broad analysis of incentives in social life. It has also massively enriched the central terrain of economics itself by providing a technique which does not require individuals to be identical or have the same information, and which can accommodate rich institutional frameworks and illuminate why in practice there might be multiple potential equilibrium outcomes. It allows economists to study interactions involving small numbers of people, as opposed to the masses who make up a market. Game theory provides a common analytical structure for the study of a huge array of social interactions. Its critics make two main points. One is that, like conventional economics, it often relies on rational choice, an assumption which we know doesn't always hold, and perhaps is especially flawed in the case of "noneconomic" decisions, which the economics profession is colonizing. However, game theory does not depend on the assumption of rational choice—for example, it can be applied to natural selection among "blind" strategies. The second

---

[8]If you've only seen the movie, read Sylvia Nasar's book too.

criticism is that it omits the social context of people's interactions when they make their choices—we saw Mark Granovetter make this point in the last chapter. However, it's in the nature of using models that they simplify away from this kind of detail. Game theory is a profoundly important and useful technique. It extends the fundamental methodology of economics to any aspect of human society.

This is a good point for a small digression on "economic imperialism." In his discussion of the extension of economic methodology to other subjects, Edward Lazear says: "It is its obsession with theories that are consistent, rational and unifying that gives economics its power" (Lazear 2000). While true, this description characterized the pre-imperialist economics of the 1960s and 1970s too. Game theory is the tool which made it possible to apply the assumptions of rationality and equilibrium, and a clear concept of efficiency, to other subject areas. But I don't think game theory is the final word in terms of techniques. I predict that economists will happily adopt other techniques, such as the agent-based computer models, and use them as tools to apply economic methodology to any area of life that arouses our interest. The development of new techniques, including game theory, is returning economics to the breadth of interest it displayed in pre-neoclassical days (Kreps 1997).

Increasing Returns to Scale

The final area of innovation I'd like to highlight, another one involving the delighted embrace of new intellectual tools by economists, is nonlinear dynamic modeling. In this book I presented the introduction of feedbacks which made models nonlinear in the context of endogenous growth theory, but nonlinearity was introduced in several different contexts at about the same time. At the same time as Paul David and Brian Arthur were introducing these concepts in innovation theory and economic history, Paul Krugman was applying them to international trade theory and Michael Spence and others to industrial organization.[9] Along with a few other economists, Krugman revived interest in the field of economic geography—whether applied to the international location of production and its consequences for international trade and

---

[9]While many readers will know Paul Krugman best for his anti-Bush polemics in the *New York Times*, many of his fellow economists think he would probably deserve the Nobel prize for his work on increasing-returns models in trade and economic geography if only he would quit dabbling in politics.

247

investment flows, or the regional location of activity within a country—and the implications for urban policy. This is an amazingly rich and interesting literature, which I didn't have the scope to cover in this book.[10]

In addition to electrifying the study of urban economics and economic geography, and completely transforming international trade theory, the same broad style of models incorporating increasing returns to scale also enriched the everyday models of industrial economics, looking at how companies compete and what kind of structure characterizes an industry. Part of the enrichment was that increasing returns, rather than the diminishing returns to scale of the old conventional model, are so evident a feature of real-life industries. Part is that the fundamental insight about growth and trade, going back to Smith and Ricardo, is the existence of gains from specialization, and the old models didn't include a mechanism or rationale for specialization. Krugman originally argued that the pervasiveness of increasing returns in industries engaged in trade justified government trade policies that intervened in the operation of markets, because the welfare benefits of competition depend on the assumption of diminishing returns. That is, when there are diminishing returns to increased output, it will be better to have more firms rather than fewer. With increasing returns, the opposite conclusions follow, and a monopoly might be the most efficient market structure, especially if you're the U.S. administration, say, and it's an American monopolist. This was controversial, to say the least. Krugman retreated from his advocacy of "managed trade," I think because it immediately became the excuse used by every special-interest group in Washington to get extra protection from competition. Besides, it was apparent that the early models would not be the last word on industrial economics, and a lot more research would be needed on questions such as incentives to innovate in an increasing-returns world.

This program of research, another area I haven't found room for here, has also flourished, and overlaps with the business economics described briefly in chapter 7. Where economists always used to work with linear models, which required the often uncomfortable assumption of decreasing or constant returns to scale, now in any specialism we can draw on an increasing-returns model incorporating nonlinear feedbacks.

---

[10]I commend Fujita et al. (1999) for a textbook introduction, and Ed Glaeser's papers on urban economics, as starting points for this area of research.

WHAT'S STILL WRONG WITH ECONOMICS?

Every so often I meet Paul Ormerod for lunch, and it's always very enjoyable because we share the same interests and agree with each other a lot. Yet Paul is highly critical of mainstream economics, whereas I'm a huge admirer of the work of the leading academic economists. He describes the reactions of his peers to his excellent books, which cover complexity, emergence, evolutionary models, and so on, as follows:

> I like to think that, in private, more of them than would care to admit had some degree of sympathy with my arguments. In public, however, the reaction was twofold. Either, "this book is completely wrong." Or, "we already know everything in it." Some reviewers managed to hold both these opinions at the same time.

So I suppose I fall into the "we already know this" camp.

Where I have to agree with him, though, is that while the leading economists are doing fantastic work—described in the earlier chapters—what we teach our students has changed only slowly over twenty-five years. About half the material covered in this book will have found its way into the basic graduate and some undergraduate courses. The rest arrives on the scene at the point when graduate students can opt to take specialized courses. What is more, the basic introduction to the subject is still the simplest version of the standard paradigm. Browsing through the latest textbooks, they've moved on a long way. Microeconomics texts include monopolistic competition, behavior under uncertainty, game theory, and asymmetric information, for example, and macro texts have started to incorporate increasing-returns models and endogenous growth theory. Still, they start from the same place as they used to, and present these areas of new research as the icing on a perfectly lovely cake.

John Sutton, a superb industrial economist at the London School of Economics, opens his book questioning conventional economic methodology by noting that the new economics student ask two obvious questions: Are people really rational? Can you really capture important points about messy reality in a simple model? He writes:

> By the time that students are a couple of years into their studies, both these questions are forgotten. Those students that remain troubled by them have quit the field; those who remain are socialized and no longer ask about such things.
>
> Sutton (2000, p. xv)

249

As he argues in the book (which focuses on the use and abuse of models), they are difficult questions and should be treated seriously by educators. It shouldn't require six years of tertiary education before young economists meet deep issues of methodology and some of the areas of the subject which are most challenging to the core methodology.

Of course, it takes many years before the best practice in any subject filters out to all those practitioners who graduated a long time ago. This isn't a problem specific to economics, and indeed most of the nonacademic economists I know are enthralled by the frontiers of research in our subject. This stuff is much, much more interesting than the proofs of the existence and uniqueness of general equilibrium and the debates about the superiority of the Brouwer over the Kakutani fixed point theorem that we all had to sit through when we were young. The arcana of general equilibrium theory should be struck out of the curriculum without hesitation. Although I hope to have persuaded some doubters that economics has made huge advances during the past quarter century, and is a ferment of intellectual excitement, I accept that critics of mainstream economics have a point until we economists teach what we preach.[11]

There are other problems in the economics ivory tower. One serious issue is the dysfunctionality of journal publishing. The leading journals are extraordinarily dominant and consequently receive many more submissions than they can publish. Some nine-tenths will be rejected, often after unacceptably long delays. No wonder many academic economists are themselves growing bitter about their subject. I know of few economists who do not rely primarily on email circulation of working papers and the principal working paper series (for example, those published by the National Bureau of Economic Research in the United States or the Centre for Economic Policy Research in the United Kingdom) to keep up to date. But this is no use to young tenure-track academics who need the formal publication of journal articles under their belt. Academic economics is also an extraordinarily male-dominated subject which I am certain skews the choice of research carried out by economists. Having said this, there can hardly be any subject which does not have its problems in the academy these days: universities are struggling to adapt to new social and economic realities just as much as any other institutions.

---

[11] See Colander (2005) for further specific concerns about U.S. graduate education in economics. He too argues that economics has changed profoundly but pedagogy has not kept pace.

WHAT KIND OF SUBJECT IS ECONOMICS NOW?

I'm optimistic that we're not too far away from a core curriculum in economics which reflects the advances I've been describing here. When I pitched up for my first ever tutorials in economics in 1978 (taught by Peter Sinclair and Tony Courakis), everything we learnt adhered to the key assumptions of the neoclassical orthodoxy:

- identical, independent agents;
- utility maximization;
- rational choice;
- complete, symmetric information;
- fixed preferences;
- unique equilibrium outcomes.

We had little access to computers, the widespread econometric techniques were statistically naive, and everything we learnt in macroeconomics was unrelated to the highly formalized microeconomics based on all the above assumptions. We also added restrictive assumptions (such as diminishing returns and simple linear relationships) to ensure we could solve models analytically. A young and eager student of my idealized new economic mainstream today would not need these additional assumptions, nor would she need to assume that individuals are all the same, make their choices independently of each other, or have access to the same information. She could accommodate multiple equilibria, and could regard macroeconomic phenomena as the emergent outcome of uncoordinated individual decisions. She would have a rich array of market design mechanisms and industry structures at her fingertips. And she would early on form the habit of interlinking theory and econometric results based on rich data sets, derived using a laptop that would fit into her handbag.

Well, it is still an ideal rather than a reality, but not all that distant. And it's the combination of new techniques and computer power, described above, which make economics today a fantastically exciting subject. Every academic journal you pick up, and the working papers available online, point to the wealth of empirical discovery taking place in economics.

The key elements of economic methodology, unchanged from the classical days, are the status of rational choice and the use of equilibrium as a modeling concept. If these are limitations, so be it: every subject has

251

core restrictions in its methodology, which in fact represent its strengths and distinctive insights. It's not that we believe that everybody chooses rationally all the time—on the contrary, the most orthodox of economists is interested in learning from behavioral research. Nor do we think the economy is always in equilibrium. That would be just as silly. Nevertheless, both elements are core to our way of thinking.

Rational choice is distinct from self-interested choice, but self-interest too is a powerful assumption. Here's how Partha Dasgupta (2005a) expresses the point about self-interest in his paper:

> Being self-regarding in the private sphere isn't the same as being immoral, nor is it the same as being amoral.... [T]o ignore the existence of the self when discussing the moral basis of a social order and thereby to neglect matters of incentives is to create social theories out of thin air.

And here's Edward Lazear:

> We may permit imperfect information, transaction costs and other intervening variables to muddy the waters, but we do not model behavior as being determined by forces beyond the control of the individual.

The assumption of self-interested, rational, maximizing behavior is often assumed by critics to imply an atomized, ultra-individualistic view of the world; but the opposite is true. Choices by one individual always have consequences for others. It's the choice-based models of economics rather than any other methodology which emphasize the opportunity costs and trade-offs arising from our social and physical existence.

The power of the assumption of equilibrium is similarly a robust framework for analyzing how individuals interact in society. We can accommodate all varieties of actual institutions in our concept of equilibrium, or large spillovers between individual decisions. We hardly ever work with the abstract and unreal "free market" of the critics' caricature, because in economics markets are institutions too and we're very empirically minded. The combination of rational maximizers and the equilibrium concept, in theories tested against a counterfactual and refined by comparison with the data, makes economics incredibly powerful.[12] For all that its practitioners criticize us, the other social sciences don't have

---

[12] Donald MacKenzie makes the interesting argument that economics is "performative," i.e., the subject's influence is shaping the world to be more like an economic model would assume it to be. His main example is the influence of the capital asset pricing model in creating today's financial markets (MacKenzie 2002, 2005).

anything remotely approaching the flexibility and strength of the economic method, nor the capacity of economic models to be honed and tested empirically. As Paul Krugman once put it: "The clarity and power of economic analysis can spoil you: once you have a taste of what it means to have a really insightful model, you tend to be inhibited about looser speculations." That's why Paul Ormerod, for all his sharp criticism of the mainstream, is an economist but John Kenneth Galbraith wasn't.

I predict that during the next ten years the astonishing mapping of our societies taking place now, using modern econometric techniques and new data sets, will start to have a revolutionary impact on public policy. The availability of solid empirical evidence on an array of social issues is, however, going to make economics very controversial. For economics is a technical subject, whose results are sometimes nonintuitive or run counter to common sense. A lot of sacred political cows are heading for the slaughterhouse. The buzz phrase in policy wonk circles these days is "evidence-based policy" (with its rather telling implication that what we had before was something else—"prejudice-based policy" perhaps). What if the evidence suggests you should overturn your old policy? What are the political implications when voters realize that the evidence says (as it clearly does in the United Kingdom) that they pay for the state education system through their taxes and then pay an extra supplement for quality, either directly in private school fees or indirectly in house prices—with the two amounts of money equal at the margin, just as an economist would predict. I suspect the policies won't go quietly.

Does this era of discovery add up to a "new paradigm" in economics? I think the paradigm is unchanged, if that means the essential elements of economic methodology, but economists are unified by a new consensus as to what economics is about. Not the study of competitive markets, but rather an understanding of society as the aggregation of millions of individual decisions, in specific contexts shaped by history and geography, and by our own evolutionary history. Partha Dasgupta says:

> It is a recognition of the commonality of human experience on the one hand and the separateness of every human being and the particularity of the circumstances she faces, on the other, that gives economics its special flavor and is a reason why it is an awesomely difficult subject.

And as Paul Seabright argues in *The Company of Strangers*, it's something of a miracle that we've achieved the level of prosperity and social complexity we see in the rich economies, so perhaps it's not surprising so many countries have failed to match it. But the "What works?" agenda of empirical economic research is one of the most pressing challenges facing the modern world today.

ECONOMICS AND POLICY

To end on a positive note, here are some of the most important areas where economic research of the past decade or two has given policy-makers a robust analysis of and evidence about what does work, and has thereby improved policy and made people's lives better. The list is potentially long, but I've selected just a few that will be uncontroversial among economists.

Transportation investment and pricing. There are many examples of the use of microeconometrics to assess the investment case for transportation projects and work out the most efficient pricing schemes. Nobel laureate Daniel McFadden pioneered this kind of work with his analysis of likely passenger numbers on San Francisco's BART system. A more recent example is the congestion charge levied on cars driving into central London. Not all transport planners make use of good economics, but where they have the efficiency and impact of the schemes has been transformed.

Auctions. Governments should allocate scarce resources—such as the radio spectrum or mineral exploration rights—through auctions. Auctions need to be tailor-made for specific circumstances but when designed appropriately they can allocate the resource in the most efficient way possible and raise significant amounts of money for the government, to the benefit of taxpayers. Auctions are somewhat vulnerable to manipulation or clever players, but the alternative of decision by bureaucrat is extremely vulnerable to inefficiency and corruption.

Monetary policy. Up until the early 1980s macroeconomics was ideologically riven (between "monetarists" and "Keynesians") and policy consequently unstable. The new professional consensus is that monetary policy (i.e., the level of interest rates set by the central bank) should aim to keep inflation low and stable over a medium-term (two-to-three-year) horizon, while using it to expand the economy and increase growth and employment is counterproductive. Inflation is lower and more stable, and growth of GDP is also more stable, in most OECD economies than in earlier decades.

Environmental and other trading schemes. The principles of market design have been applied to new greenhouse gas emission trading schemes in the United States and Europe. With some hiccups—mainly stemming from the special pleading by industry which persuaded governments to be lenient about the initial allocation of emission permits—the markets have operated smoothly and succeeded in reducing industrial emissions of greenhouse gases. The markets have been more successful than regulatory restrictions in reducing emissions.

Competition policy. The influence of economics on competition policy has grown steadily during the past twenty years, and has shaped, for example, the analysis of the effects of mergers on prices and innovation, the costs to consumers of anticompetitive arrangements, and the analysis of the existence and nature of collusion between firms and cartels. There is convincing evidence that a more vigorous competition policy has contributed to keeping prices down and improving the efficiency of U.S. and European businesses.

Contract design under imperfect information. Information economics has transformed the way contracts are drawn up in a range of important areas such as insurance, outsourcing, corporate pay schemes, and public-service provision. Economists have increased awareness of the moral hazard and principal–agent problems in business and public administration, and contributed to the spread of monitoring and targeting schemes intended to ensure that people's incentives are as closely aligned as possible to the desired outcome, whether that's a higher-quality public service or bigger profits for a company.

These are all substantial, and largely overlooked, contributions by economists to our well-being, all the result of developments in economics since about 1980. The scope for economics to improve other areas of policy is enormous, and I hope this book has helped make the case for taking economics more seriously in all areas of public policy.

References

Most of the working papers on information markets cited are down-loadable from www.aei-brookings.org/pages/index.php?id=37 and were accessed on February 20, 2006. All other web papers were accessed May 25, 2006, unless otherwise indicated.

Acemoglu, D., S. Johnson, and J. Robinson. 2002. Reversal of fortune: geography and institutions in the making of the modern world income distribution. MIT mimeo (January 2002; available at http://econ-www.mit.edu/faculty/download_pdf.php?id=613).

Adsera, A., and D. Ray. 1998. History and coordination failure. *Journal of Economic Growth* 3(3):267–76.

Aghion, P., and P. Howitt. 1998. *Endogenous Growth Theory.* Cambridge, MA: MIT Press.

Akerlof, G. A. 1970. The market for "lemons": quality, uncertainty and the market mechanism. *Quarterly Journal of Economics* 84(3):488–500.

Alesina, A., and E. Glaeser. 2004. *Fighting Poverty in the US and Europe: A World of Difference.* Oxford University Press.

Alesina, A., R. Perotti, and J. Tavares. 1998. The political economy of fiscal adjustments. *Brookings Papers on Economic Activity* Spring:197–266.

Allen, R. C. 2003. Progress and poverty in early modern Europe. *Economic History Review* 56(3):403–43.

Allen, R. C., et al. 2004. Preliminary global price comparisons 1500–1870. Utrecht Conference on Global Price and Income History (17 August 2004), Working Paper (July 30, 2004; available at www.iisg.nl/hpw/papers/lindert.pdf).

Andersen, E. S. 1996. *Evolutionary Economics: Post-Schumpeterian Contributions.* London: Pinter.

Arthur, B. 1989. Competing technologies, increasing returns and lock-in by historical events. *Economic Journal* 99:106–31.

Arthur, B., S. Durlauf, and D. Lane (eds). 1997. *The Economy as an Evolving Complex System,* volume II. Addison-Wesley.

Audretsch, D. (ed.). 2006. *Entrepreneurship, Innovation and Growth.* Cheltenham: Edward Elgar.

Axelrod, R. 1984. *The Evolution of Cooperation.* New York: Basic Books.

Axtell, R. 1999. The emergence of firms in a population of agents: local increasing returns, unstable Nash equilibria, and power law size distributions. Brookings Institute CSED Working Paper no. 3 (June 1999).

Bairoch, P. 1967. *Diagnostic de l'evolution economique du tiers-monde 1900–1966*. Paris: Gauthiers-Villars.

Baker, G., and T. Hubbard. 2000. Contractibility and asset ownership: on-board computers and governance in U.S. trucking. National Bureau of Economic Research, Working Paper no. 7634 (April 2000; available at www.nber.org/papers/w7634.pdf).

Ball, P. 2004. *Critical Mass: The Physics of Society*. London: William Heinemann.

Banerjee, A. 1992. A simple model of herd behaviour. *Quarterly Journal of Economics* 117:797–817.

Banerjee, A., S. Cole, E. Duflo, and L. Linden. 2005. Remedying education: evidence from two randomized experiments in India. National Bureau of Economic Research, Working Paper no. 11904 (December 2005; available at http://papers.nber.org/papers/w11904).

Barabasi, A.-L. 2002. *Linked: The New Science of Networks*. New York: Perseus.

Barro, R. J. 1991. Economic growth in a cross-section of countries. *Quarterly Journal of Economics* 106(2):407–43.

———. 1996. *Getting It Right*. Cambridge, MA: MIT Press.

Barro, R. J., and X. Salai-I-Martin. 1995. *Economic Growth*. McGraw-Hill.

Bass, T. 1999. *The Predictors*. Viking Penguin.

Bauer, P. 2000. *From Subsistence to Exchange*. Princeton University Press.

Baumol, W. J. 1972. *Economic Theory and Operations Analysis*. Upper Saddle River, NJ: Prentice Hall.

———. 2002. *The Free-Market Innovation Machine*. Princeton University Press.

———. Forthcoming. *Elementary Theory of Entrepreneurship, Innovation and Oligopolistic R&D*. In the press.

Bell, D. 1974. *The Coming of Post-Industrial Society*. London: William Heinemann.

Best, M. 2001. *The New Competititve Advantage*. Oxford University Press.

Beveridge, W. H. 1968. *Power and Influence*. London: Hodder & Stoughton.

Blackmore, S. 1999. *The Meme Machine*. Oxford University Press.

Blanchflower, D., and A. Oswald. 2000. Well-being over time in Britain and the USA. National Bureau of Economic Research, Working Paper no. 7487 (available at http://papers.nber.org/papers/w7487).

———. 2004a. Well-being over time in Britain and the USA. *Journal of Public Economics* 88:1359–86.

———. 2004b. Money, sex, and happiness: an empirical study. *Scandinavian Journal of Economics* 106:393–416.

Blaug, M. 1996. *Economic Theory in Retrospect* (first published 1962, by Richard D. Irwin Inc.). Cambridge University Press.

Boskin Commission. 1996. Toward a more accurate measure of the cost of living: final report to the Senate Finance Committee from the Advisory Commission to Study The Consumer Price Index (December 4, 1996; available at www.ssa.gov/history/reports/boskinrpt.html, accessed July 12, 2006).

Bourguignon, F., and D. Coyle. 2003. Inequality, public perception and the institutional responses to globalisation. *Moneda y Credito* 216:211–50.

Bourguignon, F., and C. Morrison. 2002. Inequality among world citizens: 1820–1992. *American Economic Review* 92(4):727–44.

Bowles, S. 1998. Endogenous preferences: the cultural consequences of markets and other economic institutions. *Journal of Economic Literature* 31:75–111.

———. 2004. *Microeconomics: Behaviour, Institutions and Evolution.* Princeton University Press.

Bowles, S., and H. Gintis. 1993. The revenge of Homo Economicus: contested exchange and the revival of political economy. *Journal of Economic Perspectives* 7(1):83–102.

———. 1999. The evolution of strong reciprocity. University of Massachussetts Working Paper (available at www-unix.oit.umass.edu/~bowles, accessed May 11, 2006).

———. 2002. Social capital and community governance. *Economic Journal* 112: F419–36.

Boyle, G., and S. Videbeck. 2005. A primer on information markets. Victoria University of Wellington (July 26, 2005; available at www.iscr.org.nz/documents/primerinfomarkets.pdf).

Bradley, J. 2005. Committing to growth in a small European country. In *New Wealth for Old Nations* (ed. D. Coyle, W. Alexander, and B. Ashcroft). Princeton University Press.

Braudel, F. 1985. *Civilisation and Capitalism,* three volumes. London: Fontana.

Breit, W., and B. Hirsch. 2005. *Lives of the Laureates,* 14th edn. Cambridge, MA: MIT Press.

Broadberry, S., and B. Gupta. 2006. The early modern great divergence: wages, prices and economic development. *Economic History Review* 59:2–31.

Brockway, G. 1995. *Economists Can Be Bad for Your Health.* New York: W. W. Norton.

———. 2001. *The End of Economic Man.* New York: W. W. Norton.

Browne, J. 2001. *Charles Darwin: Voyaging.* London: Pimlico.

Brynjolfsson, E., and L. M. Hitt. 2000. Beyond computation: information technology, organizational transformation and business performance. *Journal of Economic Perspectives* 14(4):23–48.

Buchan, J. 1995. The poverty of economics. *Prospect* December:29–32.

Buchanan, J. M., and G. Tullock. 1962. *The Calculus of Consent: Logical Foundations of a Constitutional Democracy.* Ann Arbor, MI: University of Michigan Press.

Burki, S. J., and G. Perry (eds). 1998. *Beyond the Washington Consensus: Institutions Matter.* Washington, DC: World Bank.

Burnside, C., and D. Dollar. 2000. Aid, policies and growth. *American Economic Review* 90(4):847–69.

Camerer, C. F. 2003. The behavioural challenge to economics: understanding normal people. Paper prepared for Federal Reserve Bank of Boston conference (June 2003).

Camerer, C. F., and E. Fehr. 2006. When does "economic man" dominate social behavior? *Science* 311:47–52.

Camerer, C. F., G. Loewenstein, and D. Prelec. 2004a. Neuroeconomics: why economics needs brains. *Scandinavian Journal of Economics* 106(3):555–79.

Camerer, C. F., G. Loewenstein, and M. Rabin. 2004b. *Advances in Behavioural Economics.* Princeton University Press.

Camerer, C. F., G. Loewenstein, and D. Prelec. 2005. Neuroeconomics: how neuroscience can inform economics. *Journal of Economic Literature* 43:9–64.

Caplan, B. 2002. Systematically biased beliefs about economics: robust evidence of judgmental anomalies from the survey of Americans and economists on the economy. *Economic Journal* 112:433–58.

Christensen, C. M. 1997. *The Innovator's Dilemma: When New Technologies Cause Great Firms to Fail.* Boston, MA: Harvard Business School Press.

Clark, C. 1940. *Conditions of Economic Progress.* Macmillan.

Clark, G. 2005. *The Economics of the Ascent of Man: A Brief Economic History of the World.* Princeton University Press.

Clements, M. P., and D. F. Hendry. 2002. *A Companion to Economic Forecasting.* Oxford: Blackwell.

Coase, R. 1937. The nature of the firm. *Economica* 4:386–405.

———. 1960. The problem of social cost. *Journal of Law and Economics* 3:1–44.

Cohen, J. D. 2005. The vulcanization of the human brain. *Journal of Economic Perspectives* 19(4):3–24.

Colander, D. 2005. The making of an economist redux. *Journal of Economic Perspectives* 19(1):175–98.

Colander, D., and A. Klamer. 1987. The making of an economist. *Journal of Economic Perspectives* 12(4):95–111.

Cole, A. H. 1974. *The Birth of a New Social Science Discipline: Achievements of the First Generation of American Economic and Business Historians—1893–1974* (available at www.eh.net/misc/birth.html). Santa Clara, CA: Economic History Association.

Cole, A. H., and R. Crandall. 1964. The international scientific committee on price history. *Journal of Economic History* 24(3):381–88.

Collier, P., and J. W. Gunning. 1999. Why has Africa grown slowly? *Journal of Economic Perspectives* 13(3):3–22.

Coyle, D. 1997. *The Weightless World.* Cambridge, MA: MIT Press.

———. 2001. *Paradoxes of Prosperity.* London: Texere.

———. 2003. Corporate governance, public governance and global governance: the common thread. IPEG Working Paper no. 3, University of Manchester (December 2003).

Coyle, D., W. Alexander, and B. Ashcroft. 2005. *New Wealth for Old Nations.* Princeton University Press.

Crafts, N. 1991. *British Economic Growth during the Industrial Revolution* (first published 1985). Clarendon.

———. 1999. Economic growth in the twentieth century. *Oxford Review of Economic Policy* 15(4):18–34.

Crafts, N. 2004. Steam as a general purpose technology: a growth accounting perspective. *Economic Journal* 114:338-51.

Crafts, N., and C. K. Harley. 1992. Output growth and the British Industrial Revolution: a restatement of the Crafts-Harley view. *Economic History Review* 45: 703-30.

Daly, H. 1996. *Beyond Growth*. Boston, MA: Beacon.

Darwin, C. 1982. *On The Origin of Species by Means of Natural Selection: Or the Preservation of Favoured Races in the Struggle for Life* (first published 1859). Penguin.

Dasgupta, P. 1998. Modern economics and its critics. Working Paper (February 1998; available at www.econ.cam.ac.uk/faculty/dasgupta/modecon.pdf).

———. 2005a. What do economists analyze and why: values or facts? *Economics and Philosophy* 21:221-78.

———. 2005b. Economics of social capital. *Economic Record* 81(S1):S2-21.

———. 2005c. Mathematics and economic reasoning. Working Paper (June 2005; available at www.econ.cam.ac.uk/faculty/dasgupta/mathematics.pdf).

Dasgupta, P., and I. Serageldin. 1988. *Social Capital: A Multifaceted Perspective*. Washington, DC: World Bank.

David, P. A. 1985. Clio and the economics of QWERTY. *The American Economic Review* 75(2):332-37.

———. 1991. Computer and dynamo: the modern productivity paradox in a not-too-distant mirror. In *Technology and Productivity*. OECD.

Davis, M. 2006. *Planet of Slums*. London: Verso Books.

Dawkins, R. 2004. *The Ancestor's Tale*. London: Weidenfeld & Nicolson.

———. 2006. *The Selfish Gene* (first published 1976). Oxford University Press.

Deane, P., and W. A. Cole. 1962. *British Economic Growth, 1688-1959: Trends and Structure*, 2nd edn. Cambridge University Press.

De Soto, H. 2000. *The Mystery of Capital*. New York: Bantam.

Diamond, J. 1997. *Guns, Germs and Steel*. London: Jonathan Cape.

———. 2005. *Collapse: How Societies Choose to Fail or Succeed*. Viking Penguin.

Dixit, A., and J. Stiglitz. 1976. Monopolistic competition and optimal product diversity. *American Economic Review* 67(3):297-308.

Dollar, D., and A. Kray. 2002. Growth is good for the poor. *Journal of Economic Growth* 7:195-225.

Dougherty, P. J. 2002. *Who's Afraid of Adam Smith? How the Market Got Its Soul*. John Wiley.

Dubner, S. J., and S. D. Levitt. 2005. Monkey business: Keith Chen's monkey research. *New York Times*, June 5, 2005.

Easterlin, R. A. 1981. Why isn't the whole world developed? *Journal of Economic History* 41(1):1-19.

———. 1995. Will raising the income of all increase the happiness of all? *Journal of Economic Behavior and Organization* 27(1):35-47.

———. 2000. The worldwide standard of living since 1800. *Journal of Economic Perspectives* 14(1):7-26.

261

Easterlin, R. A. 2001. Income and happiness: towards a unified theory. *Economic Journal* 111:465–84.

Easterly, W. 2001. *The Elusive Quest for Growth.* Cambridge, MA: MIT Press.

———. 2006. *White Man's Burden.* Penguin.

Easterly, W., and R. Levine. 2003. Tropics, germs and crops: how endowments influence economic development. *Journal of Monetary Economics* 50(1):3–39.

Fehr, E., and S. Gächter. 2000. Fairness and retaliation: the economics of reciprocity. *Journal of Economic Perspectives* 14(3):159–81.

Fehr, E., and J.-R. Tyran. 2005. Individual irrationality and aggregate outcomes. *Journal of Economic Perspectives* 19(4):43–66.

Ferguson, N. 2004. *Empire: How Britain Made the Modern World.* Penguin.

Fogel, R. 1999. Catching up with the economy. *American Economic Review* 89: 1–21.

Foucault, M. 1977. *Discipline and Punish: The Birth of the Prison.* London: Vintage.

Frank, R. 2003. *What Price the Moral High Ground? Ethical Dilemmas in Competitive Environments.* Princeton University Press.

Frederick, S. 2005. Cognitive reflection and decision making. *Journal of Economic Perspectives* 19(4):25–42.

Freeman, C., and F. Louca. 2001. *As Time Goes By.* Oxford University Press.

Frey, B., and A. Stutzer. 2002. *Happiness and Economics.* Princeton University Press.

Friedman, B. M. 2005. *The Moral Consequence of Economic Growth.* New York: Alfred Knopf.

Fujita, M., P. Krugman, and A. Venables. 1999. *The Spatial Economy.* Cambridge, MA: MIT Press.

Fukuyama, F. 1996. *Trust: The Social Virtues and the Creation of Prosperity* (first published 1995). Penguin.

Fullbrook, E. 2002. A brief history of the post-autistic economics movement (August 2002; available at www.paecon.net/#_A_Brief_History).

———. 2005. Post-autistic economics. From *Soundings* (Spring 2005; available at www.paecon.net/PAEarticles/Fullbrook1.htm).

Galbraith, J. K. 1991. *The Affluent Society,* paperback edition (first published 1958). Penguin.

Garnett, R. F. 2005. Whither heterodoxy? *Post-autistic Economics Review* 34: Article 1 (available at www.paecon.net/PAEReview/issue34/Garnett34.htm).

Georgescu-Roegen, N. 2006. *The Entropy Law and the Economic Process* (first published 1971). Cambridge, MA: Harvard University Press.

Geroski, P. 2003. *The Evolution of New Markets.* Oxford University Press.

Geroski, P., and C. Markides. 2005. *Fast Second.* Chichester: Jossey Bass.

Gerschenkron, A. 1962. *Economic Backwardness in Historical Perspective: A Book of Essays.* Cambridge, MA: Belknap Press of Harvard University Press.

Giuso, L., P. Sapienza, and L. Zingales. 2006. Does culture affect economic outcomes? *Journal of Ecomomic Perspectives* 20(2):23–48.

Gladwell, M. 2000. *The Tipping Point.* London: Little, Brown.

Glaeser, E. 2003. Reinventing Boston: 1640–2003. Harvard Institute of Economic Research, Discussion Paper 2017 (September 2003; available at www.economics.harvard.edu/hier/2003papers/HIER2017.pdf).

——. 2005. Paternalism and psychology. Harvard Institute of Economic Research, Discussion Paper 2097 (December 2005; available at www.economics.harvard.edu/hier/2005papers/HIER2097.pdf).

Glaeser, E., and J. Scheinkman. 2000. Non-market interactions. National Bureau of Economic Research Working Paper no. 8053 (December 2000).

Glaeser, E., J. Scheinkman, and A. Schleifer. 1995. Economic growth in a cross-section of cities. *Journal of Monetary Economics* 36:117–43.

Glaeser, E., B. Sacerdote, and J. Scheinkman. 1996. Crime and social interactions. *Quarterly Journal of Economics* 111:507–48.

Glaeser, E., D. Laibson, J. Scheinkman, and C. Soutter. 2000. Measuring trust. *Quarterly Journal of Economics* 65:811–46.

Glaeser, E., D. Laibson, and B. Sacerdote. 2002. The economic approach to social capital. *Economic Journal* 112:437–58.

Glaeser, E., R. La Porta, F. Lopez de Silanes, and A. Schleifer. 2004. Do institutions cause growth? *Journal of Economic Growth* 9:271–304.

Gordon, R. J. 1999. US economic growth since 1870: one big wave? *American Economic Review, Papers and Proceedings* 89(2):123–28.

——. 2000. Does the new economy measure up to the great inventions of the past? *Journal of Economic Perspectives* 14(4):49–74.

Granovetter, M. 1973. The strength of weak ties. *American Journal of Sociology* 78:1360–80.

——. 1985. Economic action and social structure: the problem of embeddedness. *American Journal of Sociology* 91(3):481–510.

Greif, A. 1994. Cultural beliefs and the organisation of society: a historical and theoretical reflection on collectivist and individualist societies. *Journal of Political Economy* 102(5):912–50.

Grossman, G. M., and E. Helpman. 1991. *Innovation and Growth in the Global Economy.* Cambridge, MA: MIT Press.

Hahn, R. W., and P. C. Tetlock. 2005. Big ideas: the market's last frontier. AEI–Brookings Joint Center for Regulatory Studies, Working Paper (February 2005).

Harford, T. 2003. All bets are off at the Pentagon. *Financial Times,* September 1, 2003, p. 14.

Hayek, F. A. 1945. The use of knowledge in society. *American Economic Review* 35(4):519–30.

Heilbroner, R. 1993. *21st Century Capitalism.* New York: W. W. Norton.

——. 2000. *The Worldly Philosophers* (first published 1953). Penguin.

Heilbroner, R., and W. Milberg. 1995. *The Crisis of Vision in Modern Economic Thought.* Cambridge University Press.

Helpman, E. 2004. *The Mystery of Economic Growth.* Cambridge, MA: Belknap Press of Harvard University Press.

Helpman, E., and P. Krugman. 1985. *Market Structre and Foreign Trade*. Cambridge, MA: MIT Press.

Hodgson, G. M. 1998. The approach of institutional economics. *Journal of Economic Literature* 36(1):166–92.

——. 2005. Generalising Darwinism to social evolution: some early attempts. *Journal of Economic Issues* 39(4):899–915.

Jacobs, J. 1985. *Cities and the Wealth of Nations: Principles of Economic Life*. New York: Vintage Books.

Jaffe, A., and J. Lerner. 2004. *Innovation and Its Discontents*. Princeton University Press.

Jaffe, A., and M. Trachtenberg. 2002. *Patents, Citations and Innovations*. Cambridge, MA: MIT Press.

James, W. 1880. Great men, great thoughts and the environment. *Atlantic Monthly* 46:441–59.

Johnson, S. 2004. *Emergence*. Penguin.

Jorgenson, D. W., and Z. Griliches. 1967. The explanation of productivity change. *Review of Economic Studies* 34:249–80.

Jorgenson, D. W., and E. Yip. 2000. Whatever happened to productivity growth? In *New Developments in Productivity Analysis* (ed. C. R. Hulten, E. R. Dean, and M. J. Harper), pp. 509–40. University of Chicago Press.

Kahneman, D. 2003a. Maps of bounded rationality: psychology for behavioural economics. *American Economic Review*:1429–71.

——. 2003b. A psychological perspective on economics. *American Economic Review, Papers and Proceedings* 93(2):162–69.

Kahneman, D., A. B. Krueger, D. Schkade, N. Schwarz, and A. Stone. 2004. Toward national well-being accounts. *American Economic Review* 94(2):429–34.

Kay, J. 1993. *Foundations of Corporate Success*. Oxford University Press.

Kenny, C. 2005. Why are we worried about income? Nearly everything that matters is converging. *World Development* 33(1):1–19.

Keynes, J. M. 1995. *The Economic Consequences of the Peace* (first published 1920). Penguin.

Kirman, A. 1993. Ants, rationality and recruitment. *Quarterly Journal of Economics* 108(1):137–56.

Klein, D. B., and C. Stern. 2005. Narrow-tent democrats and fringe others. University of Stockholm Working Paper (available at www.sofi.su.se/wp/WP05-8.pdf).

Knack, S., and P. Keefer. 1997a. Why don't poor countries catch up? A cross-national test of an institutional explanation. *Economic Inquiry* 35:590–602.

——. 1997b. Does social capital have an economic payoff? A cross-country investigation. *Quarterly Journal of Economics* 112:1251–88.

Kremer, M. 1993. Population growth and technical change: one million BC to 1990. *Quarterly Journal of Economics* 108(3):681–716.

Kreps, D. 1997. Economics—the current position. *Daedalus* 126(1):59–86.

Krugman, P. 1980. Scale economics, product differentiation and the pattern of trade. *American Economic Review* 70:950–59.

Krugman, P. 1991a. Increasing returns and economic geography. *Journal of Political Economy* 99:483–99.

——. 1991b. *Geography and Trade.* Cambridge, MA: MIT press.

——. 1991c. History versus expectations. *Quarterly Journal of Economics* 106(2): 651–67.

——. 1993. On the number and location of cities. *European Economic Review* 37:293–98.

——. 1994a. *Peddling Prosperity: Economic Sense and Nonsense in the Age of Diminished Expectations.* New York: W. W. Norton.

——. 1994b. Competitiveness: a dangerous obsession. *Foreign Affairs* March/April (online).

——. 1994c. What economists can learn from evolutionary theorists. Talk given to the European Association for Evolutionary Political Economy.

Kuttner, R. 1985. The poverty of economics. *Atlantic Monthly* February:74–84.

Landes, D. 1998. *The Wealth and Poverty of Nations.* London: Little, Brown.

——. 2003. *The Unbound Prometheus* (first published 1969). Cambridge University Press.

——. 2006. Why Europe and the West? Why not China? *Journal of Economic Perspectives* 20(2):3–22.

La Porta, R., F. Lopez de Silanes, A. Schleifer, and R. Vishny. 1997. Trust in large organizations. *American Economic Review, Papers and Proceedings* 87:333–38.

Lawson, T. 1997. *Economics and Reality.* New York: Routledge.

Layard, R. 2005. *Happiness.* Penguin/Allen Lane.

Lazear, E. 2000. Economic imperialism. *Quarterly Journal of Economics* 115(1): 99–146.

Leamer, E. 1983. Let's take the con out of econometrics. *American Economic Review* 73:31–43.

Levitt, S. 2005. *Freakonomics.* New York: William Morrow.

Legendre, T. 2006. *The Burning.* London: Little, Brown.

Leijonhufvud, A. 1973. Life among the econ. *Western Economic Journal* 11:327–37.

Licht, A., C. Goldschmidt, and S. Schwartz. 2004. Culture rules: the foundation of the rule of law and other norms of governance. Working Paper (available at www.faculty.idc.ac.il/licht/CR13.pdf, accessed May 16, 2006).

Lipset, S., and S. Lenz. 2001. Corruption, culture and markets. In *Culture Matters: How Values Shape Human Progress* (ed. L. Harrison and S. Huntington). New York: Basic Books.

Ljungqvist, L. 1993. Economic underdevelopment: the case of a missing market for human capital. *Journal of Development Economics* 40:219–39.

Lomborg, B. 2001. *The Skeptical Environmentalist.* Cambridge University Press.

Lucas, R. 1988. On the mechanics of economic development. *Journal of Monetary Economics* 22:3–42.

Macho-Stadler, I., and J. D. Perez-Castrillo. 2001. *An Introduction to the Economics of Information,* 2nd edn. Oxford University Press.

MacKenzie, D. 2002. The imagined market [essay review of Mirowski, *Machine Dreams*]. *London Review of Books* 24(21):22-24.

——. 2005. *Is Economics Performative? Option Theory and the Construction of Derivatvies Markets.* University of Edinburgh Working Paper (May 2005; available at www.sps.ed.ac.uk/staff/is%20economics%20performative.pdf).

Maddison, A. 1994. Confessions of a chiffrephile. *Banca Nazionale del Lavoro Quarterly Review* 189:1-27 (available at www.ggdc.net/maddison/personal/autobiog1994.pdf).

——. 1995. *Monitoring the World Economy 1820-1992.* OECD Development Centre Studies.

——. 2001. *The World Economy: A Millennial Perspective.* OECD Development Centre Studies.

——. 2003. *The World Economy: Historical Statistics.* OECD Development Centre Studies.

Manski, C. F. 2000. Economic analysis of social interactions. *Journal of Economic Perspectives* 14(3):115-36.

——. 2005. Interpreting the predictions of prediction markets. Northwestern University Working Paper (December 2005; available at www.faculty.econ.northwestern.edu/faculty/manski/prediction_markets.pdf).

Marshall, A. 1920. *Principles of Economics*, 8th edn (first published 1890). Macmillan. (Available at www.econlib.org/library/Marshall/marP.html.)

McCloskey, D. 1998. *The Rhetoric of Economics* (1st edn 1995). University of Wisconsin Press.

——. 2000. *How to be Human Though an Economist.* University of Michigan Press.

McKinseys Global Institute. 2001. US productivity growth 1995-2000 (October 2001; available at www.mckinsey.com/mgi/reports/pdfs/productivity/usprod.pdf).

McLaren, J. 2000. Globalization and vertical structure. *American Economic Review* 90(5):1239-50.

Menand, L. 2002. *The Metaphysical Club: A Story of Ideas in America* (first published 2001). London: Flamingo.

Meredith, M. 2005. *The State of Africa: A History of Fifty Years of Independence.* New York: Free Press.

Metcalfe, J. S. 1998. Evolutionary concepts in relation to evolutionary economics. University of Manchester, CRIC Working Paper no. 4 (January 1998).

Milanovic, B. 2005. *Worlds Apart: Global and International Equality 1950-2000.* Princeton University Press.

Milgrom, P., and J. Roberts. 1990. The economics of modern manufacturing. *American Economic Review* 80(3):511-28.

Mirowski, P. 2002. *Machine Dreams: Economics Becomes A Cyborg Science.* Cambridge University Press.

Mirrlees, J. 1971. An exploration in the theory of optimal income taxation. *Review of Economic Studies* 61:261-78.

Mokyr, J. 2002. *The Gifts of Athena: Historical Origins of the Knowledge Economy.* Princeton University Press.

Monaghan, P. 2003. Taking on "rational man". *The Chronicle of Higher Education* 49(20):A12, 24.

Myerson, R. 1999. Nash equilibrium and the history of economic theory. *Journal of Economic Literature* 37:1067–82.

Nalebuff, B., and J. Stiglitz. 1983. Information, competition and markets. *American Economic Review* 73(2):278–84.

Nasar, S. 1998. *A Beautiful Mind.* Princeton University Press.

Nelson, R. R. 1995. Recent evolutionary theorizing about economic change. *Journal of Economic Literature* 33:48–90.

——. 2006. Evolutionary theories of cultural change: an empirical perspective. Evolutionary Economics Group, Max Planck Institute, Jena, Working Paper (available at http://ideas.repec.org/p/esi/evopap/2004-22.html, accessed March 23, 2006).

Nelson, R. R., and S. G. Winter. 1982. *An Evolutionary Theory of Economic Change.* Cambridge, MA: Belknap Press of Harvard University Press.

Nordhaus, W. 1997. Do real output and real wage measures capture reality? The history of light suggests not. In *The Economics of New Goods* (ed. R. J. Gordon and T. F. Bresnahan), pp. 29–66. University of Chicago Press, for the National Bureau of Economic Research.

North, D. C. 1990. *Institutions, Institutional Change and Economic Perfomance.* Cambridge University Press.

——. 1991. Institutions. *The Journal of Economic Perspectives* 5(1):97–112.

OECD. 2000. Knowledge, technology and economic growth: recent evidence from OECD countries. Economics Department Working Paper no. 259 (by A. Bassanini, S. Scarpetta, and I. Visco; October 2000; available at www.oecd.org/dataoecd/15/39/1885659.pdf).

Olson, M. 1965. *The Logic of Collective Action.* Cambridge, MA: Harvard University Press.

——. 1996. Big bills left on the sidewalk: why some nations are rich and others are poor. *Jouurnal of Economic Perspectives* 10(2):3–24.

Olters, J.-P. 2001. Modelling politics with economic tools: a critical survey of the literature. IMF Working Paper no. 01/10 (January 2001).

Ormerod, P. 1994. *The Death of Economics.* London: Faber and Faber.

——. 1998. *Butterfly Economics.* London: Faber and Faber.

——. 2000. Death of economics revisited. Keynote address given to the Association of Heterodox Economists on June 29, 2000 (available at www.volterra.co.uk/Docs/dofer.pdf).

Ostrom, E. 1990. *Governing the Commons: The Evolution of Institutions for Collective Action.* Cambridge University Press.

——. 2000. Collective action and the evolution of social norms. *Journal of Economic Perspectives* 14(3):137–58.

Pigou, A. C. (ed.). 1966. *Memorials of Alfred Marshall* (first published 1925). New York: Augustus Kelley.

Pinker, S. 2002. *The Blank Slate.* Penguin/Allen Lane.

Piore, J. M., and C. F. Sabel. 1984. *The Second Industrial Divide: Possibilities for Prosperity.* New York: Basic Books.

Plott, C. 2000. Markets as information gathering tools. *Southern Economic Journal* 67(1):1-15.

Polanyi, K. 1957. *The Great Transformation: The Political and Economic Origins of Our Time* (first published 1944). Ashland, OH: Beacon.

Pomeranz, K. 2000. *The Great Divergence.* Princeton University Press.

Porter, M. 1990. *The Competitive Advantage of Nations.* Macmillan.

Prebisch, R. 1950. *The Economic Development of Latin America and Its Principal Problems.* Geneva: United Nations.

Pritchett, L. 1997. Divergence, big time. *Journal of Economic Perspectives* 11(3): 3-17.

Przeworski, A., and F. Limongi. 1993. Political regimes and economic growth. *Journal of Economic Perspectives* 7(1):51-69.

Putnam, R. 1993. *Making Democracy Work: Civic Traditions in Modern Italy.* Princeton University Press.

———. 2000. *Bowling Alone: The Collapse and Revival of American Community.* Simon & Schuster.

Rabin, M. 1993. Incorporating fairness into game theory and economics. *American Economic Review* 83:1281-302.

———. 1998. Psychology and economics. *Journal of Economic Literature* 36(1): 11-46.

Rajan, R. G., and A. Subramanian. 2005. What undermines aid's impact on growth? IMF Working Paper no. 05/126, p. 9.

Ray, D. 2000. What's new in development economics? NYU mimeo (available at www.nyu.edu/econ/user/debraj/Papers/AmerEcon.pdf, accessed July 12, 2006).

Rhode, P. W., and K. S. Strumpf. 2004. Historical presidential betting markets. *Journal of Economic Perspectives* 18(2):127-42.

Ridley, M. 2000. *Genome: The Autobiography of a Species in 23 Chapters.* London: Fourth Estate.

Rigobon, R., and D. Rodrik. 2004. Rule of law, democracy, openness, and income: estimating the interrelationships. Harvard University Working Paper (August 2004; available at www.cepr.org/pubs/new-dps/dplist.asp?dpno=4653).

Riley, J. G. 2001. Silver signals: twenty-five years of screening and signalling. *Journal of Economic Literature* 39:432-78.

Rodríguez, F., and D. Rodrik. 1999. Trade policy and economic growth: a skeptic's guide to the cross-national evidence. Harvard University Working Paper (May 2000; available at http://ksghome.harvard.edu/~drodrik/skepti1299.pdf).

Rodrik, D. 2004a. Rethinking growth policies in the developing world. Luca D'Agliano Lecture (October 2004; available at http://ksghome.harvard.edu/~drodrik/Luca_d_Agliano_Lecture_Oct_2004.pdf).

Rodrik, D. 2004b. Getting institutions right. Harvard University Working Paper (April 2004; available at http://ksghome.harvard.edu/~drodrik/papers.html).

———. 2005. Why we learn nothing from regressing economic growth on policies. Harvard University Working Paper (March 25, 2005; available at http://ksghome.harvard.edu/~drodrik/papers.html).

Romer, P. M. 1986. Increasing returns and long run growth. *Journal of Political Economy* 94(5):1002–37.

———. 1990. Endogenous technical change. *Journal of Political Economy* 98(5.2): S71–S102.

Rose, J. 2001. *The Intellectual Life of the English Working Classes*. New Haven, CT: Yale University Press.

Rosenstein-Rodan, P. 1943. Problems of industrialisation of eastern and south-eastern Europe. *Economic Journal* 53:202–11.

Rostow, W. W. 1960. *The Stages of Economic Growth: A Non-Communist Manifesto*. Cambridge University Press.

Ruskin, J. 2000. *Unto This Last* (first published 1860, by George Allen & Sons). Deerfield, IL: Hendon Publishing.

Sachs, J. 2000. Tropical underdevelopment. Harvard Centre for International Development (CID) Working Paper no. 57 (December 2000).

———. 2005. *The End of Poverty*. Penguin.

Schell, O. 2002. Gross national happiness. *Frontline World*, Online (May 2002; available at www.pbs.org/frontlineworld/stories/bhutan/gnh.html, accessed July 12, 2006).

Schelling, T. 1960. *The Strategy of Conflict*. Cambridge, MA: Harvard University Press.

———. 1978. *Micromotives and Macrobehavior*. Cambridge, MA: Harvard University Press.

Schumpeter, J. 1962. *Capitalism, Socialism and Democracy*, 3rd edn (first published 1942). London: Harper Perennial.

Schwartz, B. 2004. *The Paradox of Choice*. London: Harper Collins.

Seabright, P. 2004. *The Company of Strangers*. Princeton University Press.

Sen, A. 1981. *Poverty and Famines: An Essay on Entitlement and Deprivation*. Oxford University Press.

Sennett, R. 1998. *The Corrosion of Character: The Personal Consequences of Work in the New Capitalism*. New York: W. W. Norton.

Shapiro, M. D., and D. W. Wilcox. 1997. Mismeasurement in the consumer price index: an evaluation. *National Bureau of Economic Research Macroeconomics Annual* 11:93–142.

Shiller, R. 2000. *Irrational Exuberance*. Princeton University Press.

Simon, H. 1991. Organization and markets. *Journal of Economic Perspectives* 5(2):25–44.

Smith, J. M. 1982. *Evolution and the Theory of Games*. Cambridge University Press.

Smith, V. L. 2003. Constructivist and ecological rationality in economics. *American Economic Review* 93(3):465–508.

Solow, R. 1956. A contribution to the theory of economic growth. *Quarterly Journal of Economics* 70(1):65–94.

——. 1997. How did economics get that way and what way did it get? *Daedalus* 126(0):39–59.

Spence, M. 1976. Product selection, fixed costs and monopolistic competition. *Review of Economic Studies* 43:217–35.

Srinivas, M. N. 1980. *Indian Social Structure.* Somerset, NJ: Transaction Publishers.

——. 2004. *Caste: Its 21st Century Avatar.* Penguin Australia.

Stavins, R. N. 1998. What can we learn from the grand policy experiment? Lessons from SO_2 emissions trading. *Journal of Economic Perspectives* 12(3):69–88.

Stigler, G. 1961. The economics of information. *Journal of Political Economy* 69(3):213–25.

Stiglitz, J. E. 1998. The private uses of public interests: incentives and institutions. *Journal of Economic Perspectives* 12(2):3–22.

——. 2000. The contributions of the economics of information to 20th century economics. *Quarterly Journal of Economics* 115(4):1441–78.

——. 2004. Information and the change in the paradigm in economics. *The American Economist*, part 1 published in Fall 2003, part 2 in Spring 2004.

Sunstein, C. R. 2004. Group judgements: deliberations, statistical means and information markets. AEI–Brookings Joint Center for Regulatory Studies Working Paper (September 2004).

Surowiecki, J. 2004. *The Wisdom of Crowds.* New York: Random House.

Sutton, J. 2000. *Marshall's Tendencies.* Cambridge, MA: MIT Press.

Tabellini, G. 2006. Culture and institutions: economic development in the regions of europe. Bocconi University Working Paper.

Taleb, N. 2001. *Fooled by Randomness.* London: Texere.

Tetlock, P., R. Hahn, and D. Lien. 2006. Designing information markets for decision making. AEI–Brookings Joint Center for Regulatory Studies Working Paper (November 2005; updated January 2006).

Thaler, R. 2000. From homo economicus to homo sapiens. *Journal of Economic Perspectives* 14(1):133–42.

Timmins, N. 1995. *The Five Giants: A Biography of the Welfare State.* London: Harper Collins.

Transparency International. 2003. Bribe payer's survey. Transparency International Kenya (available at www.tikenya.org/documents/BribIndex02.pdf).

Uglow, J. 2002. *The Lunar Men.* London: Faber and Faber.

Veblen, T. 1898. Why is economics not an evolutionary science? *Quarterly Journal of Economics* 12(4):373–97.

——. 1994. *The Theory of the Leisure Classes* (first published 1899). Penguin.

Warsh, D. 2006. *Knowledge and the Wealth of Nations.* New York: W. W. Norton.

Weber, M. 1999. *Essays in Economic Sociology* (ed. R. Swedberg). Princeton University Press.

Weintraub, E. R. 2002. *How Economics Became a Mathematical Science.* Durham, NC: Duke University Press.

Weitzmann, M. L. 1999. Pricing the limits to growth from mineral depletion. *Quarterly Journal of Economics* 114(3):691–706.

Williamson, O. 1985. *The Economic Institutions of Capitalism: Firms, Markets, Relational Contracting.* New York: Free Press.

——. 2000. The new institutional economics: taking stock, looking ahead. *Journal of Economic Literature* 38:595–613.

——. 2005. The economics of governance. University of California, Berkeley, Working Paper (January 2005; available at http://groups.haas.berkeley.edu/bpp/oew/TheEconomicsOfGovernance.pdf, accessed May 19, 2006).

Wolf, M. 2004. *Why Globalization Works.* New Haven, CT: Yale University Press.

Wolfers, J., and E. Zitzewitz. 2004. Prediction markets. *Journal of Economic Perspectives* 18(2):107–26.

——. 2006a. Prediction markets in theory and practice. Centre for Economic Policy Research, Discussion Paper 5578 (March 2006).

——. 2006b. Five open questions about prediction markets. Federal Reserve Bank of San Francisco, Working Paper Series, 2006-06.

Wilson, E. O. 2000. *Sociobiology: The New Synthesis* (first published 1975). Cambridge, MA: Harvard University Press.

Index